TROLL

MY LIFE IN BOMB DISPOSAL

JUSTIN J. BELL QGM

Edited by
JANE HARVEY-BERRICK

HARVEY
BERRICK
PUBLISHING

Troll

My Life in Bomb Disposal

Justin J. Bell, QGM

Edited by
Jane Harvey-Berrick

Troll: My Life in Bomb Disposal
Copyright © 2019 Justin J. Bell

Editing by Jane Harvey-Berrick

Cover design by Nicky Stott

ISBN 978-1-912015-18-4
Harvey Berrick Publishing

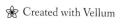 Created with Vellum

To Helen, James & Beth
Daddy loves you x

PREFACE

Justin 'Troll' Bell was an extraordinary man. He joined the British Army in the late 1980s and quickly qualified as an Ammunition Technician within the Royal Army Ordnance Corps. He completed over 20 years' service as an Army Counter Terrorism Bomb Disposal Operator seeing service in three major conflicts.

He commanded EOD operations on High-Threat tours in Northern Ireland, Iraq and Afghanistan; supporting over a decade of front line UK counter-terrorism activity including responding to the 2005 London bombings. He constituted part of the National Contingency Capability for dealing with weapons of mass destruction and undertook duties as part of the protection detail for senior figures.

During his service he received the Queen's Gallantry Medal for his EOD activities and was subsequently rewarded a second time on the Queen's New Year Honours' list on his retirement.

He left the army in 2009 to spend more time with his wife and children. He said he didn't want to be 'a father who doesn't come home'.

Troll was diagnosed with brain cancer in 2017, caused, he used to joke, "by all the nasty shit I've handled," during his time as an EOD operator. Through this final illness, his dignity and humour remained undimmed.

As his friend, and a writer myself, I rushed to collate his memoirs into a book that would make him proud. I didn't quite make it in time, and Troll died in the summer of 2019.

Unsurprisingly, it was some time before his widow, Helen, felt able to resume the task of reading and editing these memoirs on his behalf. There are occasions when we've been unsure of the timeline and have done our best to arrange his memories as accurately as possible. No doubt we have not always got it right – and we've had to edit out a couple of the most coruscating and potentially libelous sections. If you had the privilege to meet or work with Troll, you'd know exactly what we mean.

Because through his words, his love of the army shines brightly, even as he paints the most vivid pictures of military life, with its rights and wrongs, failings and injustices, all depicted with stark truthfulness and dark humour.

He was my friend, and I miss him. I feel honoured to have known him.

He was 47 when he died, leaving Helen and his two children, James and Beth. It is to them, his family after the military that he wished to dedicate this book.

His future was stolen, but his memories live on.

Jane Harvey-Berrick, August 2021

GLOSSARY

GLOSSARY

The Flaming 'A's

On e-Bay, you can buy an arm badge that represents people who work in bomb disposal. It's made in 'staybrite'.

Just saying.

I spent many years as an ATO in Explosive Ordnance Disposal, a British Army regiment. We call the insignia the 'Flaming A', for obvious reasons. Well, it's obvious when you see it. Flaming Arseholes is another term that I particularly like.

An AT is an Ammunition Technician and and ATO is an Ammunition Technical Officer.

ATO is also used for any operator soldier or officer who has led a team on bomb disposal tour in NI/Iraq/Arsecrackistan.

The 'A' in the badge stands for 'A' tradesmen. The Army had three trade standards (A, B and C).

The ATO badge has no letter in as they aren't tradesmen. They're called 'hobby badges' by ATs who spend their whole careers doing the job. Officers do a couple of years then move on.

What you're about to read is the truth, the whole truth and the whole flaming truth.

AT = Ammunition
Technician LCpl - WO1

ATO = Ammunition
Technical Officer

On the advice of my editor, names have been changed to protect the guilty as well as the innocent.

Nicknames for ATs

Albert Tatlocks* (you'd have to be a Coronation Street fan prior to 1984 to get that one), Rocket Doctors, The Operators, Felix (the cat that has nine lives), Flaming As or Flaming Arseholes (my personal favourite).

ATO Team

ATO – Sgt to Captain in rank, ammunition technician: in charge of team and makes sole approach to IEDs.

No2 – Cpl ammunition technician /driver, responsible for equipment maintenance and driving Wheelbarrow (robot).

ECM Op – Cpl Royal signals, controls electronic counter measures (called the Bleep).

Inf Escort – Historically an infantry soldier attached to the team to provide 'bodyguard' protection for operator and team.

The team has two EOD trucks for carrying the team EOD and ECM equipments. Light scale operations can be conducted with lesser scales of equipment all the way down to bergen (rucksack) mounted. However each reduction in equipment reduces capability and potentially increases risk.

Detachments

Both EOD team and WIS in a location may be referred to as Detachment or Det. While No2s and ECM soldier roles are both referred to as operators, the term 'Operator' refers to the EOD No1 or the WISWO.

REST – Royal Engineer Search Team)

7 JNCOs specialising in high risk search, the searching of areas where there is a high likelihood of IEDs being present. Their skill bringing much needed pace to a task that is inherently slow.

WIS – Weapons Intelligence Section

The section is run by an ATO sergeant major (called WISWO) selected for the post once he has completed a number of bomb disposal tours. His knowledge of IEDs and terrorist tactics provides the technical oversight for all reports originated by RMP/Intelligence corps investigations. Section will have a number of JNCOs (Junior non-commissioned officers), usually staffed from the Intelligence Corps, and Royal Military police for their background in conducting investigations and collation of intelligence. The day-to-day overt role of the section is the investigation and analysis of terrorist attacks, weapons finds, and IED related incidents. The section also provides intelligence input to the Brigade HQ, and lectures to troops about recent incidents and the threats in theatre. A less well publicised role is undertaken by the section ATO supporting covert troops and Special Forces activity. The WIS in Lashkar-Gah (LKG) had one RMP Corporal and two Int Corps Cpls. To carry out the day-to-day role, equipment includes forensic recovery kit, bags, gloves, camera equipment etc.

The offices, computers, vehicles, radios, ECM and most other support and equipment wasn't in place and had to be fought for against the system.

PART I - BEGINNINGS

PROLOGUE

ALL I WANTED to do was go shopping in Kabul.

So it might take some explaining to figure out how I ended up standing in an Afghan jail with my 'borrowed' rifle, safety off, staring at half a dozen Afghan police, looking like I was about to shoot them.

Which I was.

There are three things you need to know about Afghanistan.

It's a shithole.

It's hot in summer.

It's a shithole.

I mean, someone must like it, right? Otherwise why the fuck have we been fighting here for the last ten years? Fighting and dying.

But, back to that police jail.

I was due to be replaced. My end of tour had come, but I also felt a bit cheated. I was supposed to go and work for the Embassy in Kabul. I was almost on the plane, then we decided to invade Helmand. I say 'we', but that decision was taken by someone else. Obviously.

That being the case and Helmand looking a lot more like a shooting war, I was selected from a cast of one to be the Helmand representative, and they found someone to fill my spot in Kabul.

As it happened, that someone was Andy, a very good mate of mine. I don't begrudge him the air-conditioned brick built buildings, nor his fridges

and double bed, nor his armoured four-by-four or all of the other luxuries he
has while I'm in shitsville Helmand.

No, what I begrudge is that I wanted to go shopping in Kabul.

So I cancel my flight home, (and I've no idea why I didn't get into
trouble for this), then re-schedule it for a few weeks later, saying I need to
do a proper handover. I didn't have a real job back in the UK anyway, so
who cares?

I do my handover, this time to another good mate called Stu, and say
that I'm off to Kabul and if he has any issues to give me a call. It's a better
handover and after-support than I got. Just saying.

I fly up to Kabul and have a bit of a holiday – which isn't to say it's all
sun, sea and sangria – it just means spending some time off the military
books and being looked after by Andy.

We even do some work while I'm there.

Initially, the Ops Room staff don't take to me. Kabul is five stars
compared to Helmand, and I'm scruffy, bearded, and the fine Afghan dust
is all over my kit

I guess some of them obviously don't know what life is like further
south, but once they realise I'm with Andy, they mellow during my time
there. In fact, I'm there so long that the Ops room start referring to us as Big
WISWO and Little WISWO [Weapons Intelligence Section Warrant
Officer] when people attend asking for help.

An example of the work, we had?

Well, redacted for reasons that would get me in more trouble than you
can shake a stick at, let me just say that the bag of crystalline yellow powder
was TNT. I know because I tasted it. So did Andy. It was probably from a
broken down Russian F1 grenade. At this point, Andy returns and joins the
investigation. He eats some of the yellow powder and says, "Yep, TNT."

The other guys in the Ops room now think we're both mad, but we do
know our onions.

Anyway, Andy comes in one night with the latest news: an ex-ATO
called Bob, who is working for the UN, is in the shit.

He's been arrested by the Afghan Police for attempted murder. (Which
is another, long story.)

Did I mention that I'm an ATO with the British Army? Also known as
an Ammunition Technical Officer. Also known as a bomb disposal officer.
Also known as Troll and arrived into this world as Justin. I'd mention the
other nicknames but my wife might be reading.

ATOs are the go-to guys and girls for missiles and ammunition, the

Army's Counter Terrorism experts, and a dab hand at blowing shit up. Trade aside, the troops say I'm also a job magnet; I say it's just magnetic charm. Bob isn't his real name, of course. I could call him 'Sid', but to me a Sid is short and round and bald, and Bob wasn't. So I call him Bob.

The gist of it's that Bob has fallen out with his UN boss. We all fall out with our bosses sometimes, but in this case his boss is currently stopping any UN support reaching Bob in jail. Nice.

The UK embassy won't get involved as Bob works for the UN, and as such, that apparently causes issues. The Afghan police don't care about any of this. They will only release him on bail under stringent conditions which aren't being met by either the UN or the British embassy. If they don't get what they want – which is probably a bribe – they are going to transfer him to Pol-e-charki prison and if Bob goes in there, well he's not coming out alive.

Andy has been told by the embassy that they can't get involved, but on discussion, they have no issue if Andy, as a member of the UK military, attempts to negotiate Bob's release.

Now, this was a bit of a bluff, because technically, Andy wasn't part of the NATO mission but worked for the embassy. Andy draws up some fake military paperwork and it's at this point he comes to find me.

"Have you handed in all your ammunition yet?"

"Like fuck have I. I got rid of the grenades and explosives, but I planned to give you all my ammunition at the airport as you put me on the plane."

"Good. Get your guns and come with me."

In the four-by-four, he fills me in. The Afghan police can't be trusted, and for all we know Bob is for sale to the Taliban. Andy looks at me.

"We're not leaving without Bob."

That was it. The silent agreement between friends that we're both up for it.

I make ready my rifle: that means pulling the cocking handle back and releasing it. This draws a round out of the magazine into the chamber so my rifle is ready to fire – my pistol is always ready – and we get to the police station.

It's in a compound with a single gate at the edge of Kabul, a rundown blue building with the paint peeling off – a far cry from the police headquarters in the centre, with its sandbags and checkpoints.

I'm starting to see why we're having problems; we're not dealing with our usual ANP here.

Andy is a big lad, and he goes in and makes his way across the room to the chief police type dude sat behind a desk. The fucker has an AK against the wall with a magazine on it next to him. Andy is all smiles with the bluff paperwork in hand.

I follow. Bob is sat immediately opposite, pasty-faced and looking like he's about to crap his pants. Sorry, Bob, but you know it's true.

The room had about a dozen Afghans in it. All bar two are in shitty civilian clothes so nobody knows what the fuck they are: could be police or could be Taliban. Who knows in this shithole of a country?

Bob was silent, but you could tell he was relieved. From his point of view, we were more welcome than water in a desert after a month of living off raw camel.

Afterwards, Bob says,

"I have never been so relieved to see someone come through the door as when Andy came in ... except when he moved out of the way and you followed him. Andy came in and was all smiles. The Afghans who were talking amongst themselves pretty much ignored him and carried on. Then you came in and checked your arcs [the corners], backed yourself into the empty one with your rifle in your shoulder – a Demarco, not a shitty SA80 PoS – and the only thing missing was the order 'targets up'!"

Bob laughs so hard, he nearly chokes on the bottle of champagne he's opened now we're back at his digs.

"The Afghans all fell silent and everyone in that room knew you'd come there to kill them. The only thing missing was your safety catch clicking off."

"Bob, the safety wasn't on. Andy and I had agreed that if the Afghans looked for one second like they weren't going to release you, Andy would say the word and I was going to slot the lot of them."

There's a long silence as Bob looks from Andy to me. Do we look like we're joking? Maybe I just have that sort of face.

"Fucking hell!" says Bob. "How were you going to justify that?"

"No idea. We figured we'd just torch the place and say the Taliban did it." I shrug. "We didn't plan that far ahead."

As it happened the police released him and we didn't need to find out if I would have killed them all.

But I heard a version of that story a couple of years later.

I was running a Unit in Colchester. We had a vacancy for a driver and I asked one of my lads, Popey, if he knows any good guys in the local Units who would like to come and work with us. He said he did, and would go and see him for a chat.

He came back in the afternoon looking shifty and embarrassed.

"Well? Does he want to join us?"

"No, boss, and can I ask you a question?"

"No? Why not?"

"Well, boss, erm, because of you. Can I ask you that question?"

"Me?"

I didn't think I was a bad boss, and anyway, I had no idea anyone else in the Garrison even knew I existed.

"Go on then, what's the question?"

"Did you ever rescue a lad from an Afghan jail while you were over there?"

"Yes, buddy. Me and a mate did."

"No way!"

So I told him the story.

"We faked some paperwork and rescued a mate. Why is that such a big deal?"

"That's not what the lads over there have heard. They've all heard that the new ATO sergeant major is a head case. You blew a hole in the prison wall and machined gunned the guard towers to rescue your mate."

Huh. Good ole army rumour mill is at work.

I banned him from telling them the truth, because if they're stupid enough to listen to rumours, I'll use the intimidation factor to my advantage.

Popey said he was happy with my explanation and that he was sure that all the stories couldn't be true. He said there was a ridiculous one about me putting a head in a fridge.

"That one's true, buddy!"

CHAPTER 1

HOW I GOT INTO THE TRADE

I'M the only English boy in a Scottish family: the males being Scottish who marry English girls, by and large.

My grandfather has traced our lineage back to around the year 1600. After their sound drubbing at the hands of Sir Francis Drake, the remnants of the Spanish Armada sailed up over Scotland to make their way back to Spain. Some of those ships were wrecked on the Scottish coast, and one of the sailors married a local girl – making me Scots/Spanish by ancestry – which explains the dark hair and crappy temper. Maybe.

My grandfather asked me why I became a soldier. I told him I didn't know as it wasn't like I was from a military family. He disagreed, and told me about all my relatives who have served.

My great grandfather, Pops, was in the First World War. He was in the Royal Scots Greys. He didn't talk about the Great War, but being Scottish he was partial to the odd whiskey. Granddad said that with some whiskey in him, Pops would talk about his time in the trenches.

In one story, he said that the artillery would lift too soon, and the Germans would come out of their bunkers and man their machine guns. A plan was hatched to mount machine guns to horses, and the cavalry would charge over no-man's land as the artillery barrage started to lift, to try and beat the Germans to their guns. Pops would get animated and pull his poker from the cartridge case beside the fire, and say,

"And when your gun ran out of ammo, you'd pull a strap and dump it. Then it was out with your sabre and off with their heads."

My grandfather described ducking under the poker, and I'm left with the knowledge that my great-grandfather cut Germans heads off with his sword.

My uncle died when I was six and I inherited his air rifle. It was stored in the rafters in the garage for when I was old enough, but I used to climb up and 'borrow' it. I bought my first shotgun at 12. My mother would have gone mad if she knew, so I stored it at a mate's. It was a 4/10 with a dodgy trigger. You had to fire a couple of times to get the cartridge to work. Sometimes the pigeons would catch on and fly off.

My brother and sister were towny types. They liked discos and socialising. I grew up in the woods. I made hides to shoot from, camped out, and felt nothing for bricks and mortar. I was at my happiest under a forest canopy, smelling the scent of the forest and being tuned in to the nature around me. My preference translated well into the army for some skill sets.

But those aren't my only memories of childhood.

I sat at the top of the stairs. She was arguing with her current boyfriend. I got out of bed, looking down. The lounge is on the left and the dining room is right, with the stairs running up between. My brother is in the room opposite, asleep, I'm guessing. At least, I hope so.

She has argued with them all, there are always reasons. I sit there and listen to them going at it. I hear the slap, and see her fly from room to room across the hallway. I've had enough. He's a farm worker, and we've been shooting together with 12 gauges. I'm more than sick of this.

He's in the kitchen and I pin him to the wall, show him the shotgun cartridges out of my pocket and tell him if he touches her again, I'll kill him.

In the morning, she tells me that if she has to choose between her boyfriend and her children, she chooses him and throws me out.

I'm 15.

I move into a mate's flat. It's near college so I can continue my studies. It gets me through my 'O' Levels, but by the time I'm half way through my 'A' Levels, I have had enough.

I was 19 before I saw my father again. I was in the Army, mobile and self-sufficient. He had asked to see his children, and my mum had sent my brother and sister (biologically his), but had excluded me from the arrangement. In my whole, life my father had always treated me as his own, but my own mother was the one who made me feel like I was an outsider. She did it for her own selfish reasons.

I jumped in the car and went to meet him the same day that he arranged to see my siblings. She's hated him ever since.

We don't get on, Mum and I; she's a hate filled old woman. My father, on the other hand, has had cancer twice, five heart attacks and a triple bypass, but is the most laidback dude I know.

My wife says there is an aura of calm at my father's. He's the only man I have told everything to about my career. I'm thankful to my mother for teaching me to have manners, getting me a good education and for doing her best. If I seem disingenuous, I'm sorry. She's my mother; I just wish she could learn to move on a little bit.

My father is a down to earth plain speaking man, an engineer on oil rigs and a mechanic with haulage vehicles.

I was getting ready to go to Northern Ireland, to take over a team as the boss in 2000, when I found out my father had been diagnosed with Non-Hodgkin lymphoma. I phoned him from NI and asked him if he wanted me to come home.

"Why? Have you recently taken up cardiac surgery as a hobby?"

"No dad."

"Well, what fucking use are you, boy? You stay out there being good at what you're good at and I'll stay here with the quacks."

As I say, the most laidback dude I know.

I WANTED TO JOIN THE INFANTRY, SO I WENT INTO THE CAREERS office and took an entrance test. I scored well and was taken into the Recruiting Officer's room. He wanted me to apply as an officer, but he also told me that my housemaster at boarding school had written a damning reference, saying I would not stick at military life.

I returned to the college, quit my studies and told the housemaster what I thought of him. When I went back, the recruiting officer saw his arse: partly for me quitting and so being ineligible for officer entry, and partly for letting on that I had seen my reference.

I was then passed to a recruiting Colour Sergeant (CSgt) from the Royal Anglians, my local Regiment and the Unit I wanted to join.

I thought, I'm in here.

But he wasn't having any of it. He took one look at my test scores and told me I had to take a technical trade. He also told me I was too young and that I should get a job for six months to get a new reference, as the one from college was shit. I was given a list of jobs, and he basically pointed to Ammunition Technician and said I should consider that first.

All the applicants watched a video in three parts that showed what the jobs were like. Ammo Tech came on, then the screen disappeared in a blinding flash and I thought, that's pretty cool. The job description said we worked with ammunition and destroyed old stockpiles through demolition.

The CSgt told me that if I passed, to come back and tell him.

Six months later, with a new reference, I was on the train from Norwich to Brookwood station near Camberley in Surrey. There were a few similar looking lads on the train, so I asked two of them what they were joining as?

Ammo Tech.

There were a lot of potential ATs from Norwich recruiting at that time.

Basic training was mostly run by ex-Guardsmen who had transferred from their Regiments after the Falklands war, into the Royal Army Ordnance Corps (RAOC). I wasn't the best recruit, but I loved being there.

One day, Ptes Bell (me) and M were in the Sergeants' office making the instructors their brews. Mo M, Platoon Sergeant, is talking to Digger D, one of the instructors, and he says something along the lines of

"I'm not here to be liked; I'm here to make soldiers out of boys."

He then turns to M and says, "You hate me, don't you, M?"

He barks back a military and correct, "Yes, Sergeant!"

Mo Morris then says to me,

"You hate me, don't you, Bell?"

"No, Sergeant!"

At this, he runs over to me and leans into my face and says, "Why don't you hate me?"

(This is a man who ripped a soldier off his feet while kicking a fire extinguisher down a hallway just for looking at him wrong – the soldier, not the fire extinguisher. He's massive.) I replied that all I ever wanted to be was a soldier, and as he hadn't at that point sacked me, then I didn't hate him.

"Good point. Why do you hate me, M?"

M crumbled.

I MET CHEWY M THE DAY BEFORE YESTERDAY, AND HE REMEMBERED IT the same way.

Driver training followed, along with a staff clerks' course and a brief spell at the 11 Ordnance Battalion locations around the UK which did bomb disposal.

While I was at Colchester, one of the Sergeants loaned me his jumper (IDed with rank) while on task and sent me into the police station to collect UXO which had turned up. Technically, it was my first EOD task, and I imagine the aged police officer looked at me and thought soldiers were getting younger and younger.

We then headed to Kineton in Warwickshire to start our AT selection and training. The selection took place over two weeks and included physical assessments, command tasks, written tests and psychological assessments.

One of the psychological assessments was conducted by a computer, some old BBC-type affair with a green screen. You read questions and pressed either 'Y' or 'N' depending on whether you agreed with the statement. It had a dodgy keyboard, and one of the keys stuck so you you'd end up answering the next 20 questions 'yes' regardless as they flashed by.

You were filtered into three groups: those who were deemed suitable, those who were not, and those who were considered in need of an interview.

The pre-select filtered the applicants from 150 down to 20. As the tests were based on those currently in the trade, I think if you were normal you failed, got an interview if you were just a little strange, and only the barking mad got selected.

Luckily, I was straight in.

As a PotAT (Potential Ammo Tech – officers are called PotATOs), I wasn't in a position to comment, except that they chose me. By the time I was an instructor, I was used on the PotAT selection panel and had more impact on who was chosen for what.

Back to the careers office.

I passed my AT course. I was the only one off the train that first day, even though the Norwich careers office that had sent so many.

I returned to the office to find the Colour Sergeant and informed him of my successful completion: it had taken 15 months. He was very happy, jumped up, said some choice things and ran upstairs. It seems that they played recruit bingo: get individuals into certain job based on the job list, and I was his winning number. It was something like £10 a month each, and you sold your card to your replacement when posted.

Anyway, it explained why there were so many volunteers for Ammo Tech from that office, and it's really the only reason I became an AT.

CHAPTER 2

RE AND RLC

THERE ARE two streams of EOD in the military. I have full awareness of one side but have experience of both.

Royal Engineers EOD is taught as an addition to a core skill. RE soldiers start with a grounding in an engineering skill and then specialise into EOD & Search. The RE's expert skill set used to be in search, with combat engineering, minefield clearance and military booby traps comprising their knowledge base. It's a combat skill and driven by an acceptance of mission risk.

ATs/ATOs start with a grounding in ammunition design and explosive chemistry. However, as an officer, you will be subject to the RLC officer career management. The ATO course is one of the 'long courses' that an RLC officer must take. As a result, those who don't fancy logistics or petroleum end up on the ATO course. It's not uncommon to find more than three-quarters on the course who have no interest in being an ATO. As a 'career course', it's also problematic to fail – meaning that the standards are ignored/lowered to accommodate officers who need a long course for their career advancement. To fail the ATO course would require an officer to attend another course, which would not sit with the expectation of career promotion timelines.

Historically, the two distinct roles were separate, specialised, and expert. Having experienced both sets of instructors, they are equally expert.

RE are (were) mine experts without equal, and their military discipline exceeds that of the ATO. The drills are the drills, and they are followed for a reason. From an external perspective, I think this is best explained as, it doesn't matter how many sappers die in a minefield as long as the tanks get through.

The RE are a combat force and far more accepting of the harsh realities of war. They also have a greater percentage of soldier skills, and are more readily accepted throughout the army when they amalgamate with other units. They are a combat unit and have a can-do attitude.

The ATO were chosen for the counter-terrorism role specifically because they differ so distinctly from the RE way of doing things. Where military doctrine is set, defined and often pattern-driven, that of a terrorist is unique, individual, and prone to unseen variation. A background of first principles in ammunition design was well suited to the ever-changing aspects of terrorism. Sadly, much of the ammunition background is boring and is little more than stacking boxes and counting bullets. It's a big ask to take someone suited to this role and ask them to become combat-ready. That said, there is a high intellectual threshold for the role and most are bright enough to cope with a combat role, as well.

In the past, there was some in-fighting, much unprofessionalism, and many opportunities were lost as each side chose to undermine the other rather than concentrate on mission command.

I'm bitter about this.

In the last few years, the role has been merged. The RE took the lead in EOD/IEDD from the RLC, and now a formalised command structure exists. Instead of two differing organisations, both now have to work together. As a result, the training has been amalgamated to a single career role. The ATO course still exists, as does the RE career path, but entry into EOD is now a homogeneous single course. Both units have the same qualification. Unit roles vary, some are UK-based, NI-based, or expeditionary-based. The RLC have more day to day work, but the RE take the lead in overseas deployments with support from the RLC.

The AT course was lengthy and had regular examinations, and you were not allowed to fail more than three. Even from that early stage, you could start to filter the applicants beyond that already done by the pre-selection course. Some people you just didn't want to be near, when they're handling explosives.

The barracks where the school was located was full of Ammo Techs,

Storeman and Pioneers. It was my first experience of what was referred to as a 'Working Unit'.

We came through the guardroom and were directed to Block 6 which was for students on courses.

We were given a finger tour (which means standing in the hall with the block corporal pointing), indicating rooms upstairs, ablutions in the halls, and a TV room on the ground floor.

We stowed away our kit and made for the TV room where we could hear the noise of a football match. It was dark, with only the TV for light. The room was full of a Lance Course: basically they were being taught to handle the American-made rocket. The liquid fuel was dangerous and required special procedures for handling.

They were all sat drinking beer, an activity forbidden by the rules, but as I was to find out, ATs don't much care for the rules.

Brad L, famous for sun-burning his armpits on Bournemouth beach, continued to be a source of entertainment.

We were being given a lesson on safety fuse, which is a plastic tube filled with black powder that burns at a set rate, and can be used to initiate demolitions. The first 30cm is cut off and discarded to guard against moisture ingress.

The instructor ignited this first 30cm and threw it on the floor, then he stood on it, and the fuze started to hiss and pop as compression changed its burning rate, thus showing us that it was important not to kink or knot the fuze, or place it under rocks, and so on, as this would change the speed at which it burned: important if you're walking away from a demolition.

He then cut off a second 30cm section to use as our basis for timing how much fuze was needed for our demolitions.

As it was lit, he started a stopwatch. The instructor handed the burning fuze to Brad. We all stood around talking and watched the fuze burn. The instructor said that Brad should put it down as it would get hot soon. Brad dropped it and stamped all over it. The conversation stopped.

Brad looked up, realising all wasn't as it should be, but not knowing why. The instructor sent him to visit Bertie Basset on the hill (about two miles), while we re-ran the test with a new piece of fuze.

We had items passed around the classrooms, parts of ammunition that had been inerted. There was a bag of flechettes, small darts fired from tank shells. At one time, there must have been hundreds in the bag, but with successive courses they disappeared into potential ATs pockets.

Steve G quickly identified that they could be wrapped with toilet paper and fitted just right into the air pistol that he kept locked up in his briefcase.

The first round was test fired into a locker door. All the bullet holes fired into the walls of the block were covered up with posters at the end of our course to get us cleared from the block.

Those weren't the only items that disappeared into ATs pockets: the mercury tilt switch and micro switch that went while we were on course at the Felix centre might have well carried the death sentence when the instructors came looking for it. A right bunch of bastards they were, and in a small way I think we're lesser without that sort of rabid approach to teaching these days. Other instructors bordered on comatose. How could you make things that blow up sound so boring?

Steve G found Danny C's lesson on anti-tank mines so mind-numbing that he just burst out laughing and couldn't stop.

I recently found one of my notebooks from the course and a page had a blue ear print where I had fallen asleep on my notes and drooled. Instructors would usually wake you up, but it was down to you to pass the tests, so if you missed anything you had to revise in your own time.

The AT leadership course was designed to give young soldiers a taste of leadership skills prior to picking up their first stripe. Promotion came with successful completion of the AT course.

The course was a return to Blackdown where we did basic training, along with the associated bullshit, but it was pretty enjoyable. Instead of getting thrashed on the square, we were actually taught to do new and interesting drill moves. The patrolling was more about understanding ground appreciation and less about thrashing young lads through gorse bushes.

But the best was yet to come – the trip to Wales was an absolute hoot.

We would walk twenty miles a day over the Black Mountains and stay in camp sites near pubs. Excellent.

The first night was water logged, but the second we stayed near a pub and camped in their barn, which we nearly burnt down.

Chris told me that when his course stayed there, they set fire to the field which scared a herd of sheep out onto the local roads. The final day saw Q and his enormous bergen nearly blown off a cliff. Pity, so near and so far.

Before we did the assault course where I nearly drowned and was saved by Steve Clueless, we had to do a river crossing over a waterfall. I'm not sure how safe that was, and when Gav was the first to fall in, he nearly drowned because of a huge Arran sweater he was wearing.

THE FIRST TASK I EVER DID? THAT BRINGS BACK MEMORIES.

My Senior Ammunition Technician (SAT, our version of the Regimental Sergeant Major) says:

"You're going on your Operators' course. I know you're not promoted yet, so the boss has given you your promotion for the duration of the course. Just don't tell anyone you're not a Sergeant, especially not the RSM because you'll be staying in the Sergeants Mess."

What?

"If the OC has got me acting rank, why would the RSM care?"

"You've not got acting rank; you're just getting these tapes for the course so shhh, right?"

Brilliant. As if these courses aren't difficult enough, I'm now doing mine illegally.

The course was fantastic, taught by instructors who were all Northern Ireland veterans. What they didn't know about bomb disposal wasn't worth knowing. They even offered to coach us in their own time, if you requested it.

A fellow Sergeant on the course, Steve asked for some training and I joined him.

I really needed to pass this course. Truthfully, my career had not flown. I was told by many that I should have joined the infantry and was the wrong sort for the trade. I'd got that sick of it, I'd signed up for re-trading in 1994. I had got to within a month of completing, but something dragged me back to the trade. Unfinished business I guess: I wanted to be an Operator and for that I needed to pass the course and make Sergeant.

So, having asked for some extra training, we both arrive up at The Wing (short for Counter Terrorist Bomb Disposal School or the Felix Centre) on Saturday morning. We collect our equipment and get to a patch of grass outside the instructor's office. An AK rifle is lying on the grass near a tree, and another one close by. The idea is that there has been an attack and these have been left behind. Our mission is to recover them safely: one each. The intimation being that terrorists don't leave weapons behind so somewhere on or around the weapon is likely to be a booby trap.

"Any questions? No, good! Off you go."

The instructor disappears into his office.

Steve and I suit up in our bomb suits and start the detailed search procedure.

There are various different ways to search as an Operator, but at that level you've been shown the basics, and to be safe, you follow them to the letter. It's not rapid: when you're looking for the tiniest indication of the bomb, you don't rush. We're like the opposite of fighter pilots: they have to tell everyone they're a pilot and they say speed is life. We don't tend to tell anyone what we do and speed is death.

It's hard going: just the constant standing, kneeling, then lying, and back to standing as you examine the scene from different aspects while wearing 8olbs of Kevlar. It means you're drenched in sweat. Your visor mists up, even though you have a battery mounted fan on the top which blows air over it. It's designed to stop it steaming up, but it doesn't work well. I always used to tuck some rag down behind the blast plate. Every few minutes I would lift the visor and wipe it clean. This had the added benefit of allowing me to view the scene without looking through the visor too, although technically it meant you weren't protected if something unexpected happened.

It takes a little over two hours to get to the weapon. The closer I get to it, the more the anticipation increases that I'll spot the device. I've long since stopped noticing that Steve is working alongside me; I'm consumed in my own little world of my personal battle.

There comes a point where you start to doubt yourself. I thought I would have found it by now. The danger is that you stop being methodical and start guessing where the bomb is. Maybe I missed something? The doubt builds. Maybe it's not in the ground at all, maybe it's attached to the device? The search around the weapon is as slow and detailed as the search getting there. Nothing.

Finally, I have to move the weapon. There are numerous ways to do this safely in EOD terms, but the training is over, I only had to get there and search around it today.

Two and half hours later, I go and tap on the window. The instructor wakes from a hangover induced slumber on his desk. He's a bit bleary eyed. (We didn't know it was the night after a Regimental Dinner), and comes out to see my work. Steve is almost finished, too.

The instructor walks around our work area and asks some questions. Then he walks up to the weapons and picks them both up.

"Where's the booby trap?"

I can't help asking, professional curiosity tweaking my intellect to see how and if we'd missed something.

"There isn't one," he replies.

I failed to see the funny side of this.

"What the hell was that supposed to teach us?

You really don't have much of a sense of humour when you've been sweating your nads off for hours.

He looks at me, looks at the area I've searched which started from the point where he had stood at the beginning of the task and said,

"Start closer."

He didn't laugh. I don't think I ever did when I was instructing and passing on life-saving information, but then I can come across as a bit over focussed. Felix might have nine lives, we don't.

He never told us we had to search the whole distance; where you started, technically, the terrorist would have to consider a kill zone of over 5,000 square meters. That's not a reliable way to kill someone. You have to work out what is, work out your way around it, and when you can do that you'll be able to recover that weapon in half an hour.

That also means you're not keeping your cordon out on the ground two hours longer than you need to, so there's less chance they'll get sniped at. I'd spent plenty of time in NI by this time, so he was preaching to the choir.

Steve asked how that applied to the UK course we were on.

"It doesn't, but the UK course is a piece of piss."

The lessons continue thick and fast. Some are subtle, others not so, almost painful.

One of the instructors messed with my head so badly during one assessment – the same guy from the Saturday training.

I was questioning him about the device that had been found when the mechanic had looked at the engine. I asked if the bonnet had been left propped up. He replied that someone had ripped the stay off and thrown it onto a nearby roof. I didn't know it at the time but he was testing my ability to adapt and overcome.

As I completed neutralising the device, he started asking me detailed questions about the task. He kept asking until I doubted myself and as soon as he saw he had me, he told me to pack my kit and walked off. It seemed to me that I'd failed. Did I mention I'm grumpy?

I'm convinced I've failed and I'm now furious. I get back to the bay and the little black cloud follows me. The remainder of the syndicate run out, not wanting to suffer my wrath. The instructor comes in to debrief me. He asks how I think it went and I launch into a tirade, justifying my actions and complaining about anything and everything. I finish and he says, "Best task I've seen all course. Solid pass."

He was proving to me that I knew the regulations: I knew them inside and out, I just needed to believe in myself.

Steve's low point came during one of his assessments where he was dealing with incendiary devices. He needed to take a fire extinguisher. Halfway up the stairs, he tripped and fell on the extinguisher. He wasn't a small bloke and the added weight of the bomb suit was too much for the safety pin. Steve disappeared in a cloud of dry powder, visually impressive but clumsy isn't a trait looked for in an Operator.

We both passed though.

I RETURNED TO MY UNIT IN HEREFORD.

I was probably a bit over keen, but I offered to take over duty early. It was an August bank holiday weekend and it would release my friend Yogi early (so-called because he was a 24 stone rugby player), and he started leave the next week.

I took over on a Saturday night. My driver, nicknamed Moonhead (he had a head shaped like a crescent moon), wasn't qualified, but he had at least changed my suit. Everyone else in the Unit used a size large. I was a medium but preferred to cram myself into a small – it made me more dexterous.

About 8pm that night, the pager went off. I've got my first job. This is great. A chance to put it all into practice.

Hang on a minute. What are you doing? says the voice in my head. I'm not ready. What have I got myself into? Calm down. Now I'm talking to myself. Not a good start. I have worked, studied and sweated to get here – am I going to be any good at it? Sometimes you should be careful what you wish for.

The call was to assist police in Barry, Wales. A man walking his dog had seen suspicious activity. (Yes, that really actually happens outside of your training scenarios.) The witness saw a man in a boiler suit and wool hat, "Up to no good under a wooden board by the canal," as he walked by on the other side.

He crossed over for the walk back, and the man had gone but he had a look under the board and discovered a black box, battery and wires.

This report brought out the police who in turn called us. We respond quickly, and because it's a possible IED, we task the Bleeps (ECM team – Electronic Counter Measures). A usual response is a single van with a No1 (the Operator) and a No2 the (driver/robot operator/equipment manager); adding the Bleeps brings a second van and two more sets of hands.

It's a quick trip and we arrive in the Police Incident Control Point (ICP) in good time. Currently, only two policemen are there and, while technically they are in charge, we deploy under what's called MACP (Military Aid to the Civil Power), they defer to us on arrival and I never met one who wanted to overrule me when it came to explosives. On arrival, you try and narrow down the likely perpetrators with the police and witnesses, looking for possible targets in the area. The location was directly behind the B&Q shop who had recently sacked an employee who'd told them 'they'd be sorry'. Next door was a meat processing plant which had been targeted by animal rights, and was recently the scene of a murder. Finally, over the other side of the canal was the local TA barracks.

"So, you're saying it's everybody," says Moonhead.

Well, failure to narrow down the group doesn't change that we still have a target to go for.

"Can you get the wheelbarrow (robot) off the van and get it loaded?"

Using the robot is standard procedure, and in cases where you're not sure what's going on down the road, an invaluable aid to dealing with trouble.

"I'm not trained," he replies. "I don't even know how to turn it on."

So I'm the team number two, as well.

I take the wheelbarrow, show Moonhead how to load it (he might as well get some on the job training while we're at it), and send it down to the target. The sloping bank of the canal path runs down to a chain link fence behind B&Q, and the path along the canal is protected by two concrete bollards, probably designed to stop people cycling. I don't know how good at stopping cycles they were, but they were perfect for stopping the wheelbarrow. It can't get there.

I can see the wooden board, about 6ft square, a piece of carpet on top, but that's it. What I can also see is about 100 gas cylinders on the other side of the chain link. No-one thought to mention them in the brief. If there is a bomb down there, those cylinders are likely to get excited.

I ask for the fire brigade to attend, I want some expert advice on gas cylinder fires. It's also decided for me by way of the concrete bollards that I'm not going to be beaten at this task by a robot. It won't reach.

Bugger!

We're now into manual territory, I'll have to go and have a look myself.

I ask Moonhead to get my suit off. I'll load the EOD weapon. This is a specially designed tool developed during the early years of Northern Ireland. It fires a charge of water, but is powerful enough to punch through steel. It has saved many Operators' lives over the years and it should be your first choice on most EOD tasks.

I'll take it down the road and get some more equipment ready. I plan to have a good look at the area with a torch and then move the board using a rope. This will allow us to send the robot back in and see what's there. Again, anything that can be done remotely is safer than in person. The suit's usually in four parts, but this one is in bits – nine, to be exact. While it had been collected from the stores, no-one had seen fit to assemble the Kevlar armour into it. I'm somewhat annoyed, but what can you do? We have a saying in the ATO teams, "It's always the Number Two's fault."

Sure, Moonhead hadn't been on the course yet and no-one has trained him. It's still his fault.

We thrash it together, and Moonhead zips me into it. It's uncomfortable as we've rushed the assembly, but it will have to do. It's taken a good three hours to get to this point in the task already, and I think I need to be making some progress. The team Bleep is Chris, the Royal Signals Electronics Countermeasure expert. He hands me my ECM, a jamming module designed to stop anyone triggering a radio controlled bomb while I'm down there, and Moonhead loads me up with my equipment.

This is it for me.

They warn you it's a lonely walk. I'm feeling it, it's the most alone I have ever felt in my life. My senses are heightened and I'm taking it all in. You're insulated in the suit, remote in some ways from the outside, but I scan the whole scene with my torch as I approach. We're taught in training to put a pulley at corners to stop the wires and ropes getting tangled; it means that you have less chance of being stood on top of a bomb untangling knots.

Turning the corner, I can now see the area firsthand: it looks normal, a muddy bank illuminated by the lights of the robot. I get to the target area and lie on my belly to get a look under the board. Nothing. I set up my rope, planning how I want the board to move. Lastly, I attach the rope to the board using a clamp. I collect my ECM and head back.

It all seems so easy.

Back in the ICP, we warn the police that we're taking action; we watch the scene with the robot and pull the rope. The board slides seamlessly out of the way. We have a look with the robot, and it's as the witness described: a black box, a battery and wires. I've got the feeling we're not making much progress here. I'm not getting anywhere with the robot; I'll go have another look. Suit on, I set off back down to the target. I drop my ECM just short of the area and having decided that the grass is safe, I step onto it and move towards the black box.

I reach the target.

It looks like a black plastic case with a car battery next to it. There is a lot of wire, some of which looks like it connects the battery to the case. It doesn't look like any bomb I've seen before, but that doesn't mean it isn't one; if it isn't live, then maybe it's intended to be some sort of hoax? It certainly doesn't fit anything from the IRA that we've been shown during the course. And I know because I'm an obsessive bomb disposal expert.

So, the barracks over the other side of the river is safe.

Well, either way I've been taught to shoot first and ask questions later. I should use my EOD weapon and shoot it. But shoot what? The case or the battery? There are reasons for choosing either, and reasons to avoid both.

I'm pondering this down at the target. (I've subsequently trained numerous operators that this is your worst idea, and I was certainly told this on my course which finished the day before.)

As I stand there letting the cogs slowly turn, a stone or piece of mud that was probably dislodged when I moved the board rolls down the slope of the canal bank. It hits a loop of the wire which falls over the car battery, shorting it out. Bright blue flashes and sparks erupt and at the same time, I shit myself (not actually). I immediately decide to shoot the battery. I stick my weapon against it and half-jog, half-walk back to the corner of the building near to the ICP. Still out of sight of the ICP, I pause to get my breath back. I don't want to arrive looking like I'm panicked: it's bad form to impart panic to the troops, and besides, it doesn't look cool. Breath back, I turn the corner, tell the police there will be a controlled explosion and ask Moonhead to fire the weapon. From the darkness comes a loud boom.

Well that's that, I think.

The wheelbarrow again sees nothing of note, so suit on and another trip down the road. I check the scene and carry out a mandatory safety action which I'm not going to explain because a) it's a safety action, and b) it's secret. I mention it because as I was thinking it through, I know any ATO worth his salt would pick me up for not doing it if I didn't mention it.

I then decide the case needs to be moved next. I collect the rope from the board and attach it to the case.

The task seems back on track.

We move the case, I X-ray it, and we look at the pictures back in the ICP. We're trying to work out what's in there. It looks like machinery, maybe a sewing machine. There are some suspicious packages looking not too dissimilar to the explosive charges I've seen in training, but they aren't connected to anything, so it's certainly no bomb. It's looking more and more like a hoax. I brief Moonhead on my thoughts.

Well the case needs to be opened. I can't hand anything over as evidence without being certain it's safe.

I'm off for a walk again.

It's an old model video recorder, and the packages of "explosives" are packs of desiccant – a granule designed to absorb water. It looks like it's come from a rubbish tip, all except the case, which looks new.

It makes no sense.

Maybe it's a hoax or maybe someone was just dumping it? I've not actually been trained what to do with a hoax; all my training tasks were real bombs. I figure this all just gets handed over to the police. They'll work it out.

Have I missed anything out from training? Yep, I have to check the area where the case came from. It seems pointless here, but we get paid the same no matter how many hours we work and it won't take two seconds. I walk over to have a look.

I scan the area with a torch; just a muddy bank, some coils of wire, bits of smashed car battery. Then I spot two wires poking out of the ground. They don't belong here, and without thinking, and against procedure I grab the wires and pull them. Why do I think I did that? Because I was a fucking idiot...

The wire comes out of the ground. It's been split-locked in – a thin cut has been made and the wire pushed in and the ground closed over it. As I pull it, my vision follows the wire erupting from the turf; the wire heads in a straight line up the bank. My gaze lifts and the line of the wire is pointing exactly towards the TA Barracks.

A number of thoughts go through my head all at the same time. I only know of one terrorist group that regularly split-locks their wires into the ground. The timer used in the Brighton Hotel bombing was based on a video timer ... oh shit!

This time I do run.

I stop at the corner though – I still need to look cool.

I get back to the ICP, brief Moonhead on the change in circumstances. I'm in denial that this is a real device. Not on my first job and not with the current threat level on the mainland. This still doesn't mean it can't be real. Procedure calls for me to tell the chain of command. I have to notify someone, but instead of the SAT on duty, it's the OC. It means I'd have to wake the guy who writes my report ... at two in the morning.

I'll phone Yogi first. It's his duty anyway. So I phone my friend and brief him up.

"This can't possibly be a long delay timer targeting the barracks can it?"

"No, mate, the IRA don't bomb Wales. If they did, we'd jump on the ferry and go and fill them in."

He gives me a few words of encouragement, tells me I don't have enough to call the OC yet, and sends me back down the road to the target.

It's all different now.

I'm back at hyper vigilant. I can see, hear, feel everything and conscious of my every movement. I plan every step with Moonhead, stick to my plan and make regular returns to using the Wheelbarrow. We attack the suspicious wire which turns away from the barracks and disappears into a tangle of branches at the base of a tree. My manual approach to identify what was on the end of the wire finds that the wire runs into ... a stick. It's a hoax.

What goes through some people's heads?

On X-ray, the stick has one last surprise. It's got a circuit board inside it. Madness or design? The task comes to an end.

No matter what the reasons for it, the scene is safe.

I take the Scene of Crimes Officer (SOCO) down and hand everything over. I tell him I have heard of animal rights placing spy cameras, so wonder if this might be one, although I have no data on what they used. If it's not, then it's a hoax, but I've no idea who thought this would make any sense in a bomb way.

To say I learnt a lot with that task would be an understatement.

My training on the course had been second to none, but this task showed me there was a long way to go before I could consider myself competent, let alone expert.

Within 48 hours the answers have come out.

It was a police camera, set by CID for surveillance of the murder scene. The procedure was for them to tell the senior police when such an operation was underway, but this briefing didn't reach the rank and file for security reasons. Conversely, the suspect bomb incident never made it to anyone in the loop.

This task was my first experience with the Press. A story made the local rag was entitled, 'Bungling Cops Blow Up Own Spy Camera', with the detail that, "...equipment believed to be worth thousands of pounds had been destroyed."

Never let the truth get in the way of a good story.

PART II - NORTHERN IRELAND

CHAPTER 3

GLENANNE, 1991

THE DETACHMENT in Armagh was one of ten teams based around NI, and one of three helicopter capable Dets.

Air-portable meant that as well as the teams, two Makralon-armoured transits, a pair of lightweight vehicles called Blackboards were used to transport the team and its equipment by helicopter into areas that were too unsafe to use roads. While the team had two modes of transport, it had only one compliment of equipment, which meant that once notification of a tasking by air came in, the team had to cross-load a large portion of the equipment, strap it up for flight, then attach the slings which suspend the equipment from the helicopter. This usually took around an hour and was always a battle between the space available and the weight that the helicopters could lift. As with all drills in the Army, it becomes second nature, but you always worried that you had forgotten some vital piece of equipment in the changeover.

The weekend of 31st May 1991, I was in the detachment. The ATO office had a large, backlit map of our patch, with chinagraph pencil markings showing out-of-bounds boxes, suspicious car sightings and previous tasks. The hall had display cases with examples of recent and noteworthy IEDs, and racks with our kit ready to jump into, if tasked. The whole det had that feeling of a place ready for action. You lived in the detachment so you were totally immersed in your world.

While I was filling in the monthly paperwork, the Province Incident Net radio (PIN) was on, so you had the constant live feed of anything interesting going on around the Province.

Even so, often the first notification of a task was, as it happened that night, with the boss coming in.

"Job on."

He spotted the men with balaclavas moving up the road towards his house. They had AK rifles in hand and as they approached his house he called to his wife.

"Get the baby and get down on the floor in the bedroom!"

She hurried to the cot and lifted their infant in her arms, hiding by the bed. He drew his personal protection weapon that all off-duty RUC carried, and crouched by the window waiting for them to make their move.

I have my own issues with this: I hate terrorists.

The terrorists moved forward past his house. The policeman saw them manoeuvring a large tipper truck into position, the type that the IRA had used for attacks before. He realised that they had not come for him, and his relief for himself then became concern for those in the barracks. He phoned his station to alert the Glenanne barracks that the IRA were going to mount a mortar attack against them.

The equipment transfer was going full speed. The boss came down to get amongst it and informed us that the only helicopter available was a Wessex. This meant that the kit needed to be broken into four loads rather than two – even more work to get done. We made it around to the helicopter landing site (HLS) in record time, under 15 minutes, and the boss jumped onto the first lift.

The helicopter hovered above me in the dark in a whirl of noise and heat in the downdraft. Buzz the Bleep is with me, and touches the earthing strop on the helicopter which discharges the static before I slam the shackle onto the hook. He's an essential part of the plan as we'd had a member of the team sent home with a broken arm after being thrown off a load by the static discharge.

The load is on and the helicopter disappears into the blackness.

The terrorists line up the truck on the field by the barracks. The building is protected on two sides by lines of huge concrete blocks. The third protective line was removed after a complaint from the local farmer, who owns the field, had them removed.

The time and power units started, the vehicle is put in gear and drives on its way downhill towards the barracks. There is a function tonight, well known to the terrorists: fifty families are inside and unaware of what approaches. The terrorist jumps from the cab and the truck is sent on its way carrying two and a half thousand pounds of homemade explosives, manufactured in safety in the Republic of Ireland. The vehicle rolls through the perimeter fence and down a slope crashing into the barracks' wall. Those inside, having just been alerted by the warning from the police, start their evacuation. A characteristic burst of celebratory gunfire comes from the terrorists as they make their escape leaving the timer in the device to complete their cowardly work.

The *crump* of the explosion reaches us in Armagh. I checked the map prior to leaving the Detachment and can tell by the sound at this distance that it's not a mortar attack. The barracks is over 20km away.

The radio message reaches us soon after that the rest of the equipment will not be needed, just some forensic kit and the cameras.

We leave the kit on the field and all deploy on the helicopter. Spirits have already sunk in the team and the scene that greets us is worse than I could have imagined. The explosion has destroyed one end of the barracks.

We circle once before landing and you can see debris spread across hundreds of metres of the surrounding fields. We land and I search the scene with the boss. The explosion has blown the walls completely off one end of the barracks. Three soldiers have been killed: Paul Blakey, 30; Robert Crozier, 46; and Sidney Hamilton, 44. They were killed as they were evacuating the building, making a last sweep to ensure that everyone was safe.

I will not describe what I saw, but the smell has never left me.

There was a giant crater which, for scale, the boss had me stand in. The heat of the explosion was still there. There were broken pipes spraying water and an alarm beeping from inside what remained of the barracks.

The explosion blew out windows in houses for hundreds of metres, damaged buildings, and threw the structure of the barracks and the remains of the truck into the fields. We found a reinforced steel joist 400m away, and chunks of reinforced concrete everywhere.

A giant piece of concrete struck the policeman's house who'd called in the attack. It smashed through the roof, through the ceiling and crushed the baby's cot. The child lived, safely held by his mother next to their bed.

The husband saved lives with his warning.

I have since seen claims by the IRA that they fired the device by radio control or by firing a rifle at the bomb to detonate it. These claims are terrorist propaganda. The device was on a simple timer – they had no desire to be near such a large explosion and had already made their escape.

Evidence from the scene, collected by the team wading through fields soaked in blood from a herd of cattle killed by the explosion, prove the device to be nothing more than a timer set to a short delay.

THE MORNING SUNRISE CRESTS
THE HILLS

The morning sunrise crests the hills,
And sullen faces front the soldiers I meet,
They talk about who I could be,
And a man that's lying at my feet.

The house that's wrecked by falling iron,
With a baby alive by the hand of fate,
This family's face shows their relief,
I'm stunned to silence, again too late.

A bomb so fierce it scarred the earth,
And smashed a barracks far and wide,
I search for clues amongst debris,
And walk in blood of those who died.

This taste is failure and burns my mouth,
This smell is death, I'll not forget,
I'm haunted sometimes in my dreams,
By an Irish soldier I never met.

CHAPTER 4

ANYWHERE EXCEPT HEREFORD

I'M POSTED BACK from Germany and at last I'm going to an EOD Unit. It's the only Operational one the Army has on the UK mainland doing IEDD (Bomb Disposal).

It's been a long time coming, and although I've enjoyed a lot of the other things, this is a test I've wanted to meet. It's the reason I withdrew from my course at Hereford, to come back to the trade and prove I can do this.

I get asked by the OC in Germany where I would like to be posted and I reply, "Anywhere except Hereford."

I haven't long come back from my course, and friends could still be in the area. But I'd prefer to work somewhere else and spare myself the reminders of what I've turned down. So it's obviously no surprise when my paperwork comes through posting me to ... Hereford.

The other soldier posted at the same time as me has been told he will pick up 'Acting Rank' on his return. This means he will be a Sergeant and eligible to do courses, to go on duty as an Operator in charge of a team. I have no such notice and am posted as a Cpl. My arrival at Hereford is met with the instructions from the OC that I'm on my No1s course. Inwardly, I'm leaping. The No1s course is only available to Sgts. Has he let something slip and I'm picking up my Sgt, too?

My job is to work for the SAT in a role called 'Duty Terrorist'. It's not the most technical of roles and is more to do with mass production twice a year of all the training devices needed for validation exercises.

The camp is in a disused ammunition depot near Moreton-On-Lugg. My empire is based in the old Dog Section building, so the whole place stinks of dog. The upside is that the Senior NCO team are all good guys; some are from my course and the rest know me from Kineton. So, despite my failure to promote, I'm still treated well by the Operators, and encouraged to go out on task and start learning how the job is done.

When I say 'good guys', what I really mean is mostly reprobates – and they're not rule followers. I see many examples of how to do this job, both good and bad while I'm here.

On taking the keys over to the Dog Section/Terrorist bay, I find it's a strip building made of rooms or small offices with a larger room for a workshop at one end. I find I can't actually get into the building – the door opens but the room is full of bin bags, clutter and junk. The debris from years of training all just thrown into the building at the completion of licensing.

It takes a week just to empty and stack it all neatly in the small offices. It's filthy and stinking but at the end I have scrubbed the workshop out, fixed all the shelving and organised the tools, plotted where I'm going to store and stack stuff, and most importantly I've sourced a radio/cd player.

The components for bombs are sourced from everywhere: people bring in their junk mail to fill mail sacks, recycling bins get emptied for plastic containers, scrap cars get raided for parts, and so on. Speakers are stripped from cars to use the magnets for undercar booby traps – there is an abundance of these around the store. The wire we use for demolition is good quality, and I soon have an extension of these speakers from the stereo ringing the store. It's also important that the store has a large window at one end which looks out onto open fields and farmland. The A49 cuts through the middle, but it isn't busy. The scene is peaceful, and I often find myself lost in the moment, staring out over the fields while working on a project.

By the end of the week, I have emptied at least fifty bin bags: each is filled with general rubbish, food scraps, broken and disrupted devices. Future exercises would be organised with specific bags for the device remnants as it's not a good plan to throw bombs into the general rubbish.

I've repaired any devices that were salvageable, and stripped and saved the components from everything else.

Order has been brought to chaos, and I'm pleased with my efforts. The cleaning purge has also uncovered a stash of handguns which were behind a cupboard. Investigation suggests that they might not be de-activated, and I hand them in to the SAT who arranges for them to be destroyed the next time one of the teams uses some explosives on task.

My course paperwork comes through, and it's for a No2's course. The OC clearly can't read paperwork. This is the same course I did four years ago. I'm a little disappointed as my career is still going nowhere. The injury is added to insult when the OC tells me that as I'll be away from his Unit for more than six months, he's not going to bother writing me a CR (yearly report). I need this if I'm to have any chance of getting promoted. The SAT tells me the best thing for me would be to fail the course, return to the Unit for the year and get my report working for him. I've no doubt that if I fail the course the OC will damn me come report time. I'm 10 miles up the road from where I did my selection course and I'm wondering why I ever decided to come back to this trade.

The No2's course is virtually the same as the previous course. I can remember most of it, so I'm coasting – the robot is newer but that's about it. There is another No2, Malky, on a repeat course, and he's coasting, too. Having already done tours, we know how to be a No2 – drive the robot, run the team and so on. It's not taxing either of us, and while I take to drinking with the instructors in the evening, he takes himself home to Scotland and decides not to bother coming back. I'm so far from trying to pass that I wake up one day near lunchtime, realising I'm late and have missed the morning transport. I take my time getting ready and walk the mile to the training centre.

It's a lesson on cleaning and maintaining the robot. The instructor tells me I'm fine to just join in because he and the other instructors have covered for me. It's appreciated, but I see this as an opportunity to get myself booted off the course so I go and make my apologies to the course Sergeant Major.

He gives me a bollocking, threatens to throw me off the course but he stops when I tell him that this would be for the best. He asks me why an otherwise keen and competent soldier would wish to fail in a subject that he has proven ability from previous tours. I explain about the OC and the promotions and reports thing. The Sergeant Major calls the OC a useless cunt, and in front of me makes a phone call to the SAT in NI. He arranges for my tour to be extended by a month, and in doing so earns me a yearly report from NI. I'm doubly relieved not to be getting a report from the OC. The Sergeant Major returns to bollocking mode, and tells me to get out there and help Operators pass their course. He finishes with a message for Malky, saying I'm to tell him no matter how many doctor's notes he sends saying he's too ill to travel, if all he does is turn up at the end of the course to pick up his kit, he's passed, too, and is going to NI no matter what skives he pulls.

Second time around and with the experiences of NI behind me, the requirements of the course seems to come sharply into focus. At times, I find myself at odds with the No1s I'm working for. A command wire running under a bridge seems to me to require cutting with the robot, but the No1 is dead against it. Constantly offering him advice grates on him, and the friction builds to a head when he snaps and shouts, "Can I be in charge of the team for a change?"

Suitably chastened, I get back in my box and decide to try harder to support him, but without making any suggestions. The No1 fails the task and the DS threatened to fail me for not "making the No1 cut the wire". I learn how to do this job both by seeing how it should be done, but also by seeing how not to do it.

All eight of the No2s, and all eight ECM Operators pass the course, plus three out of twelve No1s. The successful are moved into a classroom to have the list of Detachments read out that they will deploy to. Me and Malky know already that one of us will go to Belfast and the other will go to Bessbrook, NI. It's always that way and that's just how it's.

Malky is a big drinker and out of shape, so I figure Bessbrook and its lack of facilities will be all mine. The names are read out and we're both sent to Belfast. Neither of us can believe it: with two experienced No2s in the base, life is going to be easy. The Det even has its own bar.

The tour commences and I'm chuffed to find out I'm working for Dave L. He and I served on No2 tours alongside each other in '91 – me on my first, him on his second. Dave says he's made up to have me as his No2 and I'm complimented by his faith in me. Dave encourages me to look forwards and not dwell on the poor management I've had this year. He turns me loose as his second-in-command, and says he will step in if I get it wrong, but otherwise the team is my own. Having been let down by an Operator on my first tour, this amount of faith and empowerment was appreciated.

Even during a ceasefire tour, Belfast is a busy Det.

We get tasked just as I've had my handover from Maxi-candle (so called because he accidentally blew up his own robot with an explosive charge called Maxi-candle). I still remember him on his basic course where he insisted on wiring up his robot differently to the rest of the course with the statement, "You lot have your way of doing things, I have mine."

It's fast paced, and with the patch covering the city area, we're soon on the ground. On exiting the team vehicles, I tell the team to conduct an ICP search. Nothing happens and they shuffle uncomfortably with their eyes turning to the Bleep, John. He comes over and tells me, "We don't do ICP searches anymore."

"Why not?"

I can't believe what I'm hearing. An ICP search is a mandatory safety action: it ensures that the area where we've decided to park is free from explosive devices to a distance that, should a device explode, the team would all most likely survive. What possible reason is there for this isn't to be done? Have I missed something between training and arriving here?

"It's a ceasefire tour," he says.

He's suggesting that because the terrorists have said they won't attack us, we should stop protecting ourselves. This is bollocks.

"Get your fucking arses out and get that search done. NOW!"

They sullenly leave the ICP and search the area. The task is a car clearance and I'm pretty slick opening up the vehicle with the robot. Dave dons the EOD suit and goes forwards to clear the remainder of the vehicle manually. I can see during the task that the team all defer to John's authority and that he's not happy I have undermined him in some way. The task is soon over and we pack kit to head back into camp. Hardly anyone has spoken during the task.

We get back into camp and there is little post-task admin needed on the kit. I'm happy that I can do this myself without the team helping, so I direct them all into the bar for a post-task chat. I tell them that is going to be a common occurrence – a chance to speak openly about anything, in order to make sure the team is as professional as it can be. I decide this issue is best dealt with by way of ambush.

"Right guys and girl, I get the impression that you see me as the new guy when all of you have been out here nearly a month. You all know the ground and I don't, and I should really just come to heel and do things in line with the way the team currently runs, right?"

Amazingly, I see a few nodding heads, and just before I explain the facts of life to them, I do a quick check of their operational résumés. No-one has done EOD before, some have not been to NI before, but John was in Lisburn "when the bomb went off".

He's arrogant when he tells me, but even so, I ask, "What fucking bomb? There have been hundreds!"

He's referring to a double car bomb attack carried out by the IRA in 1996 which killed one soldier and injured 31 others inside camp. He makes out he was on the team, but when pressed, admits he was in an office on camp doing another role.

I recount my résumé, my tours in NI on EOD and include the range of tasks I have seen my operators deal with. It includes a task to an up-and-running car bomb outside the RUC station in Pomeroy where the IRA had planted a 200lb device on the cordon position on a timer to catch out the unwary. I tell them that only a fucking idiot takes the word of terrorists that they won't attack us, and that if they had any grasp of history they would know that there have been numerous ceasefires, all of which ended with an attempted attack, usually a spectacular, followed by a press release saying the ceasefire was over. I tell them that the ceasefire ends tomorrow, that the spectacular planned is to kill a fucking idiot EOD team in Ireland, and that the team getting killed wasn't going to be mine. I tell them all to go to bed – they're getting training in the morning.

I then return to the EOD garage, finish the post-task admin, check over my robot that I'd used on the car, and put all the torches, X-ray and electrical kit on charge. Ordinarily, I would also head to my bed, but instead I spend a couple of hours building 10 training devices. I set my alarm to be up at 5am to plant them ready for the training.

I hate early mornings but needs must.

The Detachment is contained in three long buildings: the first contains the Operations Room, a kitchen, the Operators rooms, and their rest room; the second is the team accommodation; and the third is a high prefab construction containing most of the team's vehicles and equipment.

They form three sides of a square around a car park that has the rest of the other vehicles, and I use this area for the training.

Collecting the ten devices that I made last night, I spread them around, putting them in areas I know should get searched but are often missed. A pipe bomb is thrown onto a roof and rolls down the tiles into the gutter sitting half exposed; a time bomb is wedged in between the two sides of a road sign, again above head height where things are often missed. A coffee jar grenade gets covered up with some nettles; I put an IRA mortar up into a tree so it's pointing at where the team is going to park. I camouflage the mortar tube up but not the wire running down the side of the tree to the timer at the base. I put a device in the drain, attach one to a nearby car, and where we have a large oil tank supplying the heating with a low wall surrounding, it I put a large device in a chemical drum. I put it over the wall and scoop up some of the leaf mulch which is rotting in the base. I put this on the drum so it looks like the drum has been in here as long as everything else but it's not hidden at all.

The last device gets hidden in a place and manner where I would expect it to beat all but the most determined searchers. I plan that when the team gets put to test they may find the other nine but not this one, the lesson being that there is always risk and our procedures would protect us from such a device even if we missed it. I'm all set.

I guess I planned to let the guys get up in their own time, have breakfast and stuff before we start training, but I look at my watch and it's nearly 6am. The Detachment has an intercom linked to all of the rooms and at the press of a button you can speak across the detachment – you can also use some switches to select individual rooms. Often, I slept so lightly out there, that just hearing the click on the speaker as someone selected your room was enough to wake me. With the exception of Dave's room, I selected the rest of the Bearcat rooms and pressed the button.

"Bearcat to Ops, Bearcat to Ops!"

And with my body armour, helmet and rifle, waited for the rest of the team to catch up.

They arrive within minutes and I tell them it's a training task. The news is met with mixed responses. Murf rolls his eyes, while Teresa my driver is more annoyed that I'm 'playing games'. Rene, the Infantry Escort, looks like he's enjoying this, but John flashes me daggers as he gets ready. Oh well, out to the car park.

I explain I want them to drive around camp and then return to the Det car park, forming an ICP. Pointing out onto the main road, I tell them that we have been called to a suspicious task in a staunch Republican estate. I brief them that they are to conduct a search every time we stop, until me or the Boss tells them it's cleared. They drive in and form the ICP. Rene finds the device in the drain and the one under the car. Murf and Teresa find a device each and that's it. I'm aghast. I expected them to find eight or nine, I'd have accepted seven at a push, but four?

I tell them that there are ten devices here, and some of them have the good grace to look ashamed. I remind them that they are the experienced ones, they've been here for a month and this is their own Detachment which they walk through every day. Out there (pointing towards the camp gate), is their back yard. If you can't find devices in your own compound, what fucking use are you to the team out there?

My rant over, I calm down and take them around the area to show them what they have missed. They are surprisingly on side about it all and take the lessons well. I show them the impossible device and explain that we stay within the protection of the ICP so that a small device missed will not kill or injure anyone when it explodes.

We get to the mortar, and while they struggle to see the tube in the tree and initially think that I've made this too hard to find, when they look at the rear of the tree and see the wire, they learn another lesson. I save the large device in the oil tank until last. It was in John's arc to search, and I know I'm being hard on him when I point out that the simplest bit of camouflage was enough to fool him. He has no excuse, in my eyes – he's the only other one in the team that has done the EOD course, the same as me and the Boss – and he's the one saying the team shouldn't do searches. I didn't set out to make this about dominance in the team, but as he sullenly starts putting the vehicles back, I guess my position in the team has been asserted. We'll fall out again before the tour is over.

WORKING FOR DAVE IS RELAXED AND PROFESSIONAL, AND WE'RE happily bonding as a team. Dave earns the nick name, 'The Submarine Commander', as he lived in his room and surfaced occasionally.

Physical Training became a regular event: our team would play football against the other team when both were about. One day, 'Bobcat' (the nickname for L11 whose No1 was a Captain), are tasked as we're about to play football. As they run off to change into their combats and body armour for deployment, Dave decided we would carry on without them, and we played two-aside on the full size football pitch. This mostly consisted of sprinting the length of the field to take a shot at goal before sprinting the length back to make a save. I always felt physical fitness was an essential part of being an EOD operator.

Even though this was technically a ceasefire tour, the jobs in Belfast continued steadily. Weapons finds, car clearances following robberies or sectarian attacks, and even the occasional pipe bomb broke the calm and gave lie to the headlines proclaiming peace.

The teams came together in differing ways: the other number two had an abundance of personality, and without question, his team liked him. Mine did as I told them because it looked like I knew what I was doing. Either way, Malky and I got on well and the whole Det had a happy feel about it despite the grim living conditions.

One night in the bar, Malky and I were all that remained of the team, and we spent the night putting the world to rights. Malky had had enough of the Army and had signed off, so he was going home early to complete his resettlement training before exit. Although I knew I wasn't following the spirit of the rules, I had my two cans of beer before midnight, and deciding that after midnight was a new day, I started on two more.

Malky, on the other hand, sups steadily as we chat. I can't handle my beer as well as Malky. Before we realise, it's nearly eight in the morning. Not wanting my team to see me in the bar all night, I head to my bed. It's the weekend and we're on second team, so my team has a lie in until 10am, by which time I have cat-napped, had a shave, and am up and about for work. Malky, on first team, goes to his side of the accommodation, shaves and changes his clothes and heads to the Ops rooms – he's first on radio stag today. He passes my Operator, Dave, in the hallway, who comments that Malky must be showing his age as he can smell a bit of last night's beer on his breath. Malky replies that there is a good reason for that as he only stopped drinking half an hour ago. Dave figures that it's the Captain's problem and leaves him to it after checking that I was fit for work.

The porta-cabin that was used for the bar was being exchanged. Generations of soldiers taking a wizz up the side in the evenings had rotted it through. The memorabilia and decoration all needed removing, and a shiny new metal porta-cabin was installed. Having limited building capability within the team, we luckily get assistance from the Royal Engineer Search Team (REST). We were short on building materials, so while my team and I started scavenging through the abandoned RUC social club at the bottom of camp, the covert drivers set off to see what they could find. They returned with a van full of bricks and timber. When I asked how they'd managed to get it all, they told me they'd approached a building site and told them that they were building a children's playground for the TV programme 'Challenge Aneka'.

The REST refused to take any money for building the bar, but did accept free drinks during the building phase while Malky and I helped (with both). This total exceeded £600 in three days, and usually saw them arrive in the morning to remove the top three layers of bricks that had been laid last night asking, "Which amateur did that? Looks like they were laid pissed!"

The bar was finished in time for Christmas, painted, carpeted, decorations up and with the TV, Sky and video/porn channel all wired in. I promised to put a plaque on the bar naming and thanking them, and although it took me until my next tour in Belfast to follow through, it wasn't long in coming.

There were even enough bricks left to make a faux fireplace. This was rounded off nicely with a painted flatsword – an EOD tool. It's an armoured steel plate which is propelled by use of high explosives and is used to split or cut, and has tumble beer barrels filled with home-made explosives. This particular weapon had been fired against a Protestant Paramilitary time bomb device on the Falls Road. The members of a local Sinn Fein office had refused to evacuate their premises: this can only have been in order to watch the activities of the Operator. They would then pass this information on to terrorists; so the Operator involved had ensured that after passing through the beer keg in the device, the steel plate continued on and embedded itself in the wall of the Sinn Fein office. They were less inclined to stand at the front window watching his actions after that, and at the end of the task, the flatsword was recovered to camp and suitably painted and autographed by the team.

Numerous occurrences can trace their origin back to the Felix Bar, including the Team War between the Op Faction and the REST guys. Malky had christened his infantry escort as 'Boy' due to the fact that at 19 years of age, he didn't look a day over 16. Boy's replacement looked even younger and earned the moniker 'Embryo'. He wasn't allowed to drink beer unless there was a teat made out of a forensic glove over the can. It was a sad day when Malky was returned to UK; his replacement was a driver by trade and a good lad, but some things are just not the same.

The team was tasked to a car on the Ballysillan playing fields, an area overlooked by the Ardoyne, and a staunch republican housing estate where the military and RUC went only if they absolutely had to.

The RUC who want to get off the ground quickly. They tell Dave the car has been opened and it has nothing in it, but he isn't happy with their briefing and sends the robot anyway. The other team has parked the car half on and half off the grass. While not definitive proof that there is a bomb in or around the vehicle, it's more risky than a car parked on tarmac, so Dave wants me to clear as much as I can of the vehicle and area before he goes down.

I've already cleared a blue Ford Mondeo for him this week in under 40 minutes (a decent effort with the robot), so Dave trusts me when I tell him I can't get around the side of the vehicle due to the grass being too boggy. I do get the boot open, though – we find it's stuffed with full carrier bags; or, as the RUC now say, "Empty except for those."

I have completed everything else. Dave tells me to go back around the grass side of the car as there is a suspicious black object near the front wheel and he wants me to examine and/or move it. I remind him that I'll get stuck, but he's happy as long as I get to the object. The wheelbarrow immediately gets into trouble, but by a combination of wobbling it from side to side, shifting all the weight around and a bit of luck, I get to the object. Pulling it out from under the car, it turns out to be innocuous – just one of the foot mats, perhaps placed by someone to try and move the car off the grass? The robot it now going nowhere, and it's Dave's turn.

He pulls on the suit and disappears off into the blackness of the park. Rene is dispatched to find somewhere safe to cover the Boss, and ends up lying on the grass in the rain as there is no cover to be had for him.

Dave returns. The car is empty, just another clearance of a joyrider vehicle – not that these haven't been used to lure the unwary to be attacked before. We start to clear the kit and I find the half ton of robot buried in the soil. We end up having to use one of the vehicles to tow it out of the ground, and it's caked in clay-like mud. We return to the garage around midnight, and I start stripping and cleaning the robot. I also have to call out the 'Barrow techs', REME technicians who repair and replace parts on the robot that regularly get damaged during tasks.

By the time they arrive, the robot is clean and stripped down ready for replacement parts. I make coffee for all of us while they work. Once fixed, I have to do a functions test to ensure that all parts of the robot are working correctly and all the weapons systems will work, before I can call it a night. I get to bed around 04:30 and get a lie in to 07:30 before I get the call to the Ops Room.

The SAT is there, and gives me the good news that I'm being moved – not from Belfast, just from my Operator. The new boss coming in is an ATO called Ian (Billy). The SAT tells me that this officer needs a strong No2, and as the other lad is on his first tour and I'm on my third, he wants me to look after him. Dave, while obviously upset to lose me from his team, is laughing at me in the office. I ask the SAT if it's acceptable that I keep the remainder of the team seeing as I've got them trained. Dave does not object, so really he just jumps to the other team and we get a Captain for a Boss. How different could things be really?

Billy is a likable Irishman. In truth, he was just plain funny – a joker and a good guy – he just didn't understand how EOD worked. His first action was to ask Dave if it was okay to keep his team on duty permanently for a while, rather than do the day-on/day-off shift. Dave agreed to do it more on a daily basis, but every time Dave's team was on duty and a task came in, Billy would excitedly offer to do the job for him. Dave would grin at me and say okay. I'm glad Dave was a friend, because every time he laughed at the lunacy and at me as we got tasked, I could have got right upset.

My team were not happy while the other team laid back and enjoyed their holiday. The new Boss crossed every line: he made a mess in the kitchen then complained about the mess at the Sunday meetings, threatening to take the facility off the team. He never bothered to load his pistol, nor lock his doors on the van while travelling through any area of the city. He even opened his door to wave and shout at someone he knew while we were stopped at traffic lights – never mind that the guy in his own car might want to maintain some form of anonymity, rather than be openly acknowledged by a British Army Officer. Tosser.

For a week, my team (as I came to see them) came to me to complain about varying aspects of the new regime. For my part, I had been trying to be diplomatic about it and I already knew the reason for his over enthusiasm: desperation to defuse just one IED, and being Irish, with a father in the RUC. Why wouldn't Billy want to earn his spurs? I understood his reasons, I just didn't agree with his methods. One Saturday morning, the job came in at 08:00. Technically, our team would just be coming off a day on duty and getting the weekend lie in until 10:00. The other team would already be up, shaved, dressed and with their kit first paraded, ready to be on duty at 8:00. Any sane person would have allowed the on-coming team to deploy, but instead the intercom clicks on with, "Bearcat to Ops, Bearcat to Ops".

Bleary eyed, unshaven, and decidedly unhappy, the team deploys to a suspect car in a housing estate. The car is believed to have been used by terrorists, and requires clearing by EOD before the police can take it away for examination. Terrorists have put radio controlled devices, time bombs and booby traps in cars like this so the job is a serious one.

The robot is deployed and is making steady progress opening up the car and examining it. John-the-Bleep is doing his thing looking for radio controlled bomb signals, and Rene and the two drivers are keeping an eye on the surrounding windows and alleyways. It's not a nice area to be spending too much time in. The robot breaks: a wire which moves part of the assembly has snapped, and my wheelbarrow is stuck in a crazy salute position making it difficult to work. I wedge part of the robot under the car and drive against it; this breaks the 1000lb actuator and folds it in half. The robot is less functional but is now the right shape to carry on, and I get the rest of the car open. It's Billy's turn now, and as he's dressed in the suit by the team with his equipment getting prepared for him, I discuss what has and hasn't been cleared by the robot. While this is happening, the PIN crackles into life and a tasking message to the Everton Centre comes in. Billy is straight on it and says, "Tell them that we will take that job".

I can't believe what I'm hearing. The Everton Centre is an adult learning centre: much of the training that goes on there is for the unemployed, and it must be the most heavily bombed building in Belfast, if you go by hoaxes. I don't think there has ever been a real device there, but if you want the day off from your course, just stick a box with wires in one of the doorways and shut the place down.

I know this will be a hoax and we're only half way through clearing a serious task, but this lunatic wants to drop everything and head over to a bag-of-bollocks?

I try telling Billy that the other team will take this job and he should carry on with the car. It's a far more serious task anyway, but Billy is having none of it. He has already decided there is no bomb in the car, so he wants to go to the Everton Centre. I resist him again and tell him he needs to concentrate on what he's doing, and after a few tit for tat comments, he grips my collar and shouts that he wants to be in charge of the team. Shades of the training course return to me, and I confess I got a bit of a sulk on. Billy told me to get on the radio, and I took the microphone and pretended to press the pre-sell to speak. After trying to raise the Ops Room on a dead mic, I throw it into the van and tell him it's not working. We hear Dave's team deploying on the radio and Billy returns to the task at hand. Something really needs to be done about this and I wonder if I'll get in trouble if I raise it with the SAT. Maybe Dave can help me with him?

Billy gets on with clearing the car, and a few manual approaches later, he tells me we're done and we can pack up. John and I are down at the car collecting the robot and our equipment when John indicates to me and says, "That bit of the car hasn't been done."

I look, and he's right. In fact there are other parts too, that clearly haven't been searched. John takes one side and I take the other, and we clear the vehicle front to back. We collect our equipment, return to camp and we head to the bar for our post-task debrief.

We're now thankfully off duty as Saturday is well underway, and the other team have returned from clearing their hoax at the Everton Centre. My team isn't happy, and I know it's coming; they're ready to mutiny over the Boss who has kept us on duty for ten days straight. I tell them that in other detachments, everywhere except Belfast, is on duty every day for their whole tour. While they accept that fact, they point out that there are two teams in Belfast and they feel they are being taken for mugs. I don't like that it's causing issues between the teams. Operators might be in charge of the team, but No2s (good ones) run it.

The bar is our sanctuary, and Dave makes a point of leaving by 9pm and taking the other Operator with him because he knows that the team needs its space. I know all of their complaints before they tell me; I've watched it all happening. I tell them to stay here and I'll go have a word with him. My cheeks are still burning from being shouted at on task, so I figure it's time we had it out.

He's in his office and sees me coming. He runs and hides on the far side of his desk and in his Irish brogue asks me what's up? Try as I might, I just can't be that angry with him. I make the point that his behaviour on task was unprofessional and dangerous – and he gives as good as he gets. He's in charge and I do have to do what I'm told. He tells me that I could not guarantee that the job at the Everton Centre was a hoax, and all he cares about is defusing his first IED so he can tell his father he's done it. I tell him he won't live to defuse one if he keeps clearing cars the way he did today. He rankles at this and stands up so he's taller than me (it's not hard), and tries to intimidate me with the fact he has passed the NI course and I'm just a No2.

I've had enough and I launch into him.

"I may be the No2 but I was out here as a No2 while you were just a fucking Private soldier in the RCT. If you're that good as an Operator, why did the SAT move me to look after you?"

He's shocked that I know his history, and the SAT's lack of faith in him seems to rock him. This calms things down a little. I tell him he's losing his team and that regardless of how bulletproof he thinks he is by ancestry, he's not going to survive a tour if his team are against him. I think I'm finally getting through to him. Despite it all, I really am a loyal No2, and I really do want him to have a successful tour and survive.

I leave him to stew on the facts of life and return to the bar. It's nearly lunchtime, so I open the fridge padlock and get myself a beer. I offer the team one, as well, and some grin as they receive theirs (as it's on my flick). Things have changed between me and John; maybe it's the lunchtime pint or maybe it was the work at the car that helped. Either way, Rene tells me later that John said to the team while I was in with the Boss that he still thinks I'm too rabid about my job, but he said he thinks I'm good for the team. Malky comes into the bar, and seeing us with the fridge open, joins us for a pint.

THERE IS A SPATE OF TIT-FOR-TAT KILLINGS – MOSTLY TAXI DRIVERS, poor sods, called to collect a fare but who are met by men with guns and forced to drive to their deaths. Their bodies are left in their cars until passers-by call the police who are then faced with the possibility that in going to see if there is a chance to save life, may themselves be killed. Once it's certain there is no hope and with the body still in place, the EOD are called to clear the vehicle and the body.

It's grim work for Billy, and it's having an effect on the team, some of whom are still in their teens. I make a point of looking after my team, then drown my issues with Malky. The killings are having an effect on the atmosphere outside camp, too. We're getting stoned and petrol bombed a lot more. It's rare we make it to a task without a bang sounding on the side of the vehicle from a chunk of concrete or brick. I'm surprised the Irish aren't world champions at cricket, such is their accuracy.

The sour atmosphere takes its toll on the team, and John and I nearly come to blows over a silly ammunition issue. He has some spare rounds, and I want them put in the armoury rather than stored in his locker. He tells me to fuck off as he leaves the bar, and after finishing my pint I go to his room and read him the riot act. Back in the bar Malky says he's glad I went to fix him because if I didn't, he was going to. John comes back to the bar and throws the ammunition onto the bar and storms off. I let sleeping dogs lie.

We get tasked to the B&Q DIY store on the Westlink. Someone has found a 'suspicious box with wires'. It has been stuck in a lawnmower grass bin and taken out to the car park. We arrive and unpack in the middle of the empty car park, overlooked by the Milltown cemetery, scene of the infamous Michael Stone attack on an IRA funeral in 1988. Rene gets the car park lights turned out so we don't stand out like a spare end, and I send the robot down. The grass bin comes into view in the monitors, and I recognise it.

"That's a PIRA cassette incendiary, Boss," I tell him.

"What's that then?"

I'm beyond stunned. How did this man pass his course? This is a basic device, something that even No2s know. It's a plastic box with an electronic timer and a low explosive charge, designed to function in the dead of night and burn out commercial premises.

I tell him that the rules allow him to approach the device wearing fireproof nomex, but he insists that as I have the robot down there, I should shoot it. I oblige and there isn't much left of it afterwards.

While the Boss is unfamiliar with common IRA weaponry, he's fully aware of the Standard Operating Procedures (SOPs), regarding Incendiaries. If he shoots it, it's classed as an IED on his report; if it functions while we're attempting to defuse it, it gets classed only as an incendiary. He's determined to earn his tie – and besides, he's forgotten his nomex. His actions on this job earn him the nickname from the other Operators in the Province of 'The tic-tac man' in homage to the 2006 Terrence Strong bomb disposal novel The Tick Tock Man.

WE GET A RUN OF TASKS AT THE EVERTON CENTRE. THE FIRST COUPLE don't seem noteworthy – two hoaxes in a day. The next day, when we have two more, it's enough to get my attention, and on the big illuminated map board in the Ops Room, we start to plot the task locations, the routes taken and the ICPs used. We even start noting the timings: how long to get there, how long on target, what time of day we start and finish. Something stinks, and the paranoia rises rapidly as we try to predict what's coming.

By the end of the week, we're in double figures, and with only three roads to choose from, we're now starting to use the same ICPs and routes. Everybody is twitchy and secretly hoping the other team is on call when the attack finally comes. Luckily, Billy has been stopped by Dave from putting us on duty each day, although that hasn't stopped him from volunteering to take each job as it comes in. We're off again, the same call to the same place. This is the twelfth this week.

We use the main gate because we used the rear gate last time, and head left onto Cliftonpark Road. A swarm of kids are already running across the waste ground in front of us and the stones are already in the air. We're second vehicle, so we catch most of it. The lights and sirens are now on as we try and move vehicles out of the way to get to the Crumlin Road. I have always marvelled at how good the drivers are; the Tactica is a huge beast, and I'd have clattered half a dozen cars by now.

We follow the lead vehicle onto the Crumlin, going through the red traffic lights. Visibility is shit out of the windows covered in metal mesh, and

I'm sure we rely on the locals seeing us coming to avoid crashes. A kid, maybe a teenager, is at the side of the road near a derelict building holding a door above his head. As the Boss's vehicle approaches, he runs across the path and hurls it at the Tactica. It hits the front grills and splinters into matchsticks. I watch, fascinated, as the splinters rain down. It hits parked cars and oncoming traffic, but despite being close, it all falls between our vehicles.

I see him coming before Teresa does. Another lad comes out of the derelict door with a beer keg over his head. He hurls it towards the windscreen but it drops in front of us and goes under the vehicle. Teresa makes to brake, but I shout at her to keep going and she presses the accelerator. The keg wedges under an armoured plate at the front of the vehicle and gets belted off the road. It flies between the two youths and smashes into the wall behind them. Teresa is somewhat upset by the event and the near outcome. I tell her they all count.

We get to the ICP. It's little more than a mile to get here, and we park on the junction of the Crumlin and Ardoyne roads. Ordinarily, we'd avoid junctions as it exposes you to attack from multiple directions, but we've been here so many times that avoiding the norm isn't preferable.

The team does its search. I've taken to standing on the Boss's shoulder to listen to the arrival brief by the incident commander so I have a good idea about the task. John comes to get me and pulls me away.

He gets me out of earshot of the Boss before he says he's found something. A street bin right on the junction has a grey Royal Mail sack stuffed into it. It's tucked down at the edges or folded around something, and John says he's pressed it, and it's hard. I look at it, and it's obviously not meant to be there. I look at John then look over to where the Boss is standing.

With a nod, a silent agreement is made. John goes back to the ICP and stands by the corner by one of the Tactica, keeping an eye on me. I take hold of one corner of the bag and slowly start tugging it free. There is a lot of loose bag to pull out, and in my mind I'm alone with just me and the bin. Eventually, I get an edge and I start pulling the bag open to see inside. It's a brick, a breezeblock to be exact. I let out a sigh and realise I must have stopped breathing. John comes over with a big grin, and we laugh at each other.

We get on with the task and shoot the hoax with the robot.

The constant hoaxes stop after that and revert to intermittent. No attack occurred and maybe there never was going to be. One can only hope that if there was one planned, our drills were the deciding factor in getting it postponed. John and I never fell out again during the tour.

The other parts of this tour I've already mentioned, and I'm sure there are bits and pieces to add. The last event of note was my leaving gift to Billy.

We'd been taken to the RUC Rugby club a couple of times so Billy could play while we watched, and then he'd have a few pints in the bar before we took him back to Girdwood. I didn't have an issue with this – after all, he had family and friends out here, so why shouldn't he enjoy his time? We got taken to more than our share of RUC discos because of him, too. However, Mothering Sunday approached, and his plan was to get the guys to collect packed lunches from the cookhouse on camp and have the team sit in the car park eating 'Horror Bags' as they were called, while he sat inside having Sunday lunch with his family.

It was a bridge too far, and I ignored his instructions to book the food. Instead, when we went to the Rugby Club, I went inside and got the manger to find us a table for the team in his fully booked restaurant. As the team sat down to eat, I told them that the food was all on the Boss. My take on it was that I was returning to the UK soon and the Boss would still have to work with the team; I'd prefer they thought he was half decent rather than such an ass. The team enjoys ordering and we've soon got a table full of roast dinners. The Boss comes over and asks how the food is and the team all thank him. He looks blankly and says, "For what?"

Way to ruin a perfectly good lie.

CHAPTER 5

AN OPERATOR IN NORTHERN IRELAND

IF MY FIRST EOD Operators course had been an excellent experience, then my second had some high expectations to live up to.

The first was very well instructed, both on and off duty. I had been made into a machine; it all made sense, and the more I did it the more it made sense – it was fun.

I had since passed all my EOD validations well enough for the assessors. These were twice yearly bomb disposal assessments that often raised more terror in Operators than real devices. I'm afraid I just enjoyed them as I considered these to be the only devices I would see in my time. For the sin of passing, I had been loaded onto the Special-To-Theatre (STT) course. This was to deploy you to Northern Ireland, and was a more intimidating hurdle than licensing; it was the reason I had stopped my transfer to Hereford and come back to the trade. I was hoping that the instruction on this course would be as good as the first, and that with luck, I would have a chance of passing. (Bearing in mind it's one of the most difficult in the Army, with a first time pass rate of 12%; second attendance goes up to 38%; and if you're unfortunate enough to fail a third course, you aren't invited back for a fourth.)

The course had twelve Operators split into four bays, with a further sixteen Bleeps, and No2s, split two to a bay. This meant that each bay would have three Operators, two No2s and two Bleeps, from which they would have to field a team of four to each task. Got that?

I was amongst friends, the sun was out, and we sat on park benches surrounded by numerous models of IRA mortars in a garden outside the canteen. We were catching up on the gossip of lives spent working in small isolated Units with the usual banter: "Can I have your boots after you're gone?" and "Don't worry, I'll look after your girlfriend while you're away." Some call it humour. I actually felt pretty good about being here. What could go wrong?

The course wasn't as I had hoped; the instruction, rather than enhancing my understanding caused confusion, and often when I asked for a more detailed explanation of issues, the answer was more about the fact the instructor understood it, so if I didn't, I wasn't ready. I tried to replicate work as I had seen my bosses undertake previously on tours in NI, so I knew that on real tasks this was the way it was done – but this wasn't what the Instructors wanted to see. I wasn't successful and left the course somewhat underwhelmed.

To be honest, I think my result had more to do with my failure to be intimidated by the lead instructor who spent all his time telling the course how special he was. Sour grapes? Maybe, but years later when I returned to the school as an instructor, any doubts about my suspicions were removed. The instructor team stood in their office at the start of the first course I taught, deciding amongst them who was going to pass and fail the course. This wasn't some speculative game where you guessed how many would pass – this was an allocation of endorsement or censure. Amongst the students, it was referred to as the face gauge: if your face didn't fit, you wouldn't pass. Was it was a policy I had fallen foul of? Either way, it was something I disagreed with and felt it reflected more on the instructor than the student. As a former instructor, I apologise on their behalf.

Returning to STT for my second course, confused and without the benefit of the instructors from my Joint Service course, I stumbled through the examinations. During my long examination, I decided to err on the side of safety, as aspects of the bomb didn't make sense to me, and where things don't make sense, I'm inclined to be safe. The instructor complained that what I was doing wasn't how I would operate in Ireland. I replied that the course had taught me not to do what was done in Ireland, and that I intended to take a safe course. He said that I should change my procedure. I did, and he subsequently failed me quoting that in changing my procedure, I had been inconsistent. What a spineless weasel.

So it all came down to my last task: if selection had been the hardest physical course I had undertaken so far in the military, the mental stress on

STT far exceeded anything I had experienced. I again erred on the side of safety and the Instructor, possibly due to some conscience over my previous course result, gave me the benefit of the doubt. It was a close run thing, but I'd passed.

———

"You're shit. I don't like you, and if I had my way you'd not be out here."

My new Senior Ammunition Technician (SAT) isn't a fan. I leave his office. Chris and Geordy are outside.

"What did he say?"

"He said I'm shit."

"He knows you then," laughed Chris.

We got down to the serious business of how all three of us could go on the piss together.

There was more good news: I wasn't getting a team. I was being allocated to Province Reserve, a limbo post where you stand in for real operators who were taking R&R leave. It looked like I wouldn't get a team for three months until the next influx of successful operators – and whoever was 'shit' on the next course would take my place, and I'd be promoted and given a team.

Instead, I'm given a scratch team for Marching Season, that lovely time of year where the inhabitants of Northern Ireland temporarily let go of their sanity. The official line is parades are part of the culture. Most parades are held ostensibly by Protestant bands, but republicans have their own version and they also assert their right to parade. Parading is often controversial as each group will go to great lengths to assert their right to march in an opposing group's streets and territories. At its height, places such as Drumcree became flash points and IED attacks were common.

The Province is much busier during this period for us, so even I was allowed a team, cobbled together from reserve kits and personnel – well, at least I'm working. The lads on the team are pretty keen, too, so I'm happy. My first job is classified – by me while we're driving towards it – as an obvious hoax. Someone has put a gas cylinder with a wire on it under a bridge over the M1 near Lurgan. It's done to cause disruption and to close the motorway. To damage the bridge, it would have to be 100 times the size.

We get driven onto the carriageway by the RUC, and it's weird to see the whole motorway empty. The mandatory safety question of whether or not the police have cordoned and evacuated the area is moot. The team pulls to a stop a short distance from the bridge and set up an Incident Control Point (ICP). With three lanes to choose from, I can set up a picture perfect arrangement, and we get the robot.

Perfect, that is, if the police had put me on the correct side of the motorway. The bomb is under the bridge a hundred metres away but on the other carriageway. I still think it's a hoax, but a choice between putting the EOD suit on and going to find out for sure, or sending the robot ... I'll take the robot.

We get all the ramps off the vans and manhandle half a ton of robot over the central reservation barrier. My No2 loads the Wheelbarrow weapons, and it's sent on its merry way. It's at this point that my SAT drives up to the back of my ICP. He comments that he's pleased to see the robot going up the road and not me in my trainers. Does he really think I'm that much of an idiot? Clearly.

My No2 is a good driver, and the robot quickly pulls the items under the bridge onto the road. I put on my bomb suit and make my approach.

Inside the helmet, you are insulated from the world: you are conscious of your breathing – every exhalation briefly fogs up your visor; the whir of the fan in the helmet blowing air over your face, and clearing each breath almost as quickly. You feel everything, each pull of the cables attached to your equipment, each step you are conscious of the ground beneath. I move my head constantly, examining the world around me in a continuous scan, looking for trouble. I know from looking at the robot's camera pictures that the device is almost certainly a hoax, but that doesn't mean there isn't something else down there to catch me out. I'm hyper alert, fuel-injected on adrenaline. I can feel every pulse – but as mad as it sounds, I'm calm. I would not want to be anywhere else.

Every bit of the hoax gets examined; the area gets searched and I pack the evidence into forensic bags for the police. Only then do I step down a gear. We pack up and head back to camp, for 'tea and medals,' as they say.

My first stand-in was Armagh which was an officer's detachment. The captain there was due his two week R&R break in the middle of his tour, and I would cover the gap. As bad as things were, I wasn't unhappy. It was my birthday, and in a twisted bit of fate, I would have my 30th there as an Operator, just as I'd had my 20th birthday there as a No2. In a place where people would judge you based on whether or not you'd done any famous bombs, I'm curiously pleased that I'd grown beyond that, thanks to a former boss called Dave, who'd taught me not to go looking for trouble.

The two weeks' stand-in goes without serious incident. Except I do mount a planned operation, about half a million pounds of tax payers' money, to go and investigate a stolen car next to a derelict building – both cause for suspicion. I make my plans, and we ready to deploy. The night before I'm told by the RUC that the car has gone.

"How has it gone?" I ask, seeing as they claimed it was on a single road with police parked both north and south of the barn. How has it gone? All I get is a non-committal "don't know" from them. But it does not reassure me that they are keeping a safe eye on the area. I'm all for cancelling the operation, but the police still want me to go and clear the derelict building. I don't have an issue with this, but it would make sense that if this particular building was causing the RUC an issue.

Well, maybe it would be best if it 'fell over'; being a pile of rubble would change the problem in our favour. I plan to blow it up.

The SAT overrules me and says no. Bugger.

As the duty spare part, I'm top of the list for a thing called Exercise Galloway Cream. We deploy an operational EOD team to Scotland where we test our equipment and procedures against the latest IRA tactics. The part of the IRA is carried out by scientists from the Northern Ireland Forensic Science Laboratory (NIFSiL). The working parts of the bombs are live, and they are employed in a worst-case scenario. We're not testing if our drills work most of the time; we're testing if our drills are up to the task all of the time. Fortunately for me, the explosives aren't included. It's a controlled test, but as the SAT is coming to observe, the pressure is still there. The week starts off perfectly. I have an idiot of a Bleep and he's driving like a lunatic. I tell him repeatedly to slow down. Eventually, I tell him if he doesn't slow down, I will come over his side of the truck and fill him in. He slams the brakes and my other truck slams into the back of us. My Bleep is lucky to not get a punch for his troubles. Muppet.

The science geeks test all aspects of our work. They weigh me before I walk down the road; time how long I spend in the suit, and pin a tape recorder to me to record everything that is said. I walk over to the SAT and ask what he thinks of the cute blonde female scientist. He's halfway through his description when he sees the microphone, and unlike the state of the van, he at least finds that funny.

The week goes well. It's hard work but I'm up for it. The SAT, in close proximity, says he sees a different side to me. My last task requires repeated manual approaches up a long hill into the woods. Every time I go forwards, my Bleep follows in the truck and stops a distance away. This is to cover me with his ECM (Electronic Counter Measures), the jammers that will protect me from radio controlled devices. He gets into the back to monitor his equipment. This is to keep me safe while at the target. Up at the sharp end, I go a bit off the reservation. I don't follow convention but do it my own way. The SAT says he likes it; he says that if he didn't see that coming, then the enemy certainly won't.

It's been a better week than expected, bearing in mind the rubbish way it started. I make my way back towards the ICP, stopping at the ECM van to open the back door to tell the Bleep I'm done. He's lying back on his chair asleep. It's baking hot in there; a generator is needed to produce enough energy to do the signal jamming. That's a different story altogether – so much energy pulsing out in close proximity can't be good for you, and I think that too many former Bleeps go on to develop cancer in later life.

He's wearing his body armour (although he should have had his helmet on, too). I'm not denying that it's an unpleasant job – but even so, while I'm on target, he's supposed to be keeping me safe.

Instead, he's snoring. I close the door head back to the ICP, hand my kit to my No2 and collect one of our metal detectors. It's a long black metal pole sheathed in rubber. I return to the ECM truck, open the rear door and prod him awake. Then he gets the verbal beating he deserves, for crashing the truck, plus interest.

The team returns to NI on the ferry, and my next stand-in is at Belfast Det. I have a soft spot for Belfast.

CHAPTER 6

MISCHIEF

THERE'S a lot of mischief happening while on tour, probably more in Belfast than any of the other Detachments.

'Mischief', of course, is a broad term, and probably depends which side of it you're on.

Historically, one of my bosses got me to booby trap the RUC office while I was on tour as a Cpl. Fortunately, the RUC knew the Captain was to blame and bricked up the window of his bedroom by way of retaliation. Mind you, there was a three foot thick concrete blast wall outside the window, so the view wasn't all that special to start with.

That particular tour wasn't rife with bombs, but the killings went on just the same. We spent that Christmas pulling a number of dead taxi drivers out of their vehicles. The risk was that they had been killed to bring the RUC into an ambush or bomb.

During the quieter moments on my last tour as a No2, I'd cultivated my own entertainment within the confines of our wriggly tin fence. Shut inside Girdwood camp in Belfast, a 200m square with no escape, the EOD bar had been a magnet for many within the camp. Initially, I'd been asked by our Royal Marine contingent how to make IEDs (Improvised Explosive Devices). The Royal Marines were given to our Unit to bolster our personal protection, and I wasn't keen on alienating them, so offering them some IED knowledge was beneficial. Aware that handing out this information to all who expressed an interest was a sure road to disaster, I'd racked my brains for something 'safe' I could pass on – some small mischief that couldn't possibly be transformed into anything dangerous, placating their thirst for knowledge while at the same time protecting them from themselves.

Eventually, I decided on a booby trap across a door: a switch would cause a forensic glove filled with water to burst and soak who ever came through. It was simple mischief – what could possibly go wrong?

So I passed this idea onto the Marines who sat quietly through the demonstration. As I finished, one of the lads said, "Can we fill that with petrol?"

After some beer related trouble with some of the bigger Units in camp, we placed the bar off limits to everyone who wasn't EOD, and they had to find other places to find their beer.

The trouble had mainly been caused by other Units exceeding their nightly two-can allowance and getting into fights, damaging the camp bar and so on.

Although we had to ban the wider military from the Felix bar, we did still allow some of the smaller, more secretive Units in, on the proviso they kept it to themselves. Squaddies are well known for ruining someone else's fun if they're not invited themselves.

It was amongst these Units over a quiet 'two can' night in the bar, I set the rivalries of two groups against each other. I'd cultivated my own private little war.

Op Faction was a cadre manning a number of overt Observation Posts (Ops). They were a mix of highly professional Cpls and Ptes who manned the sangars 24 hours a day, and entered their observations into a giant computer network. This was designed to identify patterns, and spot the absence of the normal. For example, when 'Murphy', who usually drops the kids off to school every day before spending his dole cheque in the local bars, goes missing for a week, then a car bomb turns up, these things were spotted by the Op Faction teams. Confined to camp, the same as us, they were very resourceful, highly organised with a clear command structure. They had a rigid timetable for their day to day work, so fitted their mischief in around these. They used the younger soldiers as dickers, a term coined from the IRA who would use children and the lower echelons of the IRA as lookouts or 'dickers', planned their attacks well, favoured attacking with IEDs and were, on the whole, successful. Op Faction were a fair model for PIRA (Provisional Irish Republican Army).

On the other hand, the Royal Engineers Specialist Search Team, an equally professional bunch of soldiers, were a responsive Unit the same as us at EOD. With things being so quiet, they had even less work than ourselves, and would regularly only require one of the team be sober enough to drive their van. As a covert unit, they had regular access to the civilian world and they had decided their preferred weapon of choice would be super-soaker water pistols.

With the two sides set, I stayed in the middle and watched their activity progress, occasionally supplying either side with bomb-making materials if they had a particular need. Pride wouldn't let the Engineers ask for much help, but the Faction lads had no such qualms, and I refused many of their requests due to the speed their capability advanced: I felt it would be unfair.

The first attack wasn't long in coming. One of the lads waited on the roof of an accommodation block with binoculars and a radio. He was there to observe the Engineers returning to their room. The bar kicked out, the door to their room opened, the lights went on, movement was observed, and the lights went off. The young private gave his radio calls, and the Faction team went into action. With cover men sealing off the corridor so no noise would disturb the Engineers, one of the Cpls made his way up to the room and secured a bunch of party poppers against the door frame. A long length of army green string was run to the corner and handed to the trigger man. The runner then knocked on the door loudly and pegged it out of sight. Groggy from a 'two can' night in the bar, one of the RE lads opened the door and looked down the corridor as the string was pulled. He received a full dose of foot powder, which turned his head pasty white as the Faction team folded its operation back to their rooms.

One-nil to the Faction.

Within hours, one of the Faction Cpls had been ambushed on his way to take over the towers. Two men in civilian clothes wearing balaclavas, a lunatic move on a camp full of soldiers, (probably relying on the comedy value of their brightly coloured water pistols), had doused the Cpl with red food dye. With the choice of being late on stag or just living with it, he'd gone on to the OP somewhat more pink than camouflaged.

One-all.

And so it continued.

The other lads progressed quickly from rudimentary devices to some pretty complex affairs. The ringleader, Mogsy, was one of the Cpls famous for being involved in a rooftop protest in a barracks in Londonderry that made the front page of the Sun newspaper. He had a brick built enclosure in the where he would test-fire his charges, returning after the explosion to see the lads picking bits of plastic out of themselves as the smoke dissipated. I gently prodded him regarding his choice of weapons, keen that he didn't run out of talent and cause an injury – well, one that mattered – his lads and the plastic aside.

The attacks continued.

The Engineers christened themselves the SHITs (Silent Hours Initiation Team), so regularly were they caught by the devices laid for them at night.

A lot of the lower level soldiers fell victim to a soaking, but the Cpls frustrated the efforts to get them. One night of note, bolstered by the usual shed full of 'two cans', the SHITs had staked out the route back to the Faction rooms. They were after Mogsy, the head honcho. He'd been on a long shift, dishevelled from the hours cramped in a box stinking of generations of sweat, tired from constant alertness. He was walking to his room thinking of his bed. Balacava'd up, and with soakers filled with the contents of glow sticks and their own piss, they heard his feet on the stairs. Closer he came, almost to the top; knowing they'd have a height advantage attacking him just before the top, they rounded the corner and opened fire on the man in combats before him. The Captain (Operations Officer) was mightily surprised, shocked enough that the two lads made good their escape.

So, it all had to come to a head, didn't it? Eventually, they all realised I was playing both sides, sitting in the middle laughing. One night in the EOD bar, the penny dropped and they decided it was appropriate to threaten me. Mogsy had continued to ignore my warnings about his device-building – he had proved decidedly difficult to target and was probably my best friend amongst the bunch.

I decided his time had come.

Suffering the ravages of the FUCK campaign, I decided to deploy my devices by proxy. So I supplied the Engineers. The short version was a claymore under the desk where the telephone sat, and an omni-directional charge hung from the light cable in the Cpls room – thanks to some nifty lock-picking using the wire from a bulldog clip.

06:00 after a long night shift, he returned to his room. Using a small remote robot called Buckeye (the only use EOD ever got out of the crock of shit), I watched as he entered. The Engineers called the room phone.

"Hello, Cpl Mogsy speaking..."

"Got you!"

BOOM!

The bang was felt down the corridor.

Mogsy said afterwards that he didn't hear it, but just felt his bollocks super-heated as the fairy liquid and bog paper spanked out into his groin. In the time it took to ready the second charge, Mogsy managed to say into the phone,

"You Bast..."

BOOM!

The second charge sprayed mixture around the entire room. There was a silhouette of a man answering the phone on one wall.

The Engineers, excited by their success, ran down the corridor to inspect their handiwork. They were met by an enraged Mogsy who chased them out of the block.

That night in the bar, a shell shocked Mogsy could only say,

"But I've only been using party poppers!"

Both sides had a good laugh at the change in tactics. The talk turned to the previous threats to take me on – a suggestion that I'd been kind in my attack on Mogsy and that seriously no one would want to piss me off, and that anyone coming near me would feel my wrath. It was decided that the demonstration of capability was sufficient that all parties decided that they'd continue with their war, but no-one wanted to come within a mile of me.

Job done.

Having left all that childishness behind me as I became an Operator, my parting gift was to create a giant catapult made from 40m of bungee rope strung between the oil tank and a telegraph pole, with a pocket made from black tape.

John returned from his leave to take over his team. The Royal Marines – who I'm guessing enjoyed my tenure as a mad break from the norm – insisted on giving me a leaving do. The end of the night saw the Royal Marines in their traditional bar attire – that is bollock naked – catapulting a collection of items the locals had previously thrown at us, back over the fence at them.

Once the kid's tricycle and bits of assorted car parts had gone, we got to the bucket of golf balls we'd collected.

Golf balls, which historically the other team (rioters) had put nails through, were the gift that kept on giving. If they miss and land, they bounce and keep going, when you set up your vehicles for a task you angle them in towards each other in an arrow shape pointing towards the target so that any fragmentation from an explosion is shielded against. But from the rear aspect, this shape is a perfect funnel, so as the golf balls rained into the funnel in our ICP, the effect isn't anything short of magical – they just kept on bouncing, seeming to get faster.

Initially you flinch as they come in, but after the first one hits you and you realise it does nothing through your body armour, it ceases to cause worry, and you are then running about collecting them for yourselves. We had to fight the RUC for them as obviously some of them were avid golfers.

Now we dipped them in a pint pot filled with cyalume liquid, (the remainder having been splashed around the bar and over the naked party), and firing them into Cliftonville. Taff, naked and glowing in the dark, was on top of the bar shouting corrections, "LEFT 50", while looking through the team binoculars, which were liberated from Rommel's era.

The golf balls went well: Taff said they made it over the 50m of the waste ground outside, and three streets into the Cliftonville estate. When complaints were made to the RUC, the police refused to believe we were responsible. We even had the duty officer walk past the detachment, look in at the glowing naked mess, and decide it was none of his concern.

Brilliant send off. Thank you, Royals.

Lastly, and to clarify, while I was a late starter in this mischief, by the time I was an Operator, I saw it for what it was. There is no better way to grow into bomb disposal than by knowing how to make devices yourself. You often start by copying what the enemy does and in doing so arm yourself with essential knowledge of their capabilities. You get used to searching your own room for booby traps and in doing so better prepare yourself for real life risks of the job.

GIRDWOOD IS AN OUTPOST. A 200M SQUARE BOX ON THE EDGE OF A republican shithole called the Cliftonville, a grotty estate full of blind alleys, waste and hatred. Our sentries watch the perimeter from the Sangars (the armoured box-like sentry posts surrounding camp). Black curtains and blackout walls reduce the chances of anyone inside being silhouetted and shot at, but they are still regularly strafed with stray shots, and more often lasers tracing over the interior, probably from the wee scrotes outside – but who'd take the risk if it wasn't a sniper?

The camp has been mortared, proxy bombed, and grenaded, the routes in and out targeted by the IRA. Historically, it was a busy place to work. The year I went coincided with the supremely brilliant decision to legalise fireworks in Northern Ireland.

The camp is small: it's ringed by 20ft high wriggly tin (steel fencing), and the fireworks thrown over the fence rattled around camp. It was, in the words of one of my team who'd watched too many movies, "Just like Vi-et-f'cking-'Nam."

John, the lad I'm taking over from, is a quiet and unassuming family man (the opposite of me), but a highly professional lad (just like me). Fate had decided that his first trip out there would be as an Operator, as he'd missed the opportunity to tour on a team as a Number 2. We'd flown over together, and whereas the start of his tour was to be punctuated with OPTAG (a two week training package designed to bring the unfamiliar up to speed with the particular threats of Northern Ireland), I was exempt because my last tour had ended so recently.

Unfortunately, there was an arrival brief required before we could deploy – the law to be laid down by the boss and some intelligence updates. This was scheduled to occur after the OPTAG, so despite being exempt, I would not be used for anything. Personally, I would have preferred to repeat the training and stay with my friends. Instead, I had to find something to keep myself busy while left kicking my heels around HQ. John told me his only fear was getting lost around Belfast. The historical images of the two signallers, Cpls Howes and Woods, being dragged from their cars in 1988, before being beaten and executed by a baying Nationalist mob were familiar to all our generation of soldiers. So I understood his concern.

I promised him while he was on OPTAG, I would create him a 'rubics map' – a device I once saw years previously. It's a map that folded both side to side, and up and down, but was in the form of a book. It enabled you to map read through Belfast without taking your finger off the map sheet (because four map sheets is the size of a small blanket), in a product no bigger than a magazine. I had made one while I toured in Belfast as a No2, but they were not designed to last much longer than a year. I told John I'd have one made for him by the time he got back.

The map was a full 24-hour project, so it took up a good three days of my two weeks: the rest of the time I spent reading the local intelligence for the Province and trying to spruce up the dive of a room I'd been allocated – in the Mess that they were closing down.

I handed the map over to John while we were on our arrival briefs, and wished him luck in Belfast. I was somewhat forlorn as I watched them all depart to take over their teams.

A month later, I'm taking over from John. He loves the map, but also shows me that the Det has maintained the original I made. It's yellow, with layers of sellotape used to fix the splits, holes, and tears that are unavoidable. He tells me it has taken on an almost mystical reputation, as it's now believed to have been responsible for numerous exciting jobs occurring. John decided to keep his own version, preferring to make his own luck.

His first task had been an explosion in the Ballymurphy area of Belfast. Initial reports suggested an attack by Protestant Paramilitaries, but John's investigation identified that a father and son pairing had been trying to recover explosives from an IRA weapon to re-use. Their chosen method of recovery was to use an angle grinder to cut the metal casing which was filled with explosives. Those out there with training will tell you that explosives, especially detonators, aren't big fans of heat, so the action of cutting steel with a rotary tool would not be the first choice. Both survived but one left a vital part of his anatomy in the shed where the explosion occurred. No-one I know who does our job weeps for what we refer to as 'Own goals'. No tears were shed for these two geniuses.

Our handover was seamless. John, ever the professional, swiftly detailed all I needed to know, including the phone call which has arrived that night from an individual claiming to represent RIRA (Real IRA). A call from this phone informed the receptionist at the Belfast Telegraph that there is a bomb in the city. Usefully, there was no location, no timings, just a vague threat which might or might not be genuine.

John is on Second Team today – the teams take it in turns to go first in Belfast – but it means if anything does come in tonight, the Captain on the other team will respond to it. I'll have a little longer to settle in before we take over First Team tomorrow morning. John's only request was that I respect his room which I'd be using, and keep it clean. Jelly-head, (another less well regarded Operator), had done a stand-in at Belfast for the other Operator, and they had returned from R&R to find the underside of the bed strewn with used pot noodle containers, crisp packets and cigarette ends. I assure him it will be fine.

John departs in a covert car to get his flight home to his wife and family.

I settle into the bar/rest room and flick through the TV channels. In the days before digital, we're lucky to have satellite TV. Throughout my time in the Province, there was always a constant battle to find the funds just to pay for this 'treat'. With 10 detachments and 11 locations, to pay commercial rates for this would have cost the Unit thousands, so the usual routine was for one of the soldiers to make up a name and buy a private package. The costs were shared between the four team members. Belfast was different: they had a bar, and with more than 20 soldiers allowed to drink two cans of beer a night, (yeah, right), they made a tidy profit. So they had free Sky TV, and paid for posh washing powder, rather than the garbage the Army supplied. As well as Sky TV, there were the usual four TV channels, and a final channel that was linked to the video player in the Ops room. As I flicked through my choices, the video channel came on – porn.

I asked one of the lads in the bar if this was usual at six-thirty in the evening, and he replied that it was usual 24 hours a day. The detachment had a vast library of films on video, essential for keeping a captive team entertained when there was literally nowhere to go. But the library also had an equally vast quantity of porn. One of the team had his own video in his room, and was determined to copy it all to take with him at the end of his tour. He'd have had to freight it home, because he'd never be able to carry it all.

As ever with TV, when you're bored, there wasn't anything to watch.

I decided to study the history on the walls of the bar. A loose term – you'll see what I mean.

Belfast, being a city full of cars, the Unit got to blow up more vehicles than anywhere else in the Province. The Det parties were enhanced by this fact, and there was a story that historically a team had blown up a spirits lorry on the Monday, a beer truck on the Wednesday, and a van full of frozen chickens on the Thursday. Having been 'donated' goods from each incident, they had a party to end all parties at the weekend. The rule was that if you blew up a vehicle, you had to steal a number plate from it. The trophy would then be mounted with the team's name on it, and placed on the wall. These were periodically removed to make room for new ones, but there were regularly in excess of 200 number plates.

While this may seem somewhat irregular, the number plates, along with the makes of vehicle listed on them, and the locations from which they were blown up, helped an Operator to get a feel for what vehicles got stolen the most (Vauxhall Cavaliers), and where suspect cars tended to turn up (outside RUC and Security Forces bases). The souvenirs also indicated if there was a live terrorist device found in the vehicle, so you could also gauge the likelihood of devices, spot patterns and trends, or just marvel at how many people had their cars destroyed in Belfast. No wonder that insurance companies exclude NI even today.

I'm 20 minutes into my wanderings around the bar when the intercom – which is linked to every room in the detachment – clicks to life.

"Bobcat to Ops, Bobcat to Ops..."

Each team with its links to Felix the cat had a cat-linked code name – John's was Bearcat. I didn't have a team, so had no name, but while I was at Belfast, Bearcat was all mine.

The duty bod in the office would either hear of an incident building up or occurring on the PIN radio, or would get a phone call from any of the agencies that could request us through the Brigade. The call would go out over the intercom and the team would (probably) spring into action. The Boss would make his way to the Ops Room to start getting details, along with whichever member of my team was due to man the radio. The three team drivers would rush to the garage and pack any kit that was being charged back onto the vehicles, open the doors, and get the vans out.

The close protection team from our supporting Infantry Unit would man their positions in the Snatch Landrover which followed behind the two Tactica EOD vehicles. The Bleep would open the weapons safe, and start dishing out the team weapons – each member either had a rifle or a pistol depending on their job; the No2 would ensure the Wheelbarrows were on the vans, and generally run around making sure all the other business was completed.

Tonight's task for the Captain and his team was a gas cylinder with a wire running from it in Belfast Docks. Accompanied by the earlier threat of an attack, the Captain had a sense of excitement about him as the team got their body armour and weapons together. I wished them luck and good hunting as they drove from the Detachment. The big engines of the Tactica vehicles sending the heavy vehicles up the hill and out of camp, the blue lights and sirens go on as they leave. Everything about Belfast is a little different to the intermittent quiet deployments regular in rural locations.

The sirens of the Captain's team had only just faded into the night when the intercom clicked on again.

"Bearcat to Ops, Bearcat to Ops."

The pace of life here really is different to the cuds, a term for the Irish countryside or rural locations. My team mobilise, and I go to the Ops room. A member of the RUC is on the phone and says casually,

"I wonder if you'll come and have a wee look at a van that's in town."

Nothing in his tone suggests urgency, but I take the details of the location as I pull on body armour. My No2 reaches round me and fastens on a belt that holds my pistol as I write down the information and route. By the time I have done this – and had a look at the giant map of Belfast on the Ops room wall to make sure I know where we're going and what areas might be dodgy or of relevance to the task – my team is ready. I'm impressed how slick they are, and as I leave, a member of the support staff has come in to man the Ops room, so both teams will have a link back to the Detachment while they are working in the city.

I flick the switches to the lights and sirens as we leave our garages. The driver looks at me and I miss whatever hidden signal was there, but we head up the hill and out of camp all the same. The guard, on hearing our sirens, is at the gate and swings it open. As we get there, we exit onto Cliftonpark Road, only to be met by a hail of stones and missiles from a group of kids opposite the main gate. More are running across the patch of waste ground, and already forming groups at junctions in either direction. We turn right and face down the pack by the garage on Cliftonville Street.

With the exception of the odd individual (the Bleep in Scotland), I was hugely impressed with the skill of all of my drivers. This lad was no exception. At speed, he manoeuvred this giant truck down narrow streets and between parked cars. In days gone by, the military might have got away with bumping the occasional vehicle out of the way, but these days that would mean at best some paperwork, and at worst, having to stop to deal with the incident at the expense of whatever task we had been sent to. My driver was more than up to the job, even finding time to lean over the console to shout over the noise of the engines,

"We usually put the sirens on as we leave camp, Boss, not the garage. You find if you do it at the garage, the scrotes on the waste ground know we're coming and form up at the gate to brick us."

He spares me my embarrassment by going back to the task of getting us there without crashing.

Five minutes later, we've arrived. It's another adjustment to the rural locations where you could take up to an hour or more to get to your patch. Belfast is a much faster transit which gives you less time to gather your thoughts before you arrive at task.

We form our ICP on a junction near the city centre. The white transit van is obvious. It's parked on double yellow lines a short distance away. It has patches of rust showing on the paint, and it doesn't appear to be much loved. As we arrive, the phone in the call box next to our location starts to ring. It's probably just some local dickheads, but the message that they know we have arrived isn't lost on me. The RUC Officer is fairly relaxed when he starts briefing me, indicating that they just want the van cleared for removal – no rush. They would not have called me if it was just illegally parked, but the van is ringer plated, meaning the number plate on the vehicle is fake. When they ran it through their computers, it came back to a yellow van, based in Liverpool.

Taff, my No2 gets one of the Wheelbarrow robots off the van. One is primed with explosives to rapidly disrupt car bombs; the other, the one we're going to use, has smaller weapons, and a manipulator designed to do less damage and carefully open vehicles. Although illegally parked in the city centre where there have been numerous car bombs placed in history, ringer plated and parked near a government building on the only street in the city centre which isn't covered by CCTV... things aren't looking good for this van's future. It's also parked next to a derelict building which represents its own unique threat, but for the moment it's all about the van.

It's at this point that the policeman also mentions the van had only been there for 40 minutes when they found it. Why didn't he say so sooner? At this point, the possibility that there could be a timer ticking down inside the van has just gone up a notch. The RUC are still trying to get the area cordoned and fully evacuated. Currently, they have moved people only 80 meters away – we need at least twice that.

This could be an up and running car bomb and normally would result in a speedy robot delivery of an explosive charge designed to neutralise it instantly – but having the effect of blowing the vehicle to pieces and probably damaging surrounding buildings and windows. Because the vehicle isn't confirmed to contain a device and the warning earlier that evening didn't specifically identify the van as containing a bomb, I can't carry out my planned action by the rule book. In the grey area where we're supposed to excel, I'm hamstrung by the worry that if I blow the van up and I'm wrong, I will deliver my boss the proof that I am, in fact, shit, like he says.

As the conflict between my head and my gut continues, the worry that if I'm wrong my boss will second guess me, the seconds tick by.

There are two common timers out here: one-hour and two-hour timers are prevalent in IRA mechanisms. In my head, I'm adding up the lost time: 40 minutes prior to the device being found, five minutes to task us, five minutes to load up and leave camp, five minutes to drive here, and the time it has taken to set up and start questioning...

We're getting dangerously close to the first hour.

I tell Taff to put the first Wheelbarrow to the side and prepare the other version – the one with the explosive charge on. There's a sudden leap in his pulse rate – N2s love blowing up cars and claiming another number plate – and he asks if I'm sure. The answer is no, but I tell him to get it ready all the same, and return to the RUC to chase up the cordon and evacuation. It has moved out in all areas except one. Around a bend and up the street there is an old folks' home. They are struggling to clear this because many of the occupants are immobile or infirm. I tell him to get everyone he can behind cover as every second increases the pressure on me to take action, but more importantly, it brings the chance of a massive explosion a second closer. I brief him on the risk, and we discuss the evacuation. He assures me that the home will be evacuated soon.

Still not protected by the rule book, I search for any reason to tip my decision one way or the other. I go through every relevant question I can, re-examining the scene from as many view points as I can manage. I ask if the officer could see anything through the van's windows. I know, realistically, if he had, he would already have told me in his brief, but I ask it anyway. He responds that he saw nothing as he never got closer than 25 meters to the van. This in itself is unusual: many of the RUC in Belfast are famously on-side, and could usually be expected to be all over a suspect vehicle, certainly close enough to look inside.

I get the feeling this officer knows something. Maybe it's just his gut instinct, but he's the local knowledge. I consider myself brand new on this patch, despite my previous deployments to Girdwood.

We're well over the hour now. I also can't take their estimation of 40 minutes as fact. My decision is made. I tell Taff to load and send the explosives. The team has been patiently waiting but secretly hoping we'd use the explosive choice. Who doesn't love blowing up cars?

I'm back and forwards between the team and the Incident Commander, checking on the old folks' home. The robot is now at the van, poised and ready to deliver its neutralising charge. For what seems like the hundredth time, I ask the officer if the home is empty. It's not. I explain that the longer we wait the higher the chance of a possible device exploding. I also explain the risks of my explosives causing an enemy device to function. I ask if he believes the old folks will be moved in the next 30 minutes: again he shakes his head. If I fire my weapons and a device explodes, if it kills or injures anyone, even if it damages property, then I'm liable – and at 8om, the old folks' home is also inside my weapons' mandatory safety distance. If I let any device function because the cordon isn't complete, technically I'm in the clear. The 1996 Manchester lorry bomb functioned (exploded) causing millions of pounds worth of damage because of exactly this circumstance.

He says he will trust my judgement. I reply that those around the corner are old – they live in Belfast, they will have seen this all before. I ask him to get them away from the windows. I tell him to warn his cordon police that there will be two controlled explosions in one minute: a small one, followed by a larger one. While his message is being relayed over his radio, my team is relaying this over ours.

A mile away, dealing with the task at Belfast docks (which is looking more and more like a hoax), the Captain said later he heard the radio call and believed he'd gone to a hoax while the real device had turned up for me to get tasked to. He stopped his task so his team could all turn towards my location. Even my friend Yogi, who was running the team in East Belfast, heard the call, and knowing that a warning for two controlled explosions could mean only one thing, had run outside onto his heli-pad to see if he could see or hear it from where he was. Back in my ICP, we're almost there. I get the nod from the RUC and I tell Taff to fire the first charge. A small crack later and we're inside the van. He drives the charge into position. I look to the RUC once more for that final check, close my eyes, and tap Taff on the shoulder.

I immediately open them again and find a suitable position to observe the target from. It's my job to watch where that shit flies when it explodes, to see if any damage is caused and to find any significant evidence to analyse later.

Taff pulls the firing lever, whereupon an electronic signal flies from our radio transmitter to the receiver in the Wheelbarrow robot. That signal travels through the control panel, through the modular weapon mounting system firing box to the detonator leads, where the electrical charge causes the bridge-wire in the detonator to ignite the match-head composition. The message then changes from an electrical one to a chemical one: the flash causes the detonators in the charge to function, and in turn detonates the explosives in the disruption charges. Five pounds of high explosive surrounded by a top secret formula expands ten thousand times over, as it changes from a solid to gas, and rips through the interior of the van.

A miniscule percentage of the gas escapes through the hole we made, but the remainder reaches the glass of the windows, pausing only briefly at these trivial obstructions. The explosive force tears through the metal skin of the vehicle. Doors are ripped from their mounts, and the van disintegrates into parts which are thrown around the streets. The boom rattles down the walled streets towards us, channelled by the buildings. It's crowd-pleasing for the team who remain suitably British about the whole affair and let only a muted, "Yeah, sorted."

No high fives or whooping to be seen. The flash and the bang were observed at the docks, but it didn't make it all the way to East Belfast.

The old folks' home is okay, and the cordon all check in. So far, so good. It's always a 50/50 chance if your robot will survive firing this type of charge. Ours is driving, but has no cameras, so Taff brings it back to the ICP and I ask him to send the second to examine the remains of the van. There is debris strewn all over: parts of the van, rags and general smashed up rubbish – nothing that looks like it might be part of a bomb. I have a momentary sinking feeling, but I can't dwell on it. I still have to check the van in person – plus there is always the possibility the van was a bluff to get me near to the derelict building.

We clear the derelict building, and I get into my EOD suit to approach the van. In person, the scene is no different: it's all personal effects. Clothes, camping kit, a couple of smashed up guitars, piles of paperwork, and some family photos blow around the scene. It appears I have blown up somebody's life's belongings stored in a van. I spot Taff cheekily unscrewing the rear number plate with a big grin on his face. The RUC, who have seen it all before, are decidedly nonplussed. Even when I notice that the registration of the van is different to the one they gave me, and it transpires that the false number plate was in fact down to him not getting close enough to read the registration properly, their opinion is still that the owner deserved it for double parking.

A search of the area reveals my actions have only broken a single window in the surrounding buildings. Even if I'm in trouble for this, I figure I can cover a single window. It's not that I realistically expect to be held responsible, but because of my standing with the SAT, who knows? I bring the team down. They collect the debris and pile it all on top of the van chassis. They pose for a celebratory photo. I don't feel like joining in – I still have to tell the SAT what I've done.

CHAPTER 7

PROGRESSING ONWARDS

I DID STAND-INS at Antrim and Londonderry for Operators taking their well-earned R&R to go back and see their families. The three month point came, and the next batch of successful Operators, Bleeps and No2s arrive in theatre to go through the same arrivals brief and training. Historically, if you've been on Prov-Reserve, this is the halfway point through your tour, and in order that you get to run an EOD team and be reported on as regards your capabilities. This is where your time in purgatory ends and some other poor sod gets the shitty end of the stick.

I approach the SAT and ask if I'm to take over a team of my own at last. "No."

I'm obviously a bit peeved. I've done my time and not messed up; I think I should be allowed my chance to run a team. So I ask him why I'm not getting one. He replies that I'm so good at training No2s and training up the teams when I do stand-ins that he's keeping me on the reserves. He says it like it's a compliment but on reflection, training the teams and ensuring standards was his job. It's not the first time I've been damned by my efforts, and I know too many out there who were promoted away from their fuck ups.

My next stand-in is Omagh, where my best friend, Chris, is running things. The SAT had banned him, me and Geordy from being in the same room together, such was our ability to make mischief out of nothing. The SAT has briefed the driver that I'm not allowed to go drinking with Chris at the handover. We covert car our way from Lisburn down to Omagh; we're armed with pistols, as are most out here as a minimum, and I stay observant as we drive. Alert as you need to be, Ireland is a beautiful country and I fell in love with it on my first tour. I watch the scenery passing, and think I could easily live here (apart from the ever present danger of some 'fecker' in a balaclava shooting you dead on your doorstep or lobbing a grenade through your house window to explode amongst your family), but I love the place and the people (most of them) and still do.

I don't give much thought to why I do my job, but if I did, I'd say I tried to make that place a little safer for everyone, and to this day I still wish for them to find peace. I don't like people who resort to terrorism, and while I have some understanding of them and the choices they feel they have to make, I save all my pity for their victims – they had no choice at all.

I assume that the constant rain out here is what makes the whole place so beautifully green, but the closer we get to Omagh, the more boggy the land is looking.

We pull into Lisanelly Barracks and the guard approaches. I have ensured that my pistol is totally concealed under my leg before we arrive, and ready my ID card under the level of the window so he will have to approach the car and look down into the car to see it. This keeps my ID concealed from any passer-by and reduces the compromise to the vehicle.

We drive down to the Det which is next to the camp heli-pad – handy for rushing to task, less so for undisturbed sleep. I'm pleased to see Chris; he looks a little tired but otherwise is on fine form. My driver starts getting agitated, and repeats to me the SAT's instructions. He gets told to go watch TV in the Det as we're off to the bar to do our handover.

We check over the team equipment, stores and accommodation first, then we head to the Sgts Mess.

The camp is currently being run by the 'Woofers' (The Worcestershire and Sherwood Foresters). Chris says they are a good enough bunch but with things being so quiet, they are a little under employed so are constantly looking to get work for their troops. He says they have requested that when we go out on task we take the QRF (Quick Reaction Force) with us as it gets them out of camp. More troops on the ground – I certainly don't mind, and I say that I'll carry on the agreement.

One of the perks/penalties of being an ATO and on duty 24 hours a day was the accepted norm of not wearing full uniform. The boots and trousers were regulation, but since my time in NI, it was always accepted that you'd wear a T-shirt and sweatshirt. Obviously, when you go on task, you put your body armour and jacket over this so you look the same as everyone else, but in barracks this relaxed form of dress was accepted in deference to the fact you were never off duty. Even the rank and file soldiers who got caned for duty, patrols, guard stags and so on, would get down-time where they could dress in civilian clothes. Some were allowed into town. The ATO teams only came off duty to go home.

It's in this relaxed dress that we attend the Mess. We get a bottle of Budweiser each. It's like water, so technically we're not drinking so can have a few more than two; besides, it's not in cans anyway. And we talk more informally about the team, the patch, the intelligence and any other business, like how things are at home.

We take ourselves away from the crowd at the bar to do this because you never know who is listening and we might be giving unfavourable reference to someone or talking about information that is best kept within EOD circles, so it's only polite. As we're discussing this, we're approached by a lad from the bar. He's older than us, Irish by his accent and asks if we mind if he joins us? We both say he's welcome.

"I've watched you guys go up and down the road for over 25 years. I just wanted to share a drink with you and tell you I'm grateful for your efforts. You don't have to be here, and the fact you are and you do what you do ... well, words just aren't enough to say thank you."

While he's talking, I'm working backwards on the date. He's been in the UDR since 1975, transferred to the Royal Irish Regiment when they were merged and rebranded, and has been on the streets out here for 25 years. I'm in awe of him. I don't need to select a period of IED history to cover what he's seen; as far as I'm concerned he has seen it all. Both Chris and I tried to buy him a drink but he was having none of it. We shared our drink with him, he thanked us and left to go back to the bar. Chris and I looked at each other and told ourselves we were frauds – neither of us felt like we had done anything to achieve his accolade.

I never got the soldier's name, and while I doubt I will be able to find him and thank him again, he's welcome to get in touch and I'll return his gesture. I did repay his kindness to one of his brother Irish soldiers on my last tour in Ireland.

Chris and I finished our handover by discussing the usual: work politics, the SAT and our wives. Mine had been told before I deployed that we were divorcing when I got back, (not H, obviously; the ex-wife).

The internet – not long invented back then – is obviously now wholly available these days. The Bleeps (Royal Signals) with their background in communications technology are upgraded from their usual role of making sure the satellite TV is working and plumbed into all the rooms, to Satellite TV and Internet guru.

Strangely, all the Dets where I did stand-ins had the internet plumbed into the Bleeps' room. Back then, the ability to get an outside line from the military phone network was a restricted feature.

Army wide, such was the proclivity of the average soldier to kick the arse right out of such features and phone relatives in Australia or better yet the sex lines advertised in the local newspaper, that you needed a letter from God to get authorisation. However, the ATO detachment had an operational requirement for this feature, so even if such abuse took place, the only option would be to bill the individual responsible – if he could be found. You don't want to be seen as abusing the privilege though; ATO teams do get to live far more comfortably than most soldiers, so generally the team restricted themselves to phoning the local Sinn Fein councillor at three in the morning to complain about the helicopter noise. Sinn Fein, ever on the lookout for a means to complain about the Army, would be right up for taking details, anything to try and steal some more compensation for the IRA coffers, very interested, until they asked the address and would get told the barracks name and accommodation block next to the heli-pad. No sense of humour some people.

Anyway, the internet was here and the Bleeps were taking full advantage. The lad in Londonderry (whom I won't name) had been internet dating and had lined up 14 dates with 14 different girls back on the mainland for his two week R&R. The whole scheme was military in its planning, with mapping and routes to get him all around the country in time to complete his marathon.

So, suitably amused with our internet toy, we take it in turns and as a group to explore this new world – and it bites into the boredom of hours locked in a Detachment waiting for a call to come in.

It's a quiet stand-in: one of the guys is playing an online shoot-em-up game with the footage played onto a wall through the detachment lecture kit, the rest are watching a movie, and I'm just out of the gym when the phone rings.

The Brigade Ops Officer informs me that a member of the public walking his dog has found a possible weapon buried in a pipe in the woods out near Dromore. I'm told that troops have been dispatched, confirmed it looks like a weapons find, and that he will keep the troops in place and secure the area overnight until we deploy in the morning. The pace of activity in rural detachments is often much easier than the Belfast teams – perhaps that was why I didn't automatically accept the timings offered.

I'm also acutely aware that our job isn't anything without the troops that protect us, unsung heroes who put up with lousy conditions, huge amounts of boredom, abuse from the locals and being the most at risk of an attack from the IRA on a daily basis. If I can make their lives a little easier by my actions I'm all for it.

"If there is a helicopter available, sir, I'll deploy now and we can save the lads a night on the ground."

The Ops Officer is surprised and tells me he thought that ATOs didn't deploy at night. I reply that I'm aware that some don't, but this one is happy to. I know I have to seek permission from the SAT as my deployment will be light scales rather than the full EOD team, and as such he'll want to vet my plan first. I tell the Ops Officer I'll call him back while he finds out if there is a flight available.

I've grown apprehensive of phoning the SAT for anything, but it has to be done. He quizzes me on the scenario, confirming in his own mind I've got the threat level correct and that he's happy with my plan. I'm still, by his terms the lowest ranking Operator he has in theatre, qualifying as I did as a Sergeant. Operators are between Sgt and Captain out here, so I'm not surprised he wants to keep a close eye on me, but he agrees to my assessment and I call the Brigade back about getting a flight. Andy, my No2, sorts us out some bergen kits and we head off.

The flight is brief, with the usual noise and heat, and the pilot lands skillfully in a field near the task location. An infantry sergeant and a PSNI officer are waiting for us, and they take us along the Tyrone road to the forest track.

The assessed risk is low: it has to be for me to commit to this short cut in procedure, so I get them to show me right up to the find. The statement that everything had been pulled out of the pipe isn't quite as described, nor is the scene as I expected. Inside my head, I'm kicking myself that I didn't get more detail from the Ops Officer, but in truth, it's always like Chinese whispers between ground truth and tasking message.

I drop a couple of cyalume (light sticks) to mark the location and the route through the woods, (there's nothing worse than getting geographically challenged), and I set to work.

Although I'm a little more concerned by the task, I stick to my threat assessment and it's only a couple of hours before I have all the evidence cleared and handed over to a SOCO (Scenes Of Crimes Officer), a sawn off shotgun and a pistol, some ammunition, clothing and the pipe they were hidden in, all go into her van. I arrange to travel back on the same helicopter that collects the troops. Alone in my own little world, lost in the noise, darkness and warmth of the fuselage, I quietly pick my performance to pieces, self-critically analysing all the things I should have done better.

———————

CHRIS RETURNS AND THE COVERT DRIVER DROPS HIM OFF, LOOKS expectantly for me to load my kit into the car for return to Lisburn and my spell in purgatory. But I have no intention of leaving my mate. The driver starts to bleat about instructions and the SAT. I ask him if the SAT gave him instructions for my return or only for my drop off. He admits it was only the drop off, and he has no instructions about the return trip but he knows the SAT doesn't want me left down here. I know that there are at least three routine covert car journeys from the detachments back to the HQ each week, so as I have no stand-ins planned for the coming week, I'll have a couple of nights down here with my friend. The driver is clearly not convinced, but faced with senior rank he has no choice but to return to Lisburn and report in to the SAT.

Chris and I open a beer and start the post-leave debrief, then talk about more personal things. To survive in this world you need to be focussed – the more 'other' shit that is spinning around in your head, the less you have to play with. An Operator does not need to be walking down to a bomb with his head in the wrong place.

The best thing I can do for Chris is to listen and help him blot it out. The beer is finished and Chris pulls out a bottle of brandy. I'm no fan of spirits, and it's for that reason only that I lighten up on the drink. We're laughing about who will take the job if one comes in. I tell him that it's his team, so it'll be his responsibility. He replies that he has not taken the kit back over from me, so I'll have to go. Both of us have had more than we should. Chris says he's going outside for a smoke and I'm left with the team. A few minutes later, Chris comes back in laughing. He has fallen over in the dark outside his detachment (over a training mortar that he knew was there), and gashed his leg open. He has a deep, four inch gash down his shin. He laughs as he throws the pager at me and says,

"You're still on duty, buddy. I'm off to the medical centre."

I decide it prudent to have a pint of water and a coffee. Chris comes back with six stitches and we put him to bed.

The next morning the SAT is on the phone asking why I'm still on duty, and Chris tells him he arrived late last night so we're doing the kit handover today. Chris has been told to stay off his leg for three days, and I stay with the team until mid-week. We decide not to tell the SAT, and will worry about what to tell him if a task comes in and I have to deploy.

Thankfully it doesn't happen and I quietly return to Lisburn.

I'm still the only occupant of the abandoned RMP's Sergeants Mess, the remainder being moved into the new-build, but because I'm not a permanent member of the Unit and am only there for a few days between stand-ins, I don't warrant moving to the new building. I don't mind.

The new-builds, as nice as they are with their en-suite bathrooms and sterile interiors, I find soulless. The RMP building has big oak staircases, and the walls are covered with military plaques and pictures donated by the soldiers of the past; even the peeling paint and smell add to the effect for me. I'm sad to see my neighbour move out – the Intelligence Corps Sergeant was a cute girl and I'd secretly hoped to crack onto her if we were ever here together for any length of time. I also find a damn Mess bill in my room when I get back. It's trivia, but it annoys me. I'm living in the annex, I'm paying my bill at my Unit back in the UK, and none of the other Operators receive a bill because they live in their own detachment. A bit of courtesy usually sees the respective Messes waive any bill for the ATO. I go and find the RSM to beg my forgiveness and provide my mess bills to the accountant.

With no team, I have no daily routine. I'd offer to go and assist the Lisburn team, but beyond joining them for a coffee, I'd only be treading on their toes. They will have their own routine. I use the gym on camp, run around the perimeter and generally try and avoid being seen by the HQ until my next stand-ins at Antrim and Londonderry.

CHAPTER 8

ANTRIM

ANTRIM, a new-build location, is a nice clean detachment, and I'm taking over from a good lad called Jack. We do a tour of camp, hand over the kit and he's ready to go; his parting shot is to ask that I take the team to the NAAFI bingo on Thursday nights. It's clearly an age thing as Jack looks ancient (50), but I agree all the same.

Jack has really got things squared away – the detachment is on what is called half rations. It means we get lunch provided at the camp cookhouse and feed ourselves in the evenings. It's like the best of all worlds and has come about from the needs of being on-call and often away from camp during meal times if tasks come in. It means we're not tied to timings, which is a nice bit of freedom and makes the place seem all the more homely. There is a female on the team called Michelle. She's a good No2, but more importantly, having a woman in a small team always removes some of the rough edges found in an all-male environment. There is a lot less swearing and lads lifting their legs to fart while watching TV.

The detachment is positively pleasant.

Antrim is also a cushy detachment for another reason. Geographically, in the top right hand corner of the country, the majority of the tasking action is as a result of Protestant activity which reduces the threat towards ourselves somewhat and also reduces most of the devices from high or home-made explosives to pipe bombs and similar lower risk attacks. No less nasty for the recipients, but from a bomb disposal aspect, safer than taking on the IRA's efforts.

I do some training with the team to see where the strengths and weaknesses lie. Michelle does a good job of destroying a training car for me, and everything is ticking along nicely. Our first tasking comes in. The police have responded to reports of an abandoned device near a signpost on a road near Magherafelt. We load up the team kit and deploy. On the way, we get information that the report has been called in by a group naming themselves the 'South Derry Volunteers'.

The route takes us through a republican shithole called Toomebridge – a hate-filled little village with historically one of the most heavily attacked police stations in the Province. I remember from my first tour out here when the place being attacked with RPGs (rocket propelled grenades).

We pass through in our green armoured trucks, with me willing us invisible. The tasking is a little unusual as Derry is the Republican term for Londonderry. Protestants use the title Londonderry, so the group is linked suspiciously to the Republican/IRA side.

On arrival, the police brief me that they have seen the device and it's indeed at the base of the road sign further up, concealed within a cigarette packet. Really?

So this is it, my first device on Irish soil ... and it's tiny.

I follow the rules (mostly), and after a good look at it and the surrounding area with the wheelbarrow, an X-ray, and the EOD suit, I'm down there taking it to pieces so it can be handed over for forensics. It's a piece of square steel shut with welded ends. A hole in one end has a small fuse sticking out, and once opened, the inside is filled with a low explosive propellant that I recognise from my youth. Not all training was received from army sources.

All of the evidence is carefully packed and photographed; my thoughts on the task are passed to SOCO and RUC, and we head back. I try to be as meticulous as I can with my report, add my photography and email it to the SAT for its inevitable red penning and returning for correction. There is no feeling of elation, just a quiet satisfaction that I don't think I made any huge errors in procedure – my photography and reports are usually pretty close to acceptable, and I know I recovered everything I could for evidence. A nice steady task.

WE GET TASKED LATE AT NIGHT TO AN ATTACK IN A HOUSE AT THE edge of the city. A back window has been smashed, and a pipe bomb made out of a piece of metal bed frame has exploded in the hallway. The damage is minimal, and I'm quickly finished collecting evidence and handing over the scene to the RUC and SOCO. Just another intimidation attack, common out here. It's nasty how quickly you can adjust to NI, where it's accepted that a bomb attack at night is 'normal'.

We then get another abandoned device from the South Derry Volunteers – another sign post on another junction.

Again it's on the wrong side of Toomebridge and we're directed through the village. We pass the RUC station and a mental note is made as we pass, outposts of safety on our travels from base to incident. The task is a duplicate of the first – a tiny pipe bomb at the base of a road sign on a junction. The fuse, as per the last task had no signs of burning, so no attempt has been made to ignite it. It makes no sense: no damage would be caused even if it functioned, and there isn't anything in the area to target.

Warning lights start to come on in your head when things don't make sense and when there is no obvious target, you ask yourself, is it me? Could the whole purpose of these devices be to draw us into an area for an attack? Certainly, both tasks have occurred in wide open areas where we can be seen for miles around. The nagging doubts are noted, but the task is complete. We pack up and return to base.

IT'S ANOTHER BINGO NIGHT.

Dutifully, I turn the team out to the Naafi, not least because I won £200 last week. The bar isn't packed, so we make ourselves comfortable around a table and I get some drinks for the team. The environment of being on duty 24 hours a day for months on end is draining; sometimes it's better to be busy than bored, even if being busy means being at risk on task. So diversions such as the bingo aren't to be taken lightly. We fall quiet as the numbers start to be called. There are individual small prizes in each Naafi – £5 and £10 for corners and lines, then £100 for filling a whole card. Lastly, there is a live-linked game which is played out across all of the Naafi clubs in Northern Ireland for a one off prize of £500. I might be cool as a cucumber on task, but I'd be lying if I didn't admit my pulse increased a little when I had one number left on my card.

The numbers are called, and with each new number I expect the prize to be claimed. I've always been lucky, and when my number comes up, I'm also the only winner, so we claim the whole prize. I split the winnings with the team, and my total for two night's bingo while in Antrim was £780. Not bad at all, considering that if not for the management benefit of getting out of the Detachment, I would have been unlikely to attend from choice.

The 'South Derry Volunteers' are in touch once more.

It's a third call about an abandoned bomb by a road sign – another call from a Republican group drawing us into an open area. This is getting particularly twitchy, and this time we drive a circuitous route taking an hour longer to get there but avoiding Toomebridge. If this is like the previous devices, a delay to get on scene will not affect safety regarding the device itself, and we're obligated to start changing our procedures to avoid setting patterns. Once we've arrived, I take longer with the robot, examining the whole area around the road sign looking for anything else that might be waiting for me. I also have the team conduct an electronic search and deploy all our jamming equipment.

I've done as much as I can to try and find any other bomb and to guard against anything that may be down there, but with no certainty that the area is clear, it's time to go and have a look for myself. With the concerns that we're being set up for an attack, the last line of defence is the 80lb Kevlar suit. It might be cumbersome and awkward to work in, but at times like this you are happy to feel its weight on you, providing you with a degree of protection. It won't be the last time in my career, or in fact this tour, that I will seek its use with an increased expectation of needing its protection.

I'm in the process of emptying my pockets and stripping ready to put the suit on, when I spy Michelle jogging backwards and forwards between the vehicles with a concerned look on her face. I already know what the issue is, and I'm pleased to see her next come straight up to me to pass on the news affecting the task – it's the sign of a good No2 (who'd go on to be a good No1 in her own right).

We'd been training at the detachment when the task came in, and in the rush to pack the team equipment away and onto vehicle when we were tasked, one piece has been forgotten. Most things on the team you have an alternative way of achieving the same result, but you can't substitute for the EOD suit. She's already forgiven. (I'd committed a similar mistake on a stand-in years ago on my first tour as a No2, and fortunately my Operator at the time hardly ever chose to wear the suit.)

So, faced with the same choice, I had little option but to man-up and make the walk down the road in my combats. I use the EOD helmet to protect my eyes, my normal combat body armour, and for the first time on my tour, I properly break Standard Operating Procedures (SOPs) and wander off down to the target to find what awaits me.

When you wear the EOD suit, the scientists that study us claim we lose 10% of our judgmental ability due to disassociation, reduced vision, reduced ability to hear things, and a general insulation from the outside world, as I understand it. While I haven't noticed this effect first hand, as I walk down the road with a reduced level of protection, my awareness of this fact and the closeness of my surroundings is very apparent. I feel very, very alone.

What awaits me is a third small pipe bomb and nothing else. Procedures done, it's handed over and I make my way gratefully back towards camp. I'm relieved the task is over safely, but I'm growing ever more concerned that there will be another one just like it all too soon. Tasks like this have all the hallmarks of setting you up for an attack in the future. The IRA will run attack after attack to create avenues to exploit in their attempts to kill an Operator. One of my SATs had been blown up in such an incident where the IRA had set the scene for months to create the environment where they could attempt to kill him. He was lucky to survive, but the incident is described during our training as an example of how even the best of us can be targeted successfully by the other side. It makes for worrying thoughts.

JACK RETURNS AFTER A WELL-EARNED FORTNIGHT AT HOME. HE'S pleased to see the team in one piece. During the handover, I include the information about the South Derry Volunteers and he agrees the whole thing seems fishy. He also indicates that the reason we get tasked so often to the far side of Toomebridge is that the officers in Brigade won't allow the team based in Londonderry out of the city. In his opinion, he thinks it puts the Antrim team at increased risk as the terrorists will not have missed that the only team tasked is from Antrim and almost always has to transit through Toome. I tell him that my next stand-in is Londonderry and I'll have a look at the problem from the inside once there. He congratulates me on my bingo winnings and, somewhat sad to leave the detachment, I head back to the cobwebs of the abandoned RMP mess in Lisburn.

While I wait for the next stand-in, I'm back to the gym and running the perimeter again. I also get an invite over to see the new Sergeants Mess from the Intelligence Sergeant in a less than professional capacity. It's not all boring here.

Chris is coming to the end of his tour, and I'll see him in Lisburn before I go to Londonderry. He's defused a new type of IRA mortar. The dangers involved in dismantling a previously unseen IRA device are amongst the highest, not least because there is a hidden pressure from on high to maximise your forensic recovery to ensure knowledge of the new device is quickly available to others who might go on to face these devices. Such an accomplishment usually brings some form of recognition from the chain of command, if not (though usually) in the Honours list, at least some form of Commendation, but the event goes strangely un-noticed by the 321 hierarchy.

Chris arrives in Lisburn having completed eight months of his six month tour. He handed over to another Operator who has himself had his tour extended to cover the gaps in manning. By a curious bit of fate, Geordy, Chris and I have all ended up here together.

Me and Geordy are due to travel to take over teams today, and Chris has his leaving interview with the OC and his flight later that afternoon. We comment that in the old days, you would usually be given a day or two in Lisburn, kept on the Company books, but allowed to go to the bars in order to have a few beers and maybe dispel some of the stress from tour before returning home. No such consideration is given, and Geordy says we should all just have a night out, despite the SAT's position that we were not allowed to associate together.

Chris mentions that we both have stand-ins, and Geordy says that the Operators will not leave until we replace them. Chris reminds us of his flight, and I suggest that if he misses this one the Squadron would surely buy him a second, and for a moment we all grin at each other knowing we'd get in trouble but it would be worth it. Sensible heads prevail and instead of a night on the beer, we accompany Chris to the AOs office and we all buy our Operators' tie together – a hallowed garment in my eyes.

This was an entitlement earned by your service as an EOD Operator in NI. Some have protested that the right to a tie is only earned after you've defused a live device out here, but I challenge these people to ask the population of NI their opinion. I doubt if the Irish would see a difference between any Operator who took their turn guarding them from the violence, no matter the actual taskings undertaken. Indeed, some of the scariest jobs I know of turned out to have no device present at all. Chris makes his flight home on time.

The last bit of good news before I move to Londonderry comes from Jack. He has had an update from the Intelligence cell regarding the South Derry lot – apparently they have renamed themselves the South Londonderry Volunteers, so while the concept of a possible pattern of attacks to instigate an ambush isn't unknown, the prevalence of fuck-wittery amongst the Protestant groups of terrorists when it comes to bombings is far more common, especially in certain areas of operation.

So, on to Londonderry. The covert drivers ferry me and my kit to Ebrington Barracks, and on the way we pass over the Glenshane Pass, a well-known patch of land from our terrorist past. It's a beautiful and remote area, the sort of place I could imagine living when I'm older, and reminds me of the countryside I explored in my youth.

The Barracks itself is on the east side of the river with the majority of the city on the far side. Connected by two bridges, the city does not have a good feel about it, and I'm intimidated at the thought of working here.

The Detachment is run by an Officer called Steven who was on the same STT course as me. Although he has that 'proper officer' way about him, he's settled into the small Unit manner that suits an EOD team. His guys like him and call him Boss, a sure sign that he's doing okay. He offers me his room in the Officers Mess and the chance to eat there – a generous gesture which I think is a very nice touch, but as there is a transit room in the Det, I decline and say I'd prefer to stay there. It's the most god-awful room set in the rafters and above the TV room, but it's inside the team lines and I prefer to base myself there and not remote from the team if I can. I've spent enough time in a separate Mess on this tour.

Handover is pretty seamless, and we head to the Operations Room of 8 Brigade. It's from here that the issues mentioned at Antrim have been originating. The Operations Officer is obviously aware of EOD opinion on his decision to keep the Londonderry team from deploying outside the city, regardless of the fact that it puts others at risk, as he's quick to announce to me that it's his policy to keep the team in the city.

"That's fine by me, sir. I've seen enough bombs that I couldn't give a shit if I never see another. In fact I'll be quite happy if you don't bother tasking me at all."

After I left, the Ops Officer asked Steve,

"He will actually deploy if I task him won't he?"

It seems my manner had worried him.

Stage one of my plan is complete, and Steve heads off for his R&R.

Operationally, my time in Londonderry was quiet with only a handful of tasks; it was inside camp that the action really took place.

Firstly, the support staff to the Detachment. Not bound to stay inside camp on a pager, the wheelbarrow technician (barrow-tech) introduced himself to me on my first night in the Detachment by returning from a night in the local pub, drunk as a skunk with his mates. He took them to the TV room, put MTV on at full volume and made himself some toast which he forgot, burnt, and set off the smoke alarm. At one in the morning, with my team unable to join him in the pub and tied to a pager, I felt his behaviour somewhat rude. Luckily for him, aware that he had a new boss in the detachment, the No2 called Chris had gone downstairs and suggested to them that they'd be best making themselves scarce.

In the morning, I briefed Chris that as the No2, the second in command of the detachment, he was to brief the barrow-tech that the facilities of the EOD detachment were his to enjoy while he respected the team. More, that I didn't expect him to flaunt his freedom to go and get pissed in the manner that he did last night, and that if he didn't like my rules, I'd have him moved out of the detachment. The message given, and knowing as I did from my own experience that supporting your No2 is an essential trait in an Operator because it empowers him to run the team properly, I expected the message to quite simply be received and obeyed without argument.

I was irked when Chris came back to my office looking a bit sorry for himself. He'd given the message to the tech who had basically told him to get stuffed. As far as he was concerned, he worked for the QM and not me. Chris asked if I wanted him to go and try again. I replied that I didn't and that no-one gets to speak to my No2 like that. I sent Chris on his way, told him not to respond if it happened again tonight, as I would deal with it. And I carried on with my day. Sure enough, the tech went out that evening as soon as the bar opened, and I waited until my team went to bed. Then I went to work.

I was awoken by MTV, as expected, rolled over in my bed and pulled the arming pin out of a TPU that was beside my bed. The TPU is a Time and Power Unit. It's a title we gave the IRA devices. (So many were made to standard and in such quantities that we were able to give them a model number.) This particular model was called an Mk15 and had a timer that could be set for up to an hour. Mine was set for about seven minutes. I rolled over and waited.

The barrow-tech decided he fancied some toast. Hmm, he did that last night and in doing so set a pattern.

That would probably explain my decision to booby trap the toaster.

I removed the fuse, as I knew doing this would mean the toaster arm would not stay down. I then attached my booby trap to the plug. When he tried to make toast and the arm would not stay down, he tried the switch and then pulled the plug from the wall. The explosive charge I used wasn't large, but in the confines of the tiny kitchen served to augment the effect. That and his drunken state amplified the shock, and a stunned barrow-tech came out of the kitchen and sat next to his mates on the sofa.

I'm nothing if not lucky. He had been on the sofa just seconds when the timer next to my bed wound down. The wire attached to it ran from my room to the TV room, and four further charges strategically placed around the room leathered the tech and – as collateral damage – his mates. Sleep came to me with a smile.

I planned to follow this lesson up with an unpleasant one-way briefing where I was going to tell the tech he had no chances left with me – not for the rudeness and ignorance of his behaviour, but for daring to dismiss my No2. As it happened, when I got up in the morning, Chris informed me that the tech had already apologised and told him I'd put the fear of God into him. The tech was the model of professionalism from there on, and was a happy addition to the barbeque we had when I departed.

Next, I had the Ops Officer in my sights.

In short, I ran some training for him. The training was designed to test his ability to prioritise tasks. I knew from experience that it was easy for the IRA to cut the city in two by closing the bridges. My intention was to teach the Ops Officer this fact and perhaps encourage him to release the team from the city. Despite his assertions, keeping the team contained within Ebrington wasn't actually protecting the city at all.

We conducted a map exercise, with me playing the part of the 321 headquarters. I ran tasks, and the Ops room had to respond as they thought best. In a matter of an hour, he was defeated. He claimed that the scenario was unrealistic and that it would never happen in real life. It was a smug Operator that took the historical reports for him to see for himself that not only was the scenario realistic, but it had in fact happened on more than one occasion. The Ops Officer wasn't daft though, and asked if this was my way of making him release the team. I replied that I wasn't telling him his job, merely offering the benefit of my experience. I highlighted that keeping the Londonderry team confined was also putting the Antrim team at greater risk. It was his choice to make.

Stage two was complete, and although by no means guaranteed of success, I'd given it my best shot.

Steve returned, took over the team and later phoned me to say that the Ops Officer was now releasing the team outside the city. I was pleased, but while I may have helped, the decision was simply down to a professional Ops Officer who had finally listened and seen sense.

BACK TO LISBURN AGAIN.

I have two months left in my tour and I'm not scheduled to take over any more teams at the moment. It's likely that there will be one or maybe two more stand-ins before I go home, but they will be with detachments I have already served in. On the up side, I'm a young Sergeant. Maybe I will get a second tour as an Operator, or maybe a posting to NI in the Inspectorate role and get to do some more time on the teams?

I go to see the SAT to debrief him on my time in Londonderry. The SAT tells me I'm extended: I now have another three months on my tour (making five), and that I will now be given a team to take over. I have two choices: Antrim when it's available, or Omagh now. I tell him I'd like Antrim. He seems surprised; he thought a keen young thruster such as me would want the danger and possible activity of the IRA in Omagh. I viewed it differently – a detachment in swampy Fermanagh with less activity, or a shiny new Detachment with lots of simple pipe bombs was how I saw it. I had no aspirations for greatness, and just wanted to do a good job of running a detachment. I felt Antrim offered me the better chance for this.

"Pack your bags, you're off to Omagh."

The day I arrive, the Operator who took over from Chris is reluctant to hand over the pager. He has heard a task is likely to come in today and he wants it for himself.

As I'm unpacking in the Operators room, the task comes in and he's very excited. The HMSU (Headquarters Mobile Support Unit), a specialist unit of the RUC has arrested an IRA team complete with the large mortar they were transporting for an attack on a Special Forces base. A major task, and in the quieter times in NI, a significant one. The Operator later apologised to me for poaching the task, but I felt there was no need for an apology. It was his team until he handed it over, and as I have already stated, I'd learnt not to go looking for trouble. I even helped him with the graphics in his report – the mortar had a new type of fuse incorporated into it, and this information would need dissemination as soon as possible. He departed the Province on a high, and I was pleased for him.

I had my own Det at last.

I phone my father to tell him my good news. He's pleased, but then says he hasn't been well. I worry that it's his cancer but he assures me that his treatment is going fine. Instead, he has had four small heart attacks. I'm not sure what constitutes small, but I'm worried for him.

Always a down to earth man, my father. He tells me not to worry, that he's proud of me and to stay out here doing what I'm good at.

Having stood in for Chris a few weeks ago, it was an easy handover. The only point of note from the outgoing Operator before me was regards one of the team who, at the age of 19, topped the scales at 22 stone – and it wasn't a healthy 22 stone. The detachment was self-catering, meaning we cooked for ourselves. Apart from the diet mainly consisting of pie and chips, I was told that the Det had ordered a box of biscuits – Wagon Wheels. The Operator had secretly ordered the remainder of the team not to touch them as an experiment. This lad ate 48 Wagon Wheels in a single day and he was obviously in need of help. I offered to work with him in his training regime and took over the cooking to get chips off the menu.

Having had a significant task with the mortar occurring as I took over, I fully expected my time to be quiet. An arrest of IRA members would usually put a dent in their operational tempo; well, that was the general expectation.

At Omagh, I'd inherited 'Charlie' – one of those army anathemas. He didn't fit in any sort of military way, but he was perfect for the intelligence cell, and was long-term, completely in tune with the enemy activity.

The IRA had tried to assassinate him on his way to work at least twice and he'd survived. Now, I made regular stops for coffee to his office to catch up on the goings on.

I'm stood outside the detachment getting some sunshine and fresh air when my mobile rings: it's Chris. He's phoning to do a courtesy check on the detachment as really he was the Detachment commander, and the last guy was only in for a couple of weeks. He asks if everything is alright and I assure him it is, but I know something is up. He then says,

"I need a favour from someone with your unique talents."

I press him for more, but he refuses to talk over the mobile and I have to go into the detachment. (Because the Army telephone network is less monitored than a mobile.)

Anyway, on the walk in I'm speculating as to what favour he needs. The phone rings and I say to him,

"Look, Chris, I'll help you fill someone in but I'm not killing anyone for you, okay?"

"What are you on about, you idiot?"

I guess that answers the question, how far would you got for a mate.

SOMETIMES WE HAVE INTELLIGENCE THAT A TASK IS LIKELY TO COME in, but most times it's just a surprise, as it was that morning.

We're tasked to Lisnarrick, a small village to the West of Irvinestown, to a suspicious box under a vehicle. I do not make any assumptions, but it does no harm to joke, and I tell the team my guess is it's a KFC box. We drive to the RUC station and receive a more comprehensive briefing and a diagram. The box isn't under the car – it's actually stuck onto the car. That would suggest an under-car booby trap, and the diagram certainly backs this up. With all the information we need and the area checked out, we deploy to the task.

A man has been taking his eight year old girl to school. As they have come out of the house, she has seen something suspicious under the driver's side of the car and told her daddy.

What sort of country is it where a child knows to identify this to her parents?

Her father has looked under the car and confirmed he probably has a bomb attached to his car, and called the RUC. The team arrives and starts going through its usual drills, checking the area for devices first to ensure that we're in a safe area to start work. It would not be the first time an EOD has had a present waiting for them from the IRA.

I then get to talk to the witness first hand. I speak calmly and quietly to him, removing him from the others in the team and the police, and move deep into the safety of the vehicles. I start by asking the location of his daughter and family to reinforce to him that no matter what else happens today, he and his family are now safe. Even without any official psychological training, I can see this poor man is going into shock. His head is visualising what could have happened if his daughter had not spotted this on his car. Fortunately, I'm not wholly reliant on his answers, but I go through the list just the same. I make a point of looking straight into his eyes so he returns my gaze. I want to bring him away from the horror in his head and back to the here and now, where all that is going to happen is I'm going to remove the device from his car and he will be able to go back to his life. I tell him I may need to ask some more questions, but I ask that he waits in the police car next to his daughter; I know it's the best place for him to be.

I had a long history with under-car booby traps; I spotted the IRA team that was reconnoitering the garrison camp in Colchester in 1989 that subsequently put a device on an RMP Staff Sergeant's car. He got into the car to take his family shopping, sat in the driver's seat and leant over the side to look underneath. This action to check his car probably saved his life as the explosive force from the device detonating was directed upwards through his car and only claimed his legs.

Ten years prior to this task on my first tour in Northern Ireland, my team had dealt with an almost identical device. A nine year old boy had been travelling with his father on his tractor at their farm. The farmer was a part-time soldier and therefore considered fair game by the IRA. The boy had actually picked up the device that had been hidden under a paper bag beside the seat and asked his father what the box was. Fortunately, the device didn't function and two innocent lives were spared. The device was successfully dealt with by my boss, and I still remember him telling me to take the device and show the parents what we had recovered.

Numerous other tours with numerous other under-car devices had caused me to develop a personal hatred of this device and the people who employed them.

I resolve to do my utmost to protect this man and his family from this nasty little device.

The usual routine would to be to send the wheelbarrow down to the car and 'disrupt' (fire a water filled shotgun through the device), and break it up into a hundred pieces. However, I know from the diagram that this device has been manufactured from PIRA stock, the same stock that our government tells us daily on the news has been deactivated, destroyed and handed in. The RUC would be keen to recover the evidence as intact as I can manage, so I modify the plan.

I mount two weapons on my robot: one is the disruptor, the other is a tool I can use to cut wires. My plan is to attempt to cut 'the right wire' and gather the device completely whole – if this isn't possible, I can always revert to the first plan and shoot it to pieces.

My No2 drives the robot to the car, and we warn the police to take cover – just in case. The controller on the new robot is a piece of crap – there is a digital display that shows you the shape of your robot, but the monitors you watch are up in front of you, so if you use the display you have to take your eyes off the screens. The main control box that runs the robot is above the monitors, so it would have made perfect sense to put the display on that box and not the hand controller. It makes the hand controller too large and unwieldy.

I have long advised No2s to balance the damn thing on their knee to take the weight of it and allow them more dexterity with their digits to control the robot. Also, the controls are graduated: the harder/further you push the controls the faster/harder the robot moves and pushes. It's a nice technical design and an improvement, but with the old robot you had a speed dial, basically a variable resistor that you could turn up and down and very exactly control the speed of the robots movements. Very handy when your robot was in close proximity to things that might not like to be prodded.

This graduated control system meant that you had no safety net – you could not turn the speed of the robot down, you just had to press the controls very gently. One slip and it's all over. It's this fact that has my No2 stop at the edge of the car and tells me that he's a bit nervous about going for the wire. It presents me with a problem. I could just shoot the device, but I really want it intact. I could tell the No2 to give it his best shot, but I don't want him to be under any more pressure than he already is. I could take the control box off him and do it myself – I was always a bit of a dab-hand with the robots, but I'm as at risk from a slip of the controller, and the stigma of failing to defuse a device that I could have successfully defeated stays with you for the rest of your career.

Or I could put my EOD suit on, break SOPs, and go down there to do it myself. Faced with a choice between failure and death, it was an easy choice. I asked my No2 to get the EOD suit off the EOD van.

I plan to use the same equipment to cut the wire remotely, but I'll just place it myself instead of risking the robot. I rationalise that it's a small device and I will be in the suit. It's not enough to guarantee my life when I'm right next to it, but from a metre away, I'd stand a good chance. I'm aware of numerous incidents from history where the wind has blown an open door shut, or the glue holding the device together has failed, both times the device fell from the car and exploded. I'm aware of a friend who decided he would cut the wire with snips. He crawled under the car, stretched his hand to the device, extremely carefully put the cutting blades either side of the wire and snipped. As he did so, the device fell from the car, he returned to his team white faced and ashen. All of this I'm aware of, but I'm determined to capture the device intact.

I empty my pockets, strip off my jacket and body armour, remove my watch and wallet. There are numerous jokes about No2s asking their Boss for both if he doesn't come back – I made a point of leaving at least £100 in my wallet with instructions to put it behind the bar for the team.

I put the suit on: my team dress me. The trousers are referred to as 'arseless chaps' and they have no protection around the groin. The jacket is zipped at the back, just like a straight-jacket. Then there is a back plate and an armoured plate into a pocket at the front. I load my pockets with the same equipment each time – a religious habit I was taught at the Felix Centre. Lastly, I brief the police and my team. I put my helmet on myself. Usually the No2 does this, but I prefer to do it myself – they always seem to catch my ears. Suit on, ECM in one hand, weapon in the other, and I'm ready to go. It's not a game anymore.

The isolation is familiar – the weight of the suit comforting, and alone inside my cocoon all I can hear is my breathing and the helmet fan.

The device is fairly easy to see; there is a second family car on the driveway and I lie on the road to have a good look at both undersides before proceeding. My plan is to get in and out as quickly as possible. I don't want to be near this intact device any longer than I have to. I move towards the car with the device, lie on my belly and have a brief but intense stare at the device.

The wire I want is hanging tantalisingly. Away from the device and car, I set my weapon to the approximate angle I want and start to slide it towards the wire. It's only a matter of inches, but it seems much further. The stand comes to a stop, caught on some tiny piece of the asphalt. Before I have time to think, my hand has given it a shove and I stop breathing. The weapon is still a good four inches from where it needs to be, but that gap that a few moments ago had seemed much larger now seems a lot smaller. I can also see the weapon isn't at the angle I need it. I have to pull it back from under the car and reset it.

You don't do that near the device.

I slide it forwards again. This time when the stand gets stuck, I carefully lift it and move it forwards once more. I'm there, and my weapon is pointing directly at the wire. I decide I have spent enough time down here. I inch away from the car, have a look around to make sure I'm not going to bump anything as I get up, and walk slowly back to the team.

My No2 is waiting for me and removes my helmet and the jacket. I put my body armour and combats back on, and let the police know there will be a small controlled explosion. With everyone warned, I give my No2 the nod and he fires the weapon. A small crack from down near the car confirms that our equipment has worked as intended. The lack of accompanying boom means I've probably achieved my aim. We turn the robot for a look, and because I planned for my shot to cut the wire and strike the device, the under-car booby trap is laying calmly on the tarmac, as intended. I ask Dave to see if he can confirm I have cut the wire but the pictures on the monitors aren't good enough. I can't be 100% sure.

Anyway, the important bit of the task complete.

I now have a mandatory phone call to make. I call the Squadron Duty Officer and tell him I have a live IED. There is a 50/50 chance of who will be on duty as the post is shared between the SAT and the OC.

Obviously, it's the SAT, and I suspect my career in the Province would be over if I told him I had approached this device in person, so I fudge the truth a little. I tell him the shot that cut the wire was from the robot. I tell him all the relevant facts and we get to the bit where I can't be sure the wire is cut. In my head, I'm surer because I placed the weapon in person. The SAT does not want me to approach the device – he wants me to use the disruptor and take a second shot at the device. There is no way I'm losing it now, so I talk him around. He authorises me to continue and tells me to stay in touch.

Suit time again and I'm back at the car. In person, I can see the wire is cut and I gingerly reach under and tape the open ends to make sure the device can no longer function. I stand up and take a moment to look at the scene; the target car is parked very close to a hedge line. What if the terrorists expected me to shoot the device and the pieces to end up on the grass on the other side? What if there is more than one device? Should I check the other car now I know I have stopped this bomb? Why was the device so easy to see? Was it because a little girl saw it and her father didn't?

All the 'what ifs' come rushing to me while I'm stuck down there. They say you should never think in the suit, so I just start at the top. I check the second car. I do a full search around the target car and the hedge line, and eventually I'm happy that all I have left is the device under the car. Could it be booby trapped? It could. It's unlikely, but I have an X-ray machine that will prove for sure. I put an X-ray through it, and once happy with the internal make up, I pull the detonator out. It's safe, and we just have the forensics to do now.

Unknown to me, ten minutes after I have turned the phone off and started my work, the SAT has heard a rumour of an explosion down where I'm working. Initially, he's concerned that he can't get through on my phone, but a lack of radio chatter on the Province radio net suggests that I'm probably still okay.

Not only is the bomb made from a PIRA TPU, it's also filled with semtex, the stuff that PIRA sourced from Libya. While a dissident republican (as they are called) may have planted the device, it was certainly made by PIRA. The RUC officer in charge asks me to confirm my suspicions to his boss who has arrived in person to hear the details for himself. I show him the device, the explosive and the detonator, and explain how I can prove all the items are from PIRA stock (caveated that the forensic science agency are the authority on such matters), and he says that my word is good enough for him.

The device is handed over, and I go to see the father and his daughter one more time. I tell some white lies and play down the device. I tell him the device is small and suggest that his daughter would have been unharmed even if the worst had happened. I've no idea if this is the right thing to do, but it felt appropriate at the time. Anything I can do to lessen the impact of the terrorist on this family.

I remember to turn my phone back on and get a rather panicked SAT on the line almost immediately, confirming I wasn't involved in the rumoured explosion.

We pack up.

The team are jubilant, and I put on a smile so as not to spoil their excitement at having been a team that neutralised (defused) a live device. It's not that I'm not feeling happy to have dealt with another device, I guess I was just unhappy to see these things continuing to be used out there. The target wasn't even police or military. I suspect they got the address wrong – it's not uncommon. In an effort by the terrorists to try and justify their attack, they claimed he had once worked for the military, which was also wrong.

I fill in my report, send it on its way, and then perhaps fuelled by a desire to display current attacks during coming lectures, I build a copy of the device for my Detachment museum.

The following morning, the SAT comes for a visit – maybe a pat on the back or maybe to check up on me. Either way, when he asks what the device looked like, he's shocked when I go and collect my example from the museum. He asks if it's the real one. He likes it so much, he steals it for the headquarters and I have to build a second. Still, I got a pat on the back.

Rumours start circulating that I could not have shot the device from the robot. My No2, who was on a stand-in, returns to his Detachment in Holywood near Belfast, and convinced he could not have made the shot, the Operator there puts a device under a car and asks him to repeat it in training. Dave, God bless him, got the shot nine times out of nine and never told them the truth. Good lad.

Chris even phones me from the school, and when I assure him I shot it from the robot he turns to all the guys in the office and says so I can hear it:

"Troll says he used his snips."

Such goes EOD humour.

From there forwards, things start hotting up, as we say. Numerous devices, finds and explosions followed, and my team were, by my estimation, excellent. We started to gel, and I started to enjoy the freedom of running my own team. I even get some weak lager in for them one evening, telling them that the two-can rule was good enough in my day. A couple of beers are a good de-stresser in a team held captive by their job.

It's on one of these two-can nights that I get a call from the Brigade Watchkeeper.

"ATO, there's a pub on fire in Strabane."

"Good news!"

He's a bit taken aback – not everyone gets ATO humour quickly, but in my opinion if there is a place in Northern Ireland that could do with a bit of fire, it's any drinking establishment that has a staunch support network for terrorists.

I tell him he needs to phone the fire brigade, they do fire, and again I don't think he gets the joke. I must be rubbish at telling them.

He then tells me that they think the fire might have been started by a bomb. Knowing that I can do nothing with a burning building until the fire is out, bomb or no bomb, I explain this and suggest that I will deploy now if he wishes, but I may only be watching the place burn. Strabane isn't the best place to hang out as a soldier. I suggest waiting until the fire is out, deploy then, and help the fire brigade sift through the ashes to see if a bomb did cause it. He decides that this makes the most sense, puts the phone down and I go back to my second can of the night.

Any can after two is still classed as the second of the night.

About 15 minutes later he's back on the phone. He now tells me the pub isn't on fire but is smoking. It's too much to resist, so I tell him they say there is no smoke without fire. It's still the fire brigade's job. He really does seem a little flustered, so I put him out of his misery. He tells me the fire brigade responded to the fire but will not approach the pub because they have been told there are bombs in the pub. I tell him we're on our way.

An hour later, nearing midnight, we're on scene. The police explain that at about 10pm two men with balaclavas, guns and carrying a large hold-all entered the pub and forced everyone at gun point into the toilets after taking all their mobile phones from them. They were held there for about 20 minutes, brought back out into the bar, told there were bombs in the pub and they had 15 minutes. They left the bar, called police and a short time later there was an explosion and the pub caught fire. The fire brigade have been here since about 10:30 but tell me they have not been in the bar, and that's my lot.

The pub is quietly smoking but there are no flames. I'd never seen anything like this in training, although I have been to pubs that had been burnt out by bombs in my earlier tours. I wasn't really sure of the protocol, so as is always a good idea if you need some time to think, we get the robot on its way down the road. A lad called Andy has taken over from Dave (as I'm given yet another No2 to train up). We try to open the pub doors but in the end we only manage to smash one of the windows, but the smoke is quite thick so we can only see a few feet into the interior.

In this case, the timings were on my side, so there wasn't anything stopping me going for a look myself. The suit would be worn, but the smoke was causing me some concern. I was aware that the fire brigade had breathing apparatus and it was basically the same as we were trained on for Biological & Chemical Munitions Disposal (BCMD), so I asked the crew if they would lend me some. I was duly kitted out and was in the process of trying to work out how to put the EOD helmet on over the top of it when the Watch Manager wearing his white helmet comes over and says I can't use his equipment.

I'm speechless, and for a moment I consider pulling my pistol on him and telling him in no uncertain terms to "Fuck right off". I also consider that I'm dressed now and if I walk off he'd probably stay here. I guess he saw the look in my eyes and makes to step in front of me. I think about that pistol again, but just know a complaint to my HQ will see my SAT rifting me, so I guess I have to play nice. I take the breathing apparatus off and hand it back to him. The whole time his team are telling him to let me use it, so I guess they also thought he was a dick.

With no breathing apparatus and an awkward and unhelpful boss in the fire brigade, I have no choices. So, I turn to the incident commander and tell him that due to the fire brigade, I'll have to let the place burn. I've never experienced such an unprofessional lack of professional courtesy from a fellow emergency service before or since.

I know I'm putting White Helmet on the spot, but that's his problem. The RUC immediately takes issue with the Watch Manager and an argument ensues. Dispassionately, I stand on the side and watch the back and forth. The police and the fire brigade all giving the Watch Manager what for, but the tosser refuses to budge. The pub is in the middle of a terrace, so if the fire is left untended, the damage is going to be extensive and greater than just the pub itself.

After a few minutes of this, I've had enough of amateur hour. I turn to Andy and say,

"Give me my nomex, chap."

I'll just put on my fire resistant balaclava (like racing drivers wear), and go anyway. I brief the fire team that I'll go in without the BA, and ask if they are prepared to approach the pub closer so,

"If I come out on fire, you guys can put me out."

They agree and in doing so are putting themselves at greater risk, too. I brief the RUC accordingly. He glares accusingly at the Watch Manager and off I trot leaving the two of them arguing behind me.

I drop all my kit at the entrance and start working my way in, figuring I'll either find signs of the device, or perhaps just the source of the fire. Initially, it's not too hot and my suit protects me from the worst of it. The open window has let oxygen in so the fire has flared up, and behind the bar there are flames starting to appear. It's getting hot now and this forces me onto my hands and knees. I start crawling.

The fire brigade warned me about exposed electrical wiring on the walls, but no one mentioned the ones from the lights in the ceiling. They hang down in loops from the burnt plaster and wood and as I crawl, they go under my armoured plate. I can't feel them, but as I push forwards the wires pull burning embers onto the back of my suit and I get even hotter. The fire is really starting to take hold behind the bar, and I turn to make regular checks on its progress.

My breathing is shallow as the smoke is getting quite heavy this deep into the building, and I have just about given up on the search, figuring that there are no bombs in here, when I find one. It's just a bottle of petrol with a small explosive charge. I stand to take a photo of it in place. Some habits are hard to break even in a burning building. My first photo is garbage as the flash just highlights the smoke. Lower down I have better luck, and with a photo of it – and figuring it's safe to move, I pick it up. As I do so, a bottle of spirits behind the bar explodes and sends a rolling ball of flame across the ceiling. It's time to exit, and I crawl back outside, placing the device on the path before heading to the fire crew. My back is smoking so the crew give me a light hosing. The cooling relief is instant, and I then discuss the inside with them.

I explain the makeup of the device and that I have searched the bar area. I ask them if they are prepared to go inside and extinguish the fire behind the bar, and again the fire team are prepared to put themselves at risk, pull their masks on and go inside. Ten minutes later they are back out and inform me that although there are still some small fires inside, the big one behind the bar is out. They warn me that as a result the smoke inside will be worse. They suggest opening fire escapes to let them vent. BA would have been handy.

The smoke inside is intense, and I'm on my belt buckle crawling through the bar. I know on the far side is a fire escape, but even with shallow breathing, the smoke is making me cough. I get as far as I can, but have to turn around and am beaten back by the smoke. At the entrance, with the helmet and nomex off, I guess I get some of that judgement-making skill back and realise I should just open the door from the outside. An axe and a few chops later, and it's open. I look down inside, and in the soot on the floor, about six feet from the door, I can see the marks of how close I made it.

The rest of the job involves me kicking doors open and expecting back drafts. The top floor is decidedly dodgy as a lot of the floor boards are burnt, some all the way through, and in the EOD suit I must weigh a good 200lbs. By the end of the task, I have located or removed nearly 40 devices from the building. Some are on the point of exploding when I find them, and those are put separately from the others on the pavement. Some of the rooms have not been touched by the fire, so the devices are left to preserve forensics. When the fire brigade went in to confirm the fires were out, they found that the terrorists had also spread petrol through the building. They were at a loss to explain why the place had not gone up in flames.

I had to go to Omagh hospital for a check-up and the doc said I'd lost a few percent of my lung function, but that I'd be fine. The back of the suit needed replacing and the SAT demanded to know why I had not let the place burn. (He must have had the same view of republican drinking dens as I did.)

He did say he wasn't unhappy with the end result.

The only answer I could think of was that our driving ethos is to prevent the terrorist from achieving his aim; I guess they wanted to burn the pub, so I can only think my intention was to stop them.

"SGT BELL, MY OFFICE IF YOU WOULD, PLEASE."

It was the Woofers' Operations Officer.

"Certainly, sir. I'll be up presently."

I consider wearing normal uniform, but as I have a good suspicion of what is coming, I decide to exercise my right as an ATO to wear something a little different on my top. Combat trousers and boots on, I pull on a green fleece with a big Felix (our unit mascot) on the front. If I'm going to have a fight, I might as well let them know who they're messing with. I leave my beret behind; me and the rest of the Army already hate the RLC. There's no point protecting myself with Felix, only to lose the fight with the RLC.

The RLC systematically failed to support, understand or in any way show professionalism towards the AT trade throughout my entire career. As shockingly unprofessional as they were, the higher echelons of the RLC were at the front of the queue any time an AT was awarded a medal.

As I walk from my detachment to the Headquarters, I review the last 48 hours to double check my actions. Am I in the shit or not?

New Year's Eve, during a recent coffee stop with Charlie in the intelligence cell, he had passed on the information that there was going to be a rush amongst the terrorist groups in the area to be "the first of the first". Christmas and New Year historically had been times of low activity, so it was interesting to me that there may be an attempt to put in an attack on New Year's Day. I'd no idea why the rush, but it had stuck in my mind. Sitting in the Det with the team, on our second beer of the night, we get a phone call at 22:30 hours from the Brigade Watchkeeper.

"There has been a warning of a car bomb in Strabane; the car turned up outside Katy Daly's nightclub at six minutes past ten."

It's funny how fast your mind can work. Current IRA timers commonly had a two-hour timer. Allowing a couple of minutes fudge factor, the time this car was parked could lead one to imagine the timer would function the bomb at a few minutes past midnight.

"Lads, stop drinking, this one might be real."

I take my hand from over the speaker and return to the Ops Officer. He tells me that the police are currently evacuating the scene, but have not got back to him to confirm that a device is actually present. He says he does not want to task me just yet.

While I don't agree, I understand that without confirming a bomb, he doesn't want to send me out. Strabane is an hour's drive from here; the team will take ten minutes to get the kit ready and leve camp; and we'd still have to clear an ICP and get the robot down the road to neutralise the bomb. It's going to be close, even if we go now. I don't want to disagree with the Watchkeeper about deploying me, so I explain about the timings and suggest that it would not hurt for us to get on the road as soon as possible.

"I'll take the team on a Liaison visit to the RUC station in Strabane for a coffee."

He asks if I'm allowed to do that.

"Of course I can. I'm your ATO."

I don't have to tell the team anything, and while I'm still on the phone, they're on their feet. Andy phones the guardroom – we've still agreed to take their QRF (Quick Reaction Force) with us on tasks.

I tell the Watchkeeper that I should head towards Strabane. If the police decide the task isn't real then he can always get on the radio to me and cancel our visit. He's happy with this. Lastly, I mention that the routes up to Strabane have been targeted before, so I wouldn't be unhappy if he got a helicopter up to give the route a once over, and I give him the code for the route I select. He says he'll have that sorted for me.

At the garage, the flurry of activity is already over; the vans are ready, the doors are open and I just need my body armour and weapon, and we're ready to go. I jump into the lead vehicle, do a radio check with Brigade, and we head up towards the Guardroom. I hear the engine of the helicopter coming to life as I get out at the Guardroom, and it's here we run into a snag.

Short version: the QRF have drivers in sangars on the far side of camp; no drivers in the guardroom, only one of the two Land Rovers, as the Sgt on duty has taken the other to go down to the Sgts Mess. I see two soldiers arguing over whose body armour they have between them and it's all a bit naff. I go into the office and with a little bit (not much) of sternness about me, ask the Corporal where his QRF are. He starts explaining, and I tell him that it's been 10 minutes since we called – I expect them ready to go. I raise my voice, and tell him he has three minutes to get them loaded up and ready – and walk out. I turn around and tell him,

"And that was two minutes ago."

They do get one vehicle loaded but the second is nowhere to be seen. I've had enough. I tell the Cpl I'm off. I'll take the single vehicle, and I brief their vehicle driver on keeping in between our two vehicles as we have blue lights and he doesn't.

We drive off into the town, lights on but no sirens. We cross red traffic lights carefully but the roads are mostly deserted. As we exit the town into countryside, I turn the blues off. No point advertising our position for miles around. The inside of the vehicle has dim lighting, some of which I have covered with tape. It's hard enough to see out of the armoured windows with their protective grills without the glare. The vehicle has a big engine, and it turns under a cowling between me and the driver. As a result, the cab gets hot quickly. The air con is obviously cheap and doesn't do much to cool us.

Andy and I scan the road and fields as we travel; there isn't much chance of us spotting a command wire IED or main charge if there is one. The IRA are experts at emplacing such devices, but it does no harm to stay alert. I can see the lights of the helicopter up there and am happy that I have an extra set of eyes scanning the route. I discuss some ideas about options for our responses with Andy, neither of us taking our eyes off our scan as we talk.

The hour passes quickly and Strabane comes into view. I'm just starting to think about the RUC canteen and if there will be access to coffee, when the radio comes to life. The Watchkeeper is on. He gives us a formal tasking order and ICP location. We drive past the RUC station. I have time to acknowledge the task, and straight away give the call "now at task location" as we pull into the police control point. I look at my watch and it's 23:54. There's no time to think about how well that worked out for us. I notice that we have driven down the road past the nightclub, about 200m. I didn't see the car there.

The Incident Commander explains that as part of his brief, they looked in the car when they arrived and saw beer kegs and filled fertiliser bags with wires coming out. They entered the bar, informed the clientele that there was a bomb threat to the car outside, and asked them to evacuate. As the crowd started making their way out of the bar, one of them ran to the car, jumped into the driver's seat and started driving off down the street in the suspected car bomb. The RUC who had parked their car a short distance away, ran to their vehicle and give chase. The tail lights in view, they saw it swerve off the main road at the bottom of town into a large car park. They drove in behind the car and observed the doors were all shut, but the driver was nowhere to be seen. The result being that the car was in the middle of a wide open space and the nightclub stayed open. The clientele turned around and went back to their drinking.

One of the stranger starts to a task.

The drunken car theft had actually given me more options. Had the car been outside the intended target, I would have had no choice but to explosively clear it as a suspected car bomb. Here in the car park, there would be little damage if the device did function, and this allowed me a few moments to polish my response. The police give me a detailed brief of what they have seen and for various reasons they suspect the car to be a hoax. I decide that I will open the car with the robot rather than explosively disrupting it. The task takes a couple of hours and we see nothing to change our opinion of a hoax. Andy expertly opens most of the doors and pulls out the contents, laying them neatly behind the car for me to examine when I approach.

Sometime during this, a second Land Rover full of QRF joins us in the ICP. Around the time I'm checking the vehicle and contents in person, a lot of the pubs kick out. We get a lot of shouts of, "have a drink, ATO," as the bottles start raining down on the police and my team. A hoax confirmed, and with enough damage done to the vehicle to ensure the owner will be getting a new one, we finish up as quickly as possible, pack the kit, and exchange thank you's with the RUC.

As we head off, I warn the team over the intercom to ensure the dead-bolts are locked on their doors. We thread our way through the town and get a good pelting of bottles and stones as we pass the revellers. A couple even run up to try and open the doors; one gets bounced off the side armour and is knocked to the ground as we pass. His mates pick him up and stick a beer in his hand.

So overall, the only thing I can think of as I approach HQ, is that the bloke bounced off the armour and that was entirely his own doing.

The SAT had called to discuss the task and seemed very pleased that had the device been a real car bomb, we would have arrived with enough minutes to potentially defeat the timing mechanism.

I ARRIVE AT THE HQ, MAKE MY WAY UPSTAIRS, AND THE OPS OFFICER is waiting for me behind his desk. He has another couple of officers in his room. I smell an ambush.

"Come in, Sgt Bell."

I'm not invited to sit, a sure sign this is a hostile interview, but if they were expecting some sort of military stand-there-and-take-a-bollocking, they're going to be disappointed. I lean one shoulder against the door frame and ask the Ops Officer how I can help.

"We just wanted to have a chat about the riot on New Year's Eve, and your decision to leave some of the QRF behind."

Riot? We disagree from the start, and I explain it wasn't anything more than partygoers throwing bottles, mostly in good humour, as opposed to the other kind. They explain that there were only seven police officers and approximately 2000 'rioters'. Their intention is to task their OC to assess 'the tactical situation on the ground'. I respond positively – I think it's a brilliant idea to send the OC out in a helicopter to observe the scene. I might even join him, depending on the task, as an aerial view is sometimes a great asset to running EOD tasks. They stop me mid-sentence and say that they aren't planning to use a helicopter.

"Well what are you planning then?"

They are going to send him out in a normal vehicle. They even mention the duty Mini Metro – a small hatchback. I ask how they expect the Metro to beat me to task when my vehicles have blue lights. They announce that they aren't going to task me until the OC has been on scene first. I'm speechless.

Is the concept of getting to the bomb too late lost on these gentlemen?

The tragedy of the Omagh bombing was only two years ago in August 1998. I suggest that as the RUC never requested extra police assistance, that the alleged riot was well in hand. I suggest that if their OC wants to go and assess a bomb disposal situation, he needs to pass a bomb disposal course first; and I finish by politely explaining the chain of command I follow. My orders come via my Squadron OC, and I'm tasked by the Brigade, not the Battalion (the Woofers Battalion are also part of the Brigade). I answer to the Brigadier not their CO or them. I'm being polite but I can feel my personality safety catch coming off.

"Oh, come on you're just a Sergeant. We just want to get some experience on the ground."

Now that's just downright rude.

"Experience? I'll tell you about my experience."

And I do.

I explain about car bombs, and command wires, mortar attacks and land mines. I explain that I'm the ATO – if they want to change my procedures, they petition the Brigadier.

He will tell my OC what he wants, and the OC will tell me. Nothing else will see me change my procedures and I'll leave the camp when the Brigade tasks me.

I'm on the cusp of being rude.

"Well, the CO has given orders for the guard not to raise the barrier to your team until we say so."

"Well, I'll match your aluminium pole against my 14-ton armoured trucks. I fancy my chances and you'd best budget for some new poles. You've been told how it is; I'm not changing procedures. I have been taking your QRF out of courtesy, but as you can't even manage to provide that and I keep my team on 10 minutes' notice to move 24 hours a day, I'll not be taking them any more either."

I turn and leave.

I'm quietly fuming. As the fresh air hits me, I have a moment of clarity and realise I've been a little rude. Knowing the value of letting my chain of command know what's going on, I jog down the hill back to the Det and phone my OC. I brief him on the conversation and he mentions he has spoken to the SAT and has heard how well the task panned out, especially my decision to get up there in time. He tells me not to worry and he'll give the Brigadier in my brigade a call to let him know the score. I breathe a sigh of relief and think that will be an end to it.

Overly optimistic?

The phone rings: an irate Operations Officer shouts,

"Sgt Bell! My office, now!"

Hmm, we're all in our version of uniform (wearing 321 Sweatshirts). I have my boots off and I'm stretching my toes and looking at them in my socks. Some garbage daytime TV is on, and the team are relaxing. I can imagine the CO waiting alongside the other officers for round two of the ambush in the office.

"I'm sorry, sir, we're in the middle of doing some EOD training at the moment. I can probably fit you about 4 o'clock this afternoon if you'd like."

I'm being flippant, looking for a fight.

"No, we'll have to do this over the phone. I've just been on the phone to the Brigadier and he's raging about you leaving without the QRF."

He's clearly picking his position and I guess trying to force the issue of me taking the QRF at the same time. I decide I'm up to his challenge.

"Well, sir, I actually ordered the Cpl in the Guardroom to deploy half the QRF as that was all that was ready."

I've just covered the guy in the guardroom's arse. I can't save the Sgt who went to the mess as I'm only a Sergeant myself, so unfortunately he's on his own. But I have just absolved the whole guard of any wrongdoing. My tone has been penitent and I'm clearly deferring to his angry voice.

He senses victory and moves in for the kill.

"Well, the Brigadier is talking about busting (demotion) somebody over this."

I feign fear once more and further cement my position as being solely responsible for the decisions that night.

He knows he has won, and his tone softens momentarily as he makes some suggestion that he will do what he can for me but can't guarantee I won't suffer a punishment.

I ask him if he could pass a message to the Brigadier for me. He agrees, but suggests that apologising now is probably too late: what is the message?

"You tell him from me, sir, I'm his fucking ATO. If he doesn't like the way I do business, he's free to fucking sack me!"

Caught off guard, the Ops Officer splutters that he doesn't want to get me into trouble.

"Trust me, sir, you can't."

I slam the phone down, pick it up again and speed dial the OC.

"Er, Boss. I might have just overstepped the mark."

I tell him about my phone call.

The OC does what in army terms as, "Sees his arse".

He's properly angry, and I think it's aimed at me: it isn't.

"I've just finished on the phone to his Brigadier. Fine, if a Brigadier isn't good enough for him, he can answer to the bloody General," and the phone goes dead.

It's gone political. I hate politics: in my mind, there's no place for it in a professional military. It's likely that some officer's dad went to college with some General and the shit will roll downhill and land in my lap, regardless of who is right and wrong.

I wait for my inevitable punishment to arrive.

Half an hour later, the phone rings and I answer. It's the Ops Officer.

"Sgt Bell, I'm very sorry, I won't trouble you again."

The remainder of my dealings with the HQ are noticeably quiet during my time there.

THINGS EASE DOWN, AND IN THE QUIETER TIMES I DO SOME MORE training including job swapping. I make the No2 do the No1's job; the Bleep gets to do the No2's job; and the Infantry Escort gets to run the ECM instead of the Bleep. It's a good bit of fun and helps the team see things from another perspective. Andy says afterwards he doesn't know how I keep my temper while in the suit as every little snag made him angry. I just smile and tell him I have more important things to worry about when I'm in the suit.

I hope that the team is enjoying their time, and during the training we've been helping our overweight Bleep. Part of his problem is his exercise regime: he thinks nothing of spending an hour in the gym lifting weights, but does no cardiovascular work, so he regularly gets sent to do two laps of the camp by me.

It's not working though and the scales say he's not lost an ounce. Andy comes up to me and says quietly that the problem isn't being helped by the Bleep's midnight raids to the Unit's freezer. He has been eating pies in the evening. I ask him if this is true, and he swears blind he has not been eating in the evenings. I know he's lying and I'm a little annoyed by this as we have all been trying to help him.

One night I put a tripwire across the doorway, and in the dead of night as we're all in our rooms, there is a boom from the Detachment. I get up to investigate and find a shell-shocked Bleep blinking in the smoking cloud. He says he was coming for a glass of water, but there are closer taps than the ones by the oven and the splattered chicken and mushroom pie suggests otherwise. I start locking the room with the freezer in: turns out this isn't a bad thing as our No2 had also caught our Royal Engineer Search Advisor stealing the Det's rations.

I'VE BEEN IN OMAGH SIX WEEKS WHEN THE SAT DRIVES UP FOR A visit. I walk him around the Detachment and highlight the areas I've concentrated on. No-one can do it all, and I know currently my paperwork signing for my Detachment checks isn't 100% up to speed, but I've renovated the troop IED museum, playing to my strengths. The SAT says he has heard from a senior ATO who is running the Weapons Intelligence in my brigade. He attended a terrorism briefing I did for troops and felt moved to write a letter to my boss saying how impressed he had been. He walks around the Det, nodding his approval, patting me on the back, and I get the feeling he's looking for something. We get back to the lounge and I make us both a coffee.

"What would you say if I said Bessbrook to you?"

Without thinking I reply,

"Shit Det, no facilities."

Bessbrook is the senior post for an Operator in Northern Ireland. It's considered the most dangerous posting and is reserved for Sergeant Majors who have completed a tour in NI already, passed the STT course a second time, and returned as a '2nd tour Operator'. It's based in a place called Bessbrook Mill which is a converted Quaker mill, a giant grey stone building christened 'Castle Greyskull'. I've served there as a No2, and the environment is stifling.

"Would you volunteer to go down there?"

He sounds like he actually means it.

"I'm not qualified," I tell him.

I'm also thinking about the wide open camp I currently live in, the full Naafi shop, the video store, the gym, the swimming pool. I'm comfortable here. I'm also a young Sergeant; it's not my place to go to Bessbrook.

He continues and says that manning is short (the real reason comes out), and the OC wants someone to go down to Bessbrook. I'm his choice. I reply that I can't volunteer. Enough people think I'm cocksure, and if I volunteer and make a mistake, they'll be proven right. He asks, if he orders me, will I refuse to go? I say if he orders me I will not refuse, but I will not volunteer.

"Pack your bags, you leave on Monday."

The SAT promises me that if I get any big jobs while I'm there, he'll come out and back me up. I'll hold him to that.

My replacement arrives, a cocky (even by my standards) joker of a SSgt. We do our hand over and I take him into the HQ to do introductions. I smile as I imagine his interaction with the Ops Officer. As I go to leave the Ops Officer's office, he calls me back. I roll my eyes, send my replacement out to the Ops Room and turn around expecting him to start on me.

He's very polite, and explains he does know what an ATO is and he has been to NI before. I tell him I have no doubt he has, and all I have ever wanted is to provide the best and most professional support to the Units I work with. I'm sorry we fell out. He shakes his head and says he's not explaining himself properly. He says when he saw an ATO walking down the road to the bomb, he thought ATOs weren't afraid of bombs. Since he met me, he's changed that and decided that ATOs aren't afraid of anything. He says it's the first bollocking he has had from a General. He's heard that I'm being sent to Bessbrook, and he wishes me a safe time down there.

As is the way with disagreements in the military, usually professionals all want the same thing and it's frustrating when other issues get in the way. I'm pleased we're parting on better terms and say if he has any problems with the new guy, it would be my pleasure to return. I mean it: the facilities here are so much better than Bessbrook. I'm gutted to be leaving my team again. Andy even gets me a leaving present of some Tyrone crystal. It's a nice touch but just underlines that I had a good team here.

A friend of mine who had recently come back from a tour told me,

"When the bloke you're replacing finishes his handover and leaves the Det, you get the cold finger of fear running down your back as you realise you're now it."

I didn't doubt his words, but such was my familiarity with all the Dets that I had previously toured in, and because I was only doing a couple of weeks at a time, that feeling had never hit me.

THE FIRST NIGHT IN BESSBROOK, SITTING IN THE IMPOSING GREY building, feeling the damp from thick stone walls, I look at a varnished wooden board above the fire place. It's the Bessbrook role of honour, a list of those who have served in this post since 1974. There are names I recognise; in my opinion they are the stuff of legend. There are names of those who have been killed or injured in post, and the realisation that I'm now down here on my own hits me. I'm just starting the seventh month of my six month tour, and I feel very small.

The SAT sends me another temporary No2 to train up: Pete. He's atrocious, and spends most of his days on the sofa and moans whenever I tell him to get off his backside and get into the kit. It's not all bad news though as my Bleep is a good friend of mine called Paul. He's early 30s and a very calm individual – we're pleased to see each other. My infantry escort is a mad man called Bri from the Devon and Dorset Regiment (D&Ds). Historically, he went AWOL (Absent With Out Leave) and joined the French Foreign Legion. He got about two years into it and they found out he was AWOL from the British Army. They're happy to accept all sorts, but AWOL from the UK forces is a line they don't like crossing, so I heard. They get in touch with the unit he's missing from, and a deal is done. He's returned after his 'detachment' to the FFL. He's a short operationally-focussed infantry type; he isn't scared by the rules, and I like him instantly.

I get my first task in Newry, another staunch Republican town.

The job is a bit of a non-job; there has been a robbery, and the cash register that was stolen has turned up in a supermarket car park. The item itself is likely to be empty, but the job might be to get my team out on the streets and then attack them. The team in gear and everyone gets going except Pete who makes some wise arse comment about needing to take all the Detachment's guns because he's working with me. I ignore it and we finally leave.

When we arrive at the car park, I see Daisy Hill stretching up to my right; it has been known for snipers to fire from there. So I direct our vans to park one behind the other as opposed to the usual wedge formation, and we will work between them and the supermarket building.

I go to speak to the RUC officer in charge, and it's as it seems – probably nothing, but just enough to get us out to check. I ask Pete to get the wheelbarrow out, loaded, and on way to the target. I also get him to take some ECM at the same time; such is my belief that the register isn't a device, I plan to get straight down there as soon as it's shot, and clear it so we can get off the ground as quickly as possible.

Bri comes around the corner after completing his search area of the ICP and looks at me. "You're pretty scruffy for an ATO."

I've taken all my badges off my uniform and I'm wearing the same as he is: combats, body armour, a chest rig and carrying a rifle. I'm as short as him, and I look a lot like him. I tell him that my aim to look less like the ATO and more like an ordinary soldier, and if a sniper is trying to kill me, there's half a chance they'll shoot him instead.

He gives me a big grin and says, "You'll do!"

Apparently, I have his endorsement to be in charge of his team. At that moment, Pete comes around the corner of the van. He's immaculate, wearing a new smock, he has a pistol on his belt around his jacket, and if anyone looks like they are an officer in charge of the team and deserves to be shot, it's him. Bri and I look at him, then each other and burst out laughing. Pete knows something is up, but can't work it out. He jogs around the side of the van and comes back still wearing his pistol and now carrying his rifle as well. Bri and I are off again. Daftness like that I can overlook, but Pete's wheelbarrow driving was garbage. Anytime a piece of equipment wasn't prepared properly, he blamed it on the fact that, "this wasn't my kit", despite the fact that he'd been there a week. Seventy-two hours after any decent No2 takes over a team kit, he should know it inside and out.

When the job was over and we were back into the Mill, I called the SAT and sacked Pete. Despite the SATs protests, I said if Pete didn't go, I would. I also protested being given No2s to train while down there. The pressure of the job was enough without having fuckwits on my team. He promised me after the next stand-in I'd get a proper No2.

The next was Colin, and for 72 hours I didn't see him. He was buried in the back of his team kit and was a perfect No2. He went on to be a pretty perfect No1, as well.

Then came Chris M.

His arrival took the team's average age over 30, making us the oldest team in the Province. We were immediately christened 'Jurassic-Cat', and the saying was, nothing happened quickly down there.

I didn't mind. I liked the idea that we were steady and studious in our response. If there is a 'type' of Operator, some may be suited to the city and the hectic activity of such an environment. I was built for the country, and I liked the open fields and the longer tasks. I might have even started to feel settled in my post, but it was never going to happen with the spectre of South Armagh PIRA hanging over me.

CHAPTER 9

THE RAILWAY LINE

"THERE'S a bomb on the railway line."

The phone call came in from the same phone box they had used on the last big attempt to kill the ATO.

The Belfast-Dublin railway line was a regular target of the terrorists: closing it was significant to them, and causing disruption got them the publicity they wanted to symbolise their continued struggle.

In the last attack, at the same time as the phone call was received, reports started coming in of an explosion. The attack was a come-on, an attempt to get the EOD team into the area to kill them; secreted near the explosion was a radio-controlled landmine designed to catch the team out. The last Operator had found and defused it. The last Operator was a very experienced senior warrant officer.

The reports of an explosion are now coming in: the same phone box, the same scenario – it's likely the same team as well, and they have had eight months to think of a new way to kill the Operator, to kill me.

I phone the SAT and tell him I have work. The police fly a helicopter down the railway line and spot the explosion. It's near a derelict building and about 2km from where the last attack took place. I go to the Operations room and offer advice to the OC of the D&Ds about putting a cordon in, estimate the length of time it will take to clear such a task, and start thinking about the last task to see what areas I should change for mine.

The intelligence cell has on record that two IRA men have been arrested near my derelict building and they had two explosive charges on them, suggesting that the IRA had previously planned an attack in this location. It's looking more and more like there is something else going on. There is a single dirt road running down to the target area, and I speculate that in order to avoid the railway line (where the last booby trap was laid), I could drive in. I book a helicopter to fly over the area in the morning.

That night I pull out the report from the last attack. I look at all the photography, the mapping, the intelligence; I imagine myself in that Operator's shoes and look for clues as to how he was successful. I learn about the railways, how they are built. I read the historical reports and look at other attacks that have happened in the area. The RESA brings in some overhead photography and I pore over them on the Det's pool table, looking at every inch of the ground. It's early in the morning when, exhausted, I go to my room and catch a few hours' sleep.

I've just closed my eyes when my alarm goes off. I blink and the small amount of sunlight coming through the slit window in the giant stone wall hurts. I have a headache and need some water. I dress for the helicopter and go to the Det lines. I get a coffee down me and collect the team cameras, then head across the main road to the heli-pad. My pilot is called 'GFS': GS are his initials and the F was added by his friends because every other word out of his mouth is fuck.

We set off for the area of the explosion and start circling. The first thing that draws my attention is a blue car parked halfway down the dirt road leading to the area of the device. I attempt to get the registration but the vibration in the helicopter makes it impossible. GFS offers to get me a bit closer and through the binoculars I finally read the reg. I lower the binoculars and realise what he means by a little closer is actually a lot closer and I suggest we need to move away a touch. GFS is completely unafraid of any risk of explosion and is clearly barking mad.

We photograph the area even though I have some proper over-flight photography being done, as well. I have to wait for that to be processed and collected, but by doing my own I can start to make plans and refer to mine while I'm waiting. We fly back to the mill and I already know the car is going to come back as stolen. It is, and that presents me with a choice: either it's there to force me onto the railway line, or I have to go down the track and clear the car as I go. I spend another long day staring at photographs and maps; every potential hazard, area of hazard and problem is marked and plotted. When I finally have every bit of information I think I can find, I sit down and make my plan.

I have my whole team and the RESA involved and they are all encouraged to speak up: there is no such thing as a stupid comment or question, as any one of them could easily spot something I have missed. On the balance of it, I think the car is there to force me onto the railway line – it's where they hid the last device. My task is to open the railway for repair. In theory, I could clear the explosion and leave the car for another time or another team.

It's a bit close to the railway line for that, but I'm not obligated to clear it first. There are also traditional areas we avoid when flying into a task, and I spot an area that would be absolutely rubbish for our means. Telegraph wires, trees and a culvert: all things to avoid.

The team is with me, and we work out how we're going to pack, travel, and undertake our task. The SAT arrives late in the day and listens to my plan. He gives me a grin and says,

"I knew we sent the right man down here."

I'm glad he's reassured in my abilities because I'm not. This isn't some bag-of-bollocks in a supermarket car park – this is a proper PIRA task. The phone call warning is proof of that.

We have to leave the equipment on our trucks overnight. You cross-load it at the absolute last minute just in case an emergency task comes in. We'll wait for morning to do this. The SAT also has a reserve team coming down to Bessbrook to cover our patch while we're on task. He tells me he'll be back first thing in the morning along with the reserve team, and then he heads back to Lisburn for the night.

Again, it's in the early hours when I get to my bed. I'm desperate to go to sleep but it's not coming. My mind is racing, and I can see the images of all the task in my head: the aerial photography has picked up a wire running away from the explosion. Is it the command wire that was used to blow up the railway line? Is it part of another bomb? Is it a decoy? A booby trap that will cause an explosion if cut, or start a timer running? The derelict building is supposed to be fully secured and locked, but what if I get there and it's not? The hedges, streams, culverts, bales of straw, fence lines, and stolen car all swirl around in my head. What if it's not a bomb at all? What if they have a sniper out there? What if the cordon is the target? Have I done enough to make sure they are safe? *Why won't you be still and let me sleep?*

I must have closed my eyes for a second and I wake with a start. I look at my alarm and I have seven minutes before it goes off. There is no point closing my eyes for those extra minutes, I don't feel like I've slept. I shower and dress, pack some spare clothes in my bergen and make my way to the Detachment. I'm the first one down and secretly I'm pleased. I was always the first one down when I was a No2, as well. Silly, but I didn't want my team to think I wasn't working hard. They all arrive shortly afterwards. I start to help move the team kit from the vans onto the heli-portable lightweight buggies, but Chris tells me he'd prefer I didn't help. I understand: the No2 runs the team. I've told him the kit I want, and if he moves and packs it, he knows where it is and he can be sure that he has packed everything. Feeling like a bit of a spare part, Bri stuffs a coffee in my hand and tells me to go have a rest in the lounge, watch some TV.

I leave them to it and turn the TV on. The news is reporting that the railway line is closed due to an explosion. I turn it off.

I sip my coffee and stare at the fireplace on the wall. There is no fire or a flue. The bricks were just cemented in to make it look like a fireplace, and make the solid walled room seem a bit more homely. An AT has, at some point, welded brass rods together in the shape of our trade badge, and coated them in coloured crepe paper. A single bulb behind it lights up, and I'm reminded how lucky I'm to be in my trade. Above the fireplace is the imposing Honour Roll, and I'm also reminded how shit scared I am, too.

The SAT arrives and makes his own coffee.

The kit's packed, a last check behind me to make sure I haven't forgotten anything. We head over to the heli-pad. I have done dozens of planned ops as a No2 on my other tours; I have done planned ops as an Operator, but this just feels surreal.

The buggies are parked up, the team sits with the Royal Engineer Search Team (REST), and the SAT joins them. I don't know why, but I choose to sit apart, on the opposite side of the road, lost in my own thoughts. I'm going over and over my plan. I have typed the parts of my plan out in a list. A copy – without some of our more sensitive procedures – was given to the Operations room and the Ops Officer. It means, even over an insecure phone, I can reference where I am in my plan and keep everyone informed as to what is going on.

The helicopters arrive with the usual heat and noise. We pile in and the pilot then skillfully hovers over one of the buggies while it's attached for lifting. The flight is brief, and at the other end the pilot is just as skillful in placing the buggy between the wires and trees.

We then hop sideways and he lands in the field to drop us all off. Seconds later, the other buggy appears, dropped neatly, inches from the first, and the rest of the team arrive. The infantry have already cleared our drop off, and we're now cocooned inside the better part of 200 soldiers and police. Our only problem now is the explosion and whatever else is waiting for us.

The plan starts and the team gets the robot and search equipment ready.

In minutes, the robot is heading down the railway line to search and clear the first part of the plan. I split my time between the incident commander and Chris on the robot. I don't expect too much to be showing up on the pictures coming back from the robot to the monitors, so I stay off his shoulder as much as possible. The robot goes 90m forwards and stops. It should go more than three times that: it's annoying, but not fatal to the plan. We shuffle the team a bit and manage to get the robot to where we need it. There isn't anything to see, just railway lines stretching off into the distance, concrete sleepers and the gravel. The REST search expertly towards our new location, and I'm grateful they're part of the team. We move tentatively towards the site of the explosion, and the wheelbarrow is sent on its way again.

There is little to be observed, and after some more work from the REST, we confirm the wire we saw on the photos was used to cause the explosion, there is a small battery pack towards the far end that will also need dealing with. Too soon, it's that suit time again.

The whole scene has been examined by me from as many different angles and perspectives as possible. In my mind, if I was a terrorist and I was going to put a second bomb down here, the gateway near to (but not too close to) the explosion, would be my choice. It has taken us a few hours to get to this point, and every time we start a new search, secretly I hope they find something – not for the excitement of finding a bomb, but to remove the anxiety of not knowing if there is one. Even at training, when you're searching, when you actually find the bomb, the relief is palpable. I have seen many Operator's shoulders relax under assessment when they find it.

We find nothing, and it's my turn to go and look at the explosion. I suit up, brief the guys, and turn towards the target. The SAT tells me I'll be alright.

The Belfast to Dublin railway line consists of a pair of tracks that run off into the distance in front of me, appearing to join, the vanishing point.

When your faith in your skills and judgement is weakening, you start to avoid risks regardless.

As I step off, I find myself naturally treading on the concrete sleepers to avoid the gravel. It's silly, but this indicates just how aware you are of how little you know about this job.

The explosion site isn't huge, just enough to damage the railway line and close the route. I alternate between looking at my immediate surroundings and to the wider area as I'm still unsure of what else is here.

Historically, the IRA have planted booby traps in explosion craters, so that issue needs addressing. I'm soon standing in the hole.

There are bits of plastic which have obviously been in intimate contact with the explosion, probably the container. There are red and yellow detonator leads, which means I know what type of detonator it was and where they got them from.

The wider area needs searching because I know SOC will need to collect evidence.

But there is a problem.

The ground to my front needs checking: faced again with the choices of failing or just being careful and using a torch, I start carefully stepping onto the grassed area around the explosion. It's not safe, and I know that with every step I'm risking an explosion. I also know that in this case, speed kills, so I make myself count out loud after each step to give my eyes times to search every speck of ground before I take another step. I'm searching for at least an hour, and Chris gives me notice that he wants me back for a break. I hold up my hand indicating five more minutes as I'm nearly finished, and once I've marked the cleared area, I make my way back to him.

He's waiting, as ever, with a bottle of water. He takes my helmet and bomb suit jacket off. I put my body armour and combat helmet back on because there is always the sniper threat, and gulp the water down greedily. I tell the team and SAT what I have found – a drill introduced in case you don't return from your next approach.

My plan, now the explosion is clear, is to come off the railway line and clear through the steps down to a gate near the site. I need to clear the command wire and battery pack, and that will be easier using the gateway. We sweep forwards with the REST and an explosives search dog, an invaluable tool for this work.

As they approach the gate, the dog – which is in the lead – indicates on the gateway. Even though it was high on my list of suspect areas, it's still a shock for me to have my suspicions confirmed. Everybody freezes while the dog handler confirms the dog's indication, and then we slowly retrace our steps back to our ICP and safety. It's back to me to clear the gate fully now.

My rest over, my team briefed, my suit back on, I walk back towards the gateway.

There are some slab rock steps running down from the railway line. I fancy my chances on them more than down a grassy slope wearing 80lb of Kevlar, so I get down onto my front and start searching them. Down here you are focussed on the six inches in front of your face. It's different from the area-scanning you do around a target: nothing exists outside your vision, and my personal preference is to use the torch beam to guide my eyes. Even in daylight, I use it to scan every shadow under rocks and bushes.

After my visual search, I gently touch the slab of rock to see if it has any movement. It's solid: one down, just the rest to go. The steps lead to a flat patch of grass that has some signs of disturbance; it's probably footprints churning up the mud where people have been crossing a wooden stile next to the gate. It threatens to draw my gaze from the steps, as does the drystone wall between the steps and the gate, so I focus my concentration on the steps.

Every rocky step is a mission in its own right. Approached with regulation in my search pattern, the sweat is running off my head, down my nose and onto my visor. I have to stop from time to time to wipe the visor clear. I keep a check on my kit, too. I don't want anything falling out of pockets as I'm facing slightly downhill. Your vision underneath you is limited by the blast plate in your armour, so you pay extra attention. Step by step, I inch my way down the slope. I'm now close enough to the muddy grass patch that I have to clear, and I sweep a metal detector over it, one I've kept in my back pocket.

It's getting towards late afternoon now and I'm conscious of looking for a suitable part of the task to stop for the day. There are some EOD tasks you can undertake at night: but I'd rather avoid searching for booby traps in the dark, not that you can always avoid it. One of my former bosses was awarded a medal for doing just that. I have no such aspirations and I stand on the bottom step wondering if I have done enough to be sure of the grass in front of me. I stand there scanning the area: the grass, the gate, the fence, the wall, the edges where they join; everywhere, looking for any indicator of danger.

I've been standing still for some time now. My eyes keep scanning. It's like I know something is wrong: this is where I'd put it, and the dog has indicated where the gate joins the wall. It's so obvious when I see it that it scares me. I've been looking for the small stuff, but when I look at it as a whole, it leaps out at me. The drystone wall has ivy only at the ends, running down both sides. It's clear that the centre of it has been taken down and rebuilt: the clear part of the wall is about 6ft wide, and would easily fit a chemical drum full of explosives behind it. As I look down the wall, there is a stone at the base that has a hole through it. Have I missed a fishing line? I can't have. I've searched down there. I don't know what the hole is for, but I'm scared of it. I was taught that if you find something you're not expecting, you go back to the ICP to re-plan. I've grown up from my days of running away as I did on my first task, so I climb back up the steps to the railway line, pick up my equipment and walk back to the team.

Another bottle of water later and I'm rattling off my findings. It's clear the SAT is excited by my find. I'm not. I think it's a dangerous unknown, and I've decided the best way for me to clear this problem is to place an explosive disruptive charge behind the wall and blow up whatever is concealed behind it out into the field. Once broken up and scattered, I can go and find what was intended from the pieces left. The SAT overrules me and tells me I have to take the wall to pieces using a hook and line.

I put the suit back on and return to the wall. I tie numerous pieces of string to the rocks and attach them to the hook on my line. Back in the ICP, the team and all the troops around us take cover. The rope is tugged, and half a dozen rocks in the wall are pulled from it, landing on the grassy area I have cleared. Nothing. But at least I guess I was right about the grass.

I get time for one more approach before the light really has gone, and before I stop work, another six rocks join those on the grass.

Back in the ICP, Chris and Bri take the EOD suit off me. My clothing is completely soaked as if I've waded through a river. The Major from the D&Ds asks me if I'm going back into base, and the SAT joins him and tells me it's my choice. I tell the OC that as his lads are staying out, I see no reason why I wouldn't just do the same.

I unpack my bergen, put my roll mat between the railway tracks and the wheels of our EOD buggy, and that's my bed for the night. I eat a ration pack meal from its foil bag while steam rises from my clothing. Once finished, I strip my clothes off and hang them over a line between the buggies. I put on dry stuff from my pack and get into my sleeping bag. I'm asleep in seconds, on a railway line, a hundred yards from my task. Around me the police and soldiers continue their patrol, taking it in turns to sleep through the night. I know many ATOs hold these soldiers in the highest regard, and I will always say that they are unsung for their actions.

I asked to be woken at first light, and well before six in the morning, I'm given a nudge. It's truly bizarre to awake and find yourself on task.

I take my dry clothing off, and swap it for the cold and damp stuff on the line. I'm straight into my EOD suit, and have a cold cup of coffee from yesterday's flask for breakfast. The plan I give to Chris is the same as yesterday: get down to the wall and find out what it's hiding.

Another bunch of rocks join the pile, and on my next approach, I can see down into a hole behind the wall. Not for the first time in my career, there isn't anything to see. I search the hole a second time: nothing. I start searching the rocks that are left in the wall and removing them by hand. Before long, the wall is demolished. I lift my visor for a look at the scene, suck in some fresh air while I'm there, and clear my head. Maybe the explosive charge used on the railway was stored in the hole behind the wall before use? I will probably never know the answer to that.

With the gateway clear, we can use the REST to sweep forwards again, and this time the team makes it to our next control point. The derelict building is also checked out by the Engineers – it's locked and secure, just as we were told.

We're downhill from the battery pack, and that is my next task.

The SAT comes to hear my next move. I'm so convinced now that there is something more here waiting for me that my plan is to search the area around the battery pack and find the booby trap. Heads nod in agreement. I have lost count of the number of times I have walked up the road in my suit now, but I get to a point near the battery pack and start clearing my route towards it. The battery pack isn't connected to the command wire; there is a metre of wire running from it, but it has been cut and the wire running up from the explosion is just laid near the cut end. Why isn't the battery pack connected?

It's possible that the battery pack I'm looking at isn't the one that fired the explosives. If the battery is booby trapped, they could have fired the device and left the command wire here as the come-on. It's also possible that it's part of the terrorist drills to cut the wire to recover the battery pack.

Thoughts are running through my head as I continue searching. I get close and can see moss ramped up against the side of the battery. I know that it's been pulled out of the ground because I can see the discolouration of the root ends. I carefully pull it away from the pack and examine all around it looking for signs of a trap. Again, nothing, and I search a wider area, convinced I'm inches from something.

Eventually I admit defeat.

So the next part of my plan is to move the battery pack. I've done this numerous times in training, but I can't bring myself to do it here. I'm convinced that if I touch anything, I'm at risk. At last, I take the loop of string from my pocket, attach it to the hook and lay the loop like a lasso over the battery. The second my fingers let go of the string, I'm backing away, up on my feet and walking towards safety.

Normally, my team would pull the line under my instructions, but this time the item to be pulled is small, and I want to feel the line myself. I suspect that my set up won't work. With everyone under cover again, I slowly pull the line watching for movement at the firing point. I see the line move, but I think that this is all that's moving. I take my rifle, and in my suit, climb over a fence into the field beside the railway line for a look. The battery pack hasn't moved. I kind of knew it. I have to approach it again, this time with a better attachment – and I make sure this time that it will move.

The next pull is done by Chris, and I watch the battery bobble across the grass away from its resting place.

There is no explosion.

An X-ray confirms the battery pack is clear. A final search of the area finds nothing. It was just a device to blow up the railway line.

Something doesn't feel right, but there isn't anything more I can do here. The helicopters come back for us, the kit's packed up, picked up and moved 100 yards off the high bank of the railway line and into the field next to it. Chris gets the wheelbarrow off and we load it up with an explosive charge. I still have the stolen car to clear, but with the explosion on the railway line cleared as a priority, I'm not wasting time fannying about with the car. The charge is dropped into the car, the robot is pulled back, and with everyone taking cover, Chris fires the charge. The car is opened up, doors flung wide, roof peeled back, and my job of clearing it's made that much easier.

The area around the car is cleared first, then the car is searched, and lastly we move the remains of the chassis. SOCO come in for the explosion, the cordon steps down and prepares to collapse in and return to camp. A man in civilian clothes is let through by the police and comes towards us. Apparently he's the owner of the car, a Catholic from Newry – it's possible he may not be too friendly. I offer my hand and an explanation. The car had been crashed into a large rock on the track. The damage wouldn't have written it off, but my explosives certainly have. I offer that I thought he might prefer a new car rather than the bill to repair a damaged one, and he smiles, thanking me.

The SAT says he has seen it all now.

We pack to lift back to camp, and after two days of work, my team doesn't rest. While I go to the office to write up my report, they unpack the kit from the heli-portable buggies, check it, clean it and pack it away on the vans, so we're ready for another task if it comes in. It's a lot of work, and I'm grateful to them for their activity. Bri helps between the two vans, and intermittently brings me coffee and a sandwich.

My report takes a couple of hours, and long before I'm finished, the team has sorted the kit. I send them to their beds, but before they go Chris and Paul both ask me what was up with the task. I tell them I don't know: the SAT says before he leaves that sometimes the IRA just blow up the railway line. Paul says it still doesn't explain the reason for the warning beforehand, and there is a nagging doubt hanging over us all that something wasn't right. The SAT tells me "well done", and heads back to Lisburn with my report and photos. I take a copy to the Ops Room for the Ops Officer. He tells me his Ops Room were able to get a remote camera from one of the border watchtowers onto our task. One of the staff had recorded how long I had been in the EOD suit – 18 hours in two days. If anyone feels the need to lose a few pounds, I can recommend it.

For the next couple of days, it plays on my mind, but by the end of the week it's behind me. Friday comes and we're looking forward to the rugby over the weekend.

It's about 8pm and we're relaxing as best you can in Castle Greyskull.

The phone rings: you grow to hate or love the phone ringing in this job, depending on how you are set.

The Ops Officer tells me we have had a phone call from the phone box again – about a bomb on the railway line. Within minutes, there are reports of four explosions occurring on a 400m long railway viaduct north of Newry called the Eighteen Arches. Paul looks up and says, "that was what they were doing last week, they were 'dicking your drills'."

He means that a simple task was put in as a practice run to see if they thought they could kill me with the real job. The fact that this second job has now commenced means that they think they can get me.

I have another job on the railway line.

The preparation for this task is as bad, if not worse, than the last. The Int Cell has reports of men with balaclavas under the bridge. An over-flight by helicopter identifies explosion craters at either end of the bridge. There is a patch of suspiciously disturbed earth in the centre of the bridge, and while I'm in the helicopter, one of my ECM alarms goes off. The viaduct is approximately 200m from Kilnasagert Bridge. Even with my limited time in Bessbrook, I'm aware that there have been dozens of IRA attacks around there.

After landing, I report the ECM alarm to the headquarters, and an electronics expert comes down to examine the findings. A second helicopter ride later, and he has confirmed that I have expertly identified and localised onto the ECM transmitter at Bessbrook mill. I feel like a complete arse, and am aware that I'm already overly paranoid.

When I have spoken to other ATOs about my moment of stupidity much later, I find that it's surprisingly common.

It's still an ignominious start to my task and I'm embarrassed by my mistake.

Everything is pointing towards this attack being linked to the previous one a week ago. The same team, the same phone box, and the same MO.

I call the SAT to let him know I have another job and I'd like his attendance. He tells me he's not on duty this week and he's going on leave instead. The duty roster can obviously not be manned by just one person, and traditionally the cover is provided by the OC and SAT taking turns. The OC is also a capable and knowledgeable EOD operator, but the SAT is a soldier. The OC promised that he'd be on every task. Again, I'm feeling too young and too inexperienced for this post.

I have a large clean wall in my detachment room, 15ft high and 20ft across. I start to plan my task on it. My mind goes into overdrive. I take my last task apart in minute detail. I look at every picture again, and I put a huge map on the wall and tack pictures and notes to it. I then duplicate the set up for this new task and examine similarities and differences. I get my team to look through the last 30 years of reports looking for any tasks that have occurred in this location. I get them to look at railways – anything and everything that might have anything to do with the enemy plans for this attack. I ask Chris to get the technicians down for a second time to examine the robot and find out why it would only go for 90m before failing. They were obviously brought down by Chris after the last task, but they could find nothing wrong with the robot. I want the problem fixed.

I close my eyes and visualise myself as a terrorist watching my last task. I imagine how I would plan and implement an attack. Worryingly, I come up with dozens of ways to kill soldiers because I know their procedures.

Slowly, the intelligence picture builds. It comes in from RUC who were on duty, witnesses calling in the explosions, and our flights and photography. Everything is pointing to a major amount of activity by men wearing balaclavas centring around the 18 arches of the railway bridge.

I pore over the photographs, putting a template of every type of attack on top of the bridge. Many are mercifully impracticable and are ruled out, but with each evolution and discussion with my team, we keep coming back to one type of attack that just seems right. I try not to be too focussed on this, but despite the fact it's not the only possibility, it keeps coming back as most likely. If ... and it's a big if ... if this is the attack they're planning, will my drills and equipment be enough to defeat it? The simple answer is no. The location is difficult, the bridge is a good 100ft high in the middle, and anyone approaching is channelled onto either end. Also, in an environment where so many things are looked at in two dimensions, my plan in three dimensions. A distance that would be safe on any other task, now has to be looked at with trigonometry. A jammer that would keep me safe normally, does not have the range. I have to make a plan to cover at least 400m of railway line in electronic jamming.

This is going to be tricky.

Chris comes in with an idea: there is an ancient piece of kit in the garage that was scheduled to be back-loaded (returned to stores for disposal) as it had not been used in years. Basically a wooden pallet with a pair of railway wheels on and a small electric motor. It was designed to run a robot along a set of railway lines before dropping ramps and allowing the robot to deploy at a target. It avoided the difficulty of driving over railway sleepers and lines. It was called 'Belfast Belle'. We don't even know if it would work because it hasn't been subjected to any servicing and maintenance like the rest of the kit.

But batteries are plugged in and it's fully functional. It now becomes the subject of one of the quickest research and development projects in EOD history.

It was designed to be operated by the radio control pack on the robot, but as my robot's radio seems to want to stop 90 cm from us, will the Belle have the same problem? I wonder if it can be controlled by a command wire. We cut up parts of an old wheelbarrow cable drum, modify a firing cable from our team kit, and a couple of hours later we give it a test in the garage. It works.

I now have the means to drive the Belle as far down the railway line as I want to run cable: I have miles of cable. The next problem is how to know when I'm in the right spot on the railway line. Again, a piece of little-used equipment is modified.

'Houston' is a cable-controlled video camera. It replaces a piece of kit called Jack-in-the-box, and has been cursed as a piece of shit since it came in. The old kit could run off wheelbarrow batteries and feed through the monitors on the van kit. It meant all you had to carry was the camera and the cable. The new kit is a self-contained piece of flash nonsense. It can't be used through the van kit, and requires its own monitor, power supply and control system. Basically it's over-engineered and isn't used for anything except as a TV camera. It's bulky, too.

It finds itself having holes drilled into it and being bolted to the Belle.

I now have a cable-controlled railway trolley with video pictures. I can see the railway as I drive forwards for as long as the video system cable, which is at least 200m. This might just work.

We have no idea how far the Belle will travel on a set of batteries, but I figure it was meant to deploy and recover a robot, so if it only gets to the target for my task, that will be enough to get my jamming in place.

I turn my attention to another hole in our procedures in case the enemy had been watching the last task.

I need to modify how I use the REST team to search the railway line. So, I explain my plan to their boss, the Royal Engineer Search Advisor (RESA), the Army's expert on all things search. Ginge, the lad I worked with on the last task, has gone on his R&R, and I have a lad called Norman instead. My plan would require the use of a second REST, but I know they had two in the Province and the means to call up a third if required.

The IRA had historically used a device called a remoted-rc, and on my first tour, I had seen one first hand because I was used by my Operator to help him manually pull a half ton of explosives out of a drain at the side of the road – part of a land mine that had been designed to kill the Engineers returning from building military bases on the Irish border. If it hadn't been found and neutralised by us, it would certainly have been successful against the convoy of vehicles coming up the road. So tight was the time scale for completing their evacuation that the bomb had only been made partially safe by the boss as the convoy rolled past.

The RESA was having none of it.

My plan wasn't what it said in his rule book, so he wasn't prepared to change anything. I go from pointing to the pictures on the wall and explaining my concerns, to making a model on top of the Detachment pool table using an army blanket. I'm trying to keep my temper but I'm tired, and this bloke, Norm, just doesn't seem to understand what I'm talking about. We go from talking about it, to arguing. He says that his drills are his drills, and I say that the IRA don't follow drills, and that following drills blindly gets people killed.

"Look, fella," I say. "I understand your procedures, and on the last job this is what we did. This time, I'm telling you we need to guard against a remoted-rc. If they run a wire this way, I need to have searchers looking for it down here."

I'm pointing with a pool cue, and I explain that if we have his team in the places I want, they are still safely under my ECM cover but will find the enemy bomb before we're close enough to be killed by it.

He tells me that this procedure isn't in his drills, and in his opinion, his boss won't go for it. He wants to use one team and do the same drills as last time.

"Norm, if you do that, you'll find the device at the same time as you're standing on top of it. The IRA will let you fucking know because they'll kill your team."

He's looking blank.

"You do know what a remoted-rc, is don't you?"

He doesn't.

He describes a type of device that has never been seen anywhere in Northern Ireland. In fact, it was just a load of made-up shit, and I realise that this guy doesn't have a fucking clue. I'm so angry that I want to punch his lights out. Luckily, he's around the far side of the table and I'm able to calm myself momentarily as the rage ebbs just a touch.

I smash the cue onto the table and it splinters to pieces as I storm out. I pass through the garage, and I see Paul. With my fists still clenched, I tell him to go in there and explain to Norm what a remoted-rc is. I head off to the Ops Room to make my call to his boss.

His boss is completely okay about it.

I explain my idea: he endorses it and tells me that if I want a second team, I can have one. It really was that simple. Somewhat calmer, I return to the Det and see Paul. He explained the device to Norm repeatedly, but had given up. On returning to the garage, he checked his explanation with Chris just to make sure he hadn't lost his mind. Norm has gone, and I don't see much of him before the start of the task.

I make my plans for using the two REST without him. It's my operation anyway: he's only included out of courtesy, and because you never know, he might know something I don't. But I doubt it.

We delay responding to these types of devices for days or weeks, depending on the threat. Something like this, I'd have wanted to leave weeks, but you can't leave the railway shut down for so long. We have to go and clear it sooner rather than later.

Again, I'm not sleeping.

I make and remake my plan. I get the lads to 'red team' – to play the part of the IRA and see if I have missed anything. My team is fantastic. An Operator could not ask for a better bunch of lads to have his back, and even though they know I'm worried, they say nothing about it, just keep sorting kit and helping me with the plan.

We cleared the last task after two days. This time I asked for four, but the Ops Room and the RUC have pushed me to a compromise of three. Two nights of lying in the darkness and staring at the ceiling has not improved my general fluffy demeanour, so by day three, I'm sure I was an absolute joy to be around.

It's the last day before my task. The troops that will protect me have already deployed, and I worry for their safety as they take up their positions. Their OC has seen this concern adding to my burden and told me not to – that was his job. I'm grateful for the support, but I'm still relieved to hear that everyone has taken up their positions safely.

Both REST arrive. I have been sending briefings their way over the last two days but I'm pleased to meet them in person. I'm also relieved to find that both the Cpls in charge of the teams know far more than the RESA. I watch their faces as I explain the task to them. A typical task would see them search a perimeter of perhaps 800-1000m: in this case, they would be doing at least two-and-a-half times that. We were also breaking their current drills and putting in new ideas. Both the team leaders listen to my explanations as to why I want changes, and they're both happy that I'm not putting them or their boys at any greater risk than usual. One of them points to a spot on the map and says that this area has been missed in their sweep. I tell him I know, and that I think the risk to his lads going there is too great. I'll be going there in my suit without them.

He lets out a whistling laugh, and says, "Better you than me, buddy!"

I laugh.

"I know, mate, but once I've cleared this end, my plan is to put you guys onto the other end."

It's a bit of bravado on my part, but I know confidence is contagious, as is fear.

The plan is agreed.

The evening before the operation, I'm visited by our Chief Bleep, a big lad called Chunky. He and the OC (who is coming out on the task) arrive together. They let me talk them through my plan and my fears. I point out that there were two big areas of risk in my plan: one at the north and one at the south ends of the task. I felt that the south end – with three explosion craters – seems to be less risky than the north end with a single explosion. Therefore, my plan is to put myself to the north end first, and if I survive that, I might put the REST to the south.

Obviously, if the REST hadn't been happy with the plan, I would have just done both ends. Chunky tells me he thinks the plan is good and he can't suggest any improvements. He then tells me he's come down so we can use a bit of equipment for the first time. I've seen things like this before: when we have intelligence that something new is coming, we build a response to combat the threat. It doesn't get used until right at the last minute. Chunky explains what it does, and I slot its deployment into my plan. The OC tells me it's a good plan and that he knew the SAT had sent the right man to Bessbrook.

I've no faith in that statement, but I try not to show it.

The OC is particularly interested in the modifications I have made to the equipment and my plan to cover the viaduct in ECM. He looks at the Heath Robinson contraption, sees the bits of team equipment I've cut up and bolted together, and says, "Of course you've submitted the correct paperwork to allow you to conduct in-service modification of equipment then?"

He's joking, but for a second I don't realise. When I catch up, I join in his laughing.

"Of course I have. I love paperwork."

The OC then tells me he'll shoot off now and be back at zero-dark-thirty in time to join me on task, but he won't be flying out with me. He'll catch up before I make my first manual towards the target.

Within minutes of the OC leaving, the CATO (Chief Ammunition Technical Officer) arrives at the Det. It's rare to see this particular Colonel out of his office, let alone down here. It's as if they all smell something big in the offing and want to make sure they don't miss out on the action. He asks me to go through the task and my plan with him, and amongst the crowd of my team, both RESTs, Ops and Int staff, RUC liaison, dog handler and everyone else who now seems to crowd my Detachment, I find space to sit on a pair of comfy chairs in front of the fireplace and roll of honour, lay my map onto the coffee table, and repeat my plan to the Colonel.

Towards the end of my briefing, he interrupts me and in a mocking tone he says, "Oh Come on, Sgt Bell. I've only been sat here five minutes and I can see holes in your plan."

I guess tiredness and stress got to me in that moment, and I cuttingly hiss back at him that I know there are holes in the plan. I've been sat here looking at them for the last three days. I've made my plan to only leave these specific holes, and that I'm taking the risk to go and clear them, not him.

Before he can respond – and luckily for me Chunky, who has been watching – leans over and says it's as good a plan as could be made in the circumstances. Somehow, he deflects the Colonel from me, and I don't remember him leaving.

It's dark now and I tell my team I want them to go to their beds. I know I'm not going to sleep, and I guess I need them as rested as they can be. There is just me and Chunky left in the Det. Over a coffee, he asks me if I'm okay. I shrug my shoulders. I have no idea.

My room is sticky, airless and hot.

Army single beds are especially crap, and I recommend buying your own mattress. I must have woken up around three. The team will be up before five to start cross-loading kit onto the heli-vehicles.

For nearly two hours, I can think of nothing else: the railway lines stretching off into the distance, the high gravel banks that mean you can be seen from miles around, the explosions, the risks in my plan, the muppet RESA, and the damn CATO turning up at the end to rubbish my work. I'd prayed that something would turn up by now – some bit of intelligence, some image on the photography spotted and identified, anything … something … so it wasn't just the IRA versus me. Nothing had come.

I lie on my bed and realise how scared I am. It's pointless trying to sleep, so I shower and dress, lock my room and take the spiral stone steps down to the outside. It's right next to my Detachment.

I make myself a coffee and stand outside looking at the grimness of the mill in the pre-dawn light. The first glimmer of sunlight is starting to crest the horizon, and to one side of the mill there is a large tree. Stripped of its leaves for winter, the sun's rays are playing through its skeletal form. I know deep down that I'm not good enough, and that despite my best efforts, I'm not coming back alive today.

The sun in the trees reminds me of the farmland where I grew up. I realise that I'm never going to see my family again, and I think of how much my death will upset my father who is ill. My eyes well up. My thoughts are all of regret, for all the things I will never get to do and for the sadness I have caused my family.

The door next to me opens and I hold my hand up as if I'm shielding my eyes from the sunlight.

Chris says, "Morning Boss," as he passes, and I reply in kind, while turning my back to him.

He opens the door to the detachment, and I stick my boot in to stop it from closing as he goes through. I dry my eyes. The time for selfish thoughts is over. I sip my coffee and to go to work. If Chris noticed, he never said anything.

We land short of Kilnasaggart Bridge.

I have to clear past that to get to the viaduct. The task is the same as last time, but I can see people looking at us from the fields and farms either side of the railway lines. There are two people, a man and a woman, standing in a farmyard. While I'm on task, the man spends nearly the whole time on the phone.

We get ourselves to our start point and the railway stretches off into a lazy left-hand bend over the arches. Periodically, I scan the bridge with my binoculars, but I'm unlikely to see anything more than I could on the photography taken by the over-flight. Chris deploys the robot to the start of the bridge to examine the first site of explosion. There isn't anything except the crater. The OC arrives in plain clothes and an unmarked car. He climbs up the steep bank to the railway line over an uncleared route. This does not go un-noticed by the team.

As he gets to the ICP, Bri pulls a spare combat jacket out of his pack and tells him to put it on – no point sticking out like a sore thumb, exposed for the world to see. The REST are next and depart on their mammoth task. I watch their progress, knowing that when they get back to the ICP it will be a step closer to my turn. They disappear from view as they track across the far end of the search area. I know that they'll be stopping as they cross the tracks to add shunts to the railway lines. Previously, the IRA had nearly killed an Operator using two of the railway lines to send a firing signal to a bomb. We now routinely cut or shunted the railways anywhere we worked. It was an old and unlikely way to fire a bomb, but you could be sure if we stopped combatting it, the IRA would go back to using it again. Once a threat, always a threat was the mantra.

Over an hour later, and the REST are back.

They drop their kit and gather at the back of the ICP. Chris and Paul get the Belfast-Belle out and onto the tracks. The camera is attached and the ECM systems are all strapped onto the wooden platform. We operate it through a controller wired directly to the wheelbarrow: from there through a cable connecting the wheelbarrow to the modified firing cable, and through that cable to the controller on the Belle. Chris presses the buttons and the Belle rolls seamlessly down the railway line. So far so good. As we roll, I watch the monitor and scan the image looking for anything out of the normal. The contraption is past the first explosion at the entry to the bridge and now onto the viaduct. In the cameras, I can see the far end of the bridge and even some of the troops guarding the area. I'm looking for the patch of disturbed earth we saw from the helicopter – the hidden controller for the bomb they have planted.

We get to the end of the cable on the camera before we get to the target. There is still cable left on the firing cable drum, but from here on we'll have no camera pictures. I zoom in and search for the patch of earth. After what seems like ages, we spot it. Carefully, I pull the picture back on the camera and count the number of railway sleepers between the square mark in the stones and the trolley. It's 48 sleepers away.

I get Paul to measure the sleepers behind us and tell me the distance. He comes back to me and we're too far away. I then ask him to pull out the same distance on the firing cable we're using to control the Belle. He lays this behind us, and after disconnecting the camera cable, Chris sends the little trolley forwards. The cable runs out and I use it to position the trolley. I can't see if it's in the right place, but this is as good as it's going to get for me. Chunky then deploys the new-fangled piece of kit and normal transmission in hundreds of Northern Irish homes is suddenly interrupted. Our electronic jamming has played havoc with Irish TV for generations.

It's time.

The suit comes out and the team helps me into it. My equipment is loaded onto me, and Chris carries my EOD helmet. For a change, I let him put it onto my head rather than doing it myself. He folds both of my ears down onto the side of my head, and I have to get him to hold it still while I wriggle my head around and sort myself out.

"Good luck, boss."

The team is briefed: everything that can be done has been done. All I have to do is go and have a look at the explosion.

I'm completely detached as I walk forwards. I can remember imagining being outside myself looking down from behind as I walk forwards. I'm on the sleepers again, and I take my time getting to the explosion. As I walk, I scan around me: the couple in the farm are still there, he's still on his phone. There is a dead fox in a tree, probably launched there after being hit by a passing train, but being unusual (by my terms), it gets a good looking at on my way past. The explosion is just a hole in the ground, no sign of anything, no evidence of what caused the explosion or in fact evidence of it being an explosion at all. I search carefully around the hole and the area. I find nothing. It's not difficult to make a bomb that would leave so little sign, but it's unusual in IRA terms. I don't feel any easier for not finding anything.

I stand at the entrance to the bridge I can see the Belle halfway across the viaduct parked where I know the patch of disturbed earth is. I pick up my kit and start towards it. I'm sweating inside the suit and I'm conscious of everything in minute detail. As well as scanning where I'm going, I also turn around periodically to scan the area behind me, in case something hidden as I approach is visible when I pass. Each time, I look back towards my team who are getting further and further away.

I get to the Belle and put my equipment down carefully. I make sure to put each piece on a railway sleeper rather than the stones between. I search an area up to the disturbed earth and lie down. My face is inches from the stones now and I carefully start lifting them one at a time. The pile grows as each new stone is examined, gently lifted, examined again and then slowly pulled to my side. The hole gets deeper, and eventually I have to accept defeat, there isn't anything here. If there is, I can't find it. I walk back to the ICP and the OC is keen to know what I have found. He's positively excited.

"There's nothing there, sir," I tell him.

I've no idea about the hole in the ground. I can find no indications of an explosion, let alone any parts of a device. In my opinion it's nothing, at best a hoax. The OC can't believe it.

"What about the explosions?"

What explosions? No matter where the four actual explosions heard on the night were, I doubt they were here. I expect the holes seen at the far end are nothing, too.

The clearance takes another 24 hours and, as I predicted, the holes at the other end of the bridge aren't explosions either. I suspect they were caused by railway work. We had the railway workers into the Det (after covering up everything on the walls), who swore blind the holes photographed were new and definitely not from railway maintenance.

Where were the explosions from that night? I have no idea. We used to have a system of sensors that would triangulate explosions so we could narrow down search areas. When I asked about this system at the start of the task, I was told that a decision had been made to stop paying to have them maintained and calibrated. I'd like to weigh the cost of that maintenance against the half a million pounds per day that an EOD Planned Operation costs.

After another two days on the railway, I'm exhausted.

My team tell me that they didn't think I'd make it through. To repay them in kind, I told them that if I was the IRA, I'd have targeted the whole team. That made them quiet down. Chris said afterwards that he's petrified of heights, so being on top of the railway viaduct with a low wall around his knees to trip over wasn't much fun for him either. I'm just relieved it's all over, and each time I hear from the SAT/OC and HQ that they're sorry there wasn't anything down there for me, I bite my tongue instead of telling them that they're fucking idiots. If there had been something, I might not have made it home.

I didn't realise the damage that I had done to myself that day.

You have to account for your actions in all areas of your work, and this day would come back to me numerous times over my career in both good and bad ways.

FOR A WHILE, BESSBROOK QUIETENED DOWN.

I did a clearance of a suspect postal item which turned out to be an appointment for a barium enema. Nice.

Then after the calm, it all started ramping up again.

The briefing room in Bessbrook had a fantastic scaled 3D model of the area of operations. Every road and house was modelled in minute detail, and the daily briefing was accompanied by an assistant with a laser pointer who would highlight the areas as they were discussed.

"Kevin O, who lives at... [point with laser] ... has been leaving his house in Cullyhanna [point] in the mornings, picking up Peter R from here [point], and driving down the A29 [point following road], and crossing the border at H21 [point] and into the South [wave around on carpet representing Southern Ireland]. It's assessed that as KO is an explosives manufacturer, and PR is known as part of the fabrication department, it's our assessment that a mortar attack is likely within the next two to four weeks. Intelligence suggests that their most likely target is Bessbrook. All personnel are to wear helmet and body armour when not in hardened accommodation.

I plod back to the detachment, and warn the team about the good news and the new dress code. I'm now 10 months into a six month tour. I'm ready to go home, but all that's waiting back there is a divorce. What is there to go home for? As I'm mulling over my choices, the SAT phones: I'm being replaced. Excellent news. Matt will be down to take over in two weeks. He puts the phone down.

The briefings continue.

The terrorists are clearly progressing – notable absences, presumably to make the mortar bomb. This is the same mortar that PIRA have been using for years.

It's clearly coming.

Matt arrives by covert car which pulls to a stop outside the Det. After shaking my hand, he says,

"Just a second," and calls the SAT. As he answers, Matt says, "Are you fucking kidding me?"

He's not impressed with the Det. To be fair, it's going to be grim after the plush existence in the Officers Mess up in Londonderry. He's more impressed as I show him his bunk, the perimeter fence, central cookhouse, and what passes for an Officers Mess here. Then I brief him on the patch.

"You've got a mortar attack coming."

He replies he's already had one. He'd been woken from his sleep by a bang in Ebrington one morning. Wondering what had woken him, he thought it was a dream and then told himself that if it was anything important, someone would come and tell him. He closed his eyes only to have a knock at the door and one of the mess say, "There's been a mortar attack on camp."

He opened the window of his room and leant outside. There, on the floor next to his room, was a 120kg IRA mortar.

They almost managed to deliver it to him personally.

"Well you've got another one coming," I said.

I packed kit, did my handover, said my farewells, and gave my team each of their leaving presents. I thanked Matt for letting me go home, and got into the covert car. The driver took me back towards Lisburn, and as we drove north, we passed the 18 arches.

The SAT and OC wrote me a nice report and that was my lot.

Back via Belfast airport to Birmingham, and a train and taxi ride to my UK base. Four days after I got home, the IRA fired a mortar bomb into Bessbrook SF Base. Fortunately, the damage was minimal and Matt got to defuse the second mortar of his tour. He was later awarded a Queen's Gallantry Medal for his time in NI.

I didn't want to be at home, and within twenty four hours, I'd had enough. I unpacked my kit from Ireland, re-packed a single civilian bergen, and got on the train to Heathrow. I stood in the airport, looked at the flights that were departing and decided.

"That one."

I'd fill the visa in on the plane.

I WAS STILL THINKING ABOUT THE RAILWAY JOB WHEN I RANDOMLY happened to find myself in contact with a former AT who'd served in Bessbrook. His name was on the role of honour in front of me. Over a few cagey questions, we confirmed we knew the same people and accepted the other as genuine. He told me he was scared while he was out there, and that helped me a little.

His name was one of the old guard, a legend from my history, and I appreciated his support. I had nightmares about the under-car job, the burning pub and the railways for years afterwards.

I dreamed that I'd lost both my hands under the car and woke crying; I dreamed the wires caught around my jacket stopped me escaping the, and I watched third party as my hands burned and shrivelled like the corpses I'd seen in NI already. But the railway ones were beyond all that. I'd wake crying in my sleep, but the relief that it was a dream was quick to kick in.

Eventually, I was able to accept the dreams were the same as scars and earned by my own actions, so I could blame no one else. I learned to live with them, even though I still have flashbacks on railways stations and I still have the occasional night sweat, panic attack, or just depressed grumpy mood for no reason.

At the time, I saved myself by concentrating on the little girl I'd saved who would now grow up to have a life. It was worth everything to know I'd made that difference. She'll be 18 about now. The little boy from my first tour will be 31.

CHAPTER 10
I DIDN'T VOLUNTEER

I WAS at our Army School of Ammunition (ASofA) as an instructor, a teacher on our 'A Team' that trained bomb disposal operators for operations against the IRA in Northern Ireland. I had a real passion for that work.

All the instructors were assembled and told that it was likely we would go to war in Iraq in the New Year. I didn't ask to go to Iraq – for the first time in my career, I didn't volunteer. I thought the second I heard it was on the cards, it was a bullshit story, and that any dealings in it would also be shit. I have no interest in going.

Then Chris, my best friend, sticks his hand up excited like a kid saying, "Send me, send me, send me ... and send Troll, too."

Yeah, thanks.

The Unit we're sending has been under supported for decades. It was traditionally a dumping ground for muppets, but all of a sudden it's going to war. When they actually looked at what they had, it was 50 ammo techs under strength. Five instructors from the ASofA are nominated to deploy and make up the numbers. We spend some time with 821 EOD Squadron, but we're made to feel like outsiders. No kit arrives, the vehicles are late getting to us and what we get is mostly the shit other units are happy to get rid of. It's badly organised, it's going to be shit.

We'd keep arrive at the airport then keepgetting turned back. Our SAT gets through to us on the phone and tells me and Chris we have to be on the next flight. Chris and I are back at HQ in Didcot (also known as Deadcat).

Chris spies a copy of Big Boys Rules on the bookcase and says he'll have that to read on the plane. We've no civvies to wear, so we go to a charity shop in town and buy trousers and luminous tops. We look like a pair of lunatics. We go for a curry and sleep in the stores wrapped up in a vehicle camouflage net. We attend Brize Norton again. The RAF say we can't get on the flight as it's a Press Flight, full of reporters. Chris sees his arse, and we get told we can fly.

At the main building, the journos are all laying on the comfy seats, spread out relaxing, while the few soldiers who are flying are either standing or sitting on hard, plastic seats.

I bought my deserts as I knew we'd never get our issue in time. Chris is still in green DPM (disruptive pattern material) and leather boots. He goes up to one of the prone journos and measures his boots against the journo's desert boots. He wakes up and thinks Chris is going to nick them. We go along the line making them all wake up, feel uncomfortable, or just plain poking them to move over. We clear a line of seats then go and tell the soldiers to go sit and relax. They do.

Chris says he's spotted someone. Who? A woman. He says she's a news reporter, then runs off to the free book stand and picks up some sci-fi paperback. He stands behind her shoulder and says nothing. She has a crowd of lackeys, hanging on her every word, but one of them can't help but keep looking at Chris over her shoulder. She realises someone is there and turns. Chris thrusts his book at her and shouts, "Sign this, please!" She's properly startled and jumps; the lackeys laugh. She snorts but does sign his book. I'm behind him and think, in for a penny. I offer my book and she takes the copy of Big Boys Rules off me and signs it. Chris says, "I've got a copy of that in my ... you bastard!!!"

"It's mine now."

We get to theatre and are told the rush is that we're being allocated to American Units to invade the night before the Brits. We have to do some training with the American EOD, but the Royal Engineer chain of command have insisted that the Americans take their EOD teams, as well. I was tasked with running some EOD training for the Royal Engineer (Engineers are referred to by me as Wedge, The Wedge, The Stinking Wedge and the Borg. In some areas, there's a little animosity between our trades.)

There is a Lt H who has a story all of her own and a guy called Si Cullingworth, a Staff Sergeant (SSgt). He's clearly the brains of the operation and keeps Lt Hardwick in check.

We get given an area to use that has some chicken huts and a single building. We give the Americans the house and we use the huts. I arrange a training task (options are limited), but I set up an obvious tool on a release wire so if he moves it the device will function. He searches into the location and finds the wire running from the tool. He stands up and says, "Over to you ATO."

I ask him if he wants to search any more – the item might be attached to a military booby trap rather than an IED (military booby traps are Wedge territory), but he says, "Nope, you guys can have it and send your little robot in."

"You sure I can't get you to go check?"

Nope, besides there's a RCIED over there, (Radio Controlled device), which I'd hidden on an oblique angle, often missed by the unwary hadn't fooled him. Yep I like this guy.

We run some more training with Lt Wegde; the short version is she manages to set off the booby trap and gets a face full of Kuwaiti chicken dung propelled by a small simulator change for her troubles.

We go to collect our ammunition. There isn't any.

We get one box of explosives and one roll of detonating cord (like explosive washing line), but no detonators – without which it's virtually useless.

I scavenge around the depot and start stealing stuff. We get a box of detonators with the quantity 35 written on the side. I throw it into the cab and we head off. I open it after we're outside the depot and it only has 10 in it – someone has already beaten me to it. They're electrical ones, so anything we blow up will have to be connected to us by a cable. I have 200m of that in the vehicle.

We have no ammunition for our pistols and little for our rifles. We then get co-located just inside the Kuwait border with the American EOD team we're supporting ready for the invasion, and I get some ammunition from them and, crucially, five plain (non-electric) detonators, some burning fuse and six firing devices which will start the fuse burning.

We have all been put into chemical weapon suits. The British only have the woodland camouflage version (which made buying your own desert combats a pointless exercise).

The area is like a moonscape. The burning sun combined with this flat featureless desert do a cracking job of baking us in our black, brown and green camouflage suits.

We put up cam nets on our vehicles for shade and dig 'shell scrapes' next to them (shallow pits for taking cover and sleeping). We're there for about 36 hours and during this time we have regular alerts. Every 15 minutes the alarm goes off and we have to get into our holes. Fifteen minutes later and it's Gas! Gas! Gas! as the chemical alert drill goes, and we have to put our respirators on and lie there. Another fifteen minutes, and it's all clear. This goes on for hours, and eventually the Brits have had enough. We're having an O Group (giving out orders), and the alarm goes off. We all sit around the nearest shell scrape but just put our feet in, sitting in a circle. The Gas! Gas! Gas! alarm goes off and we all put our respirators on the top of our heads but don't pull them down. One of the lads has a burner going in the middle, brewing up so we can have a cup of tea. An American patrol making their way around the location in their full chemical suits and respirators see us not in our holes and come over.

"Hey, you guys, you need to get in your holes," they mumble through their face gear.

"We're in it," comes the reply, and one of the team points to our feet which are clearly in the hole.

"You guys also need to have your respirators on."

"We can't wear our respirators we need to be able to drink our tea."

"You guys can't be drinking tea during an alert," he says.

"Not drink tea? We're having our O Group and you lot and your exercise drill will have to wait."

The patrol look at each other...

"Exercise drill? We've been getting shot at with Scuds for the last six hours."

"Well, they'll have to be a fucking good shot to hit me in the middle of the desert," says Colin.

The patrol walk off and I hear one of them say to his mate, "Those Brits are crazy, man."

The American EOD ask us for a team photo. They exclude the Wedge. I'd have invited Si, but he'd have brought that muppet with him.

We invade.

The Americans shoot an Iraqi civilian for, "Not stopping when we shouted STOP."

I ask them if they knew whether he spoke English in the first place, and what would they do as a civilian if they saw another nation's army coming down the road. They shrug and send him to the medics. The Americans are heading off to Baghdad; we're going to be left at the target on our own until the Brits arrive. The American EOD guys offer email addresses, and knowing that I'll lose any bits of paper, they stick them in the book next to the woman journalist's signature. Their comments are better than hers.

On the morning of 23 March, a report comes in of explosives under a bridge.

"Sounds like a military demolition to me," I say.

Si replies, "Nah, it's definitely an IED."

In an environment where some people were 'poachers' and would be unprofessional to try and gain jobs, we had a laugh at how neither of us cared. Then his Captain, Mick E, turned up and started arguing that this was definitely an Engineers' task. Oh, you're one of them.

Si and I offered to both deploy and whoever the task belonged to would take it, but he wasn't having that. I offer Si a bottle of Port (well, he's a fellow senior NCO), and ask him to sign my book. He says he'll sign it later and heads off to have another go at convincing the idiot captain that we should both deploy.

Both of them return to the CP; the Wedge Captain (SO3) is smiling. Fortunately for him, a routine ammo task came in and he deploys me to the Black Watch in an instant.

PART III - IRAQ

CHAPTER 11

AZ ZUBAYR – 23 MARCH 2003

MY TEAM DEPLOYED to dispose of the ammunition which the Black Watch called in. We went to their HQ where we were handed a British 51mm Illuminating Round that had been shut in a warrior door and damaged. The Black Watch then said they had more ammunition to be disposed of. I said they would need to ask the Engineers as I was technically under their control. I was about to tell them to get on the radio when the Wedge SO3 drove past with the EOD team. The issue that seemed to have delayed our deployment to the bridge appeared to have evaporated and he couldn't get himself there fast enough.

He was flagged down, and they started to explain about his other task, some ammunition and some vehicles needed destroying. He waved them off with a, "whatever, but the ATO isn't allowed to blow up vehicles," and pulled his door shut.

Really?

The Black Watch took that to mean they could use my ATO team. The truck was a Duro, a six-wheel un-armoured vehicle built for us for the operation. With my ECM support in a lightly armoured Saxon, we were escorted to the task area by two Black Watch Warriors. I had been given a bum steer in my history with all the ATO officers I had worked for who could read a map, and the Lt in charge of the front warrior got us geographically confused three times whilst trying to find the way out of the oil facility.

We headed down main road past the last Challenger Tank and into Az Zubayr, just south of Basra.

As we arrived in the first street, the small arms fire started. From a history of peace-keeping operations, I was used to having a protective cordon around me when I worked. The protection of the infantry is appreciated by all decent ATOs and I always made sure I helped them out whenever I could. I looked at my number two, Colin, and said, "Sounds like the cordon's getting shot at."

Colin, who was ex-infantry and had more of a clue about these things having been involved in the first Gulf war, replied, "What cordon, dickhead? It's us."

The Warriors began engaging enemy left and right down alleyways, firing main armament at RPG gunners, and we made our way through town with the Warriors leap-frogging past us at each junction. The lead Warrior would drive forwards and stop on a junction, engage down the road, then leap forward with the commander beckoning us to sprint across.

As we made our way through town, Col had an Iraqi run up to his door and attempt to engage him with an AK rifle. The door isn't armoured, so the 7.62mm ammunition is going to slice straight through it. The rifle jammed and we drove forwards. As we did so, the lead Warrior fired its main armament past us and a 30mm round took out the gunman, painting him across the side of our truck.

As we drove through the marketplace in the centre of town, the gunfire died off. The faces of the Iraqis in town showed their surprise, and it was so crowded we really had to work to push through. We exited the far side of the market and turned right.

As we left town, we had buildings on our right, with open ground on our left leading to more buildings that we later found out were barracks. The lead Warrior stopped, the commander came out of his turret and spread his map out to try and unfuck our position.

The only way to describe it is in Col's words: BANG – WHOOSH.

We could hear the rounds flying past us. I initially thought it was a tank engaging us. I was looking out of the driver's side trying to identify the firing point. There were more rounds fired at us and my ECM Operator, Glenn, got on the radio.

"Can we move? Not trying to be a girl or anything but we've just had three RPG rounds fly between our vans."

I instructed my No2 to drive our van onto the gardens beside the

Warrior in front, protecting us from our left flank ... and so I could shout at the Warrior Commander to drive on.

He asked me where to.

"Anywhere, just fucking drive!" He was resistant to my advice, so I pointed to his left and shouted, "Tank!"

That got his attention, and we set off. Col used the lead Warrior as a shield until we were out of town on a dust track. A crowd of people were running up to a bank on our right and they came around a building on the hill as we approached. The taller guy at the back had a tube held in his hands – an RPG? I wasn't able to be sure. (To this day, I still can't be sure.) I opened fire on them with my rifle which I'd cleaned and oiled that morning, and had two stoppages in five rounds: piece of shit. But they all scattered and there was no-incoming rocket.

We continued at speed down the track a short distance and found a lone Challenger tank pointing menacingly back towards the town, so we stopped beside it.

We de-bussed, the lads took cover, and I have the opportunity to get a cheeky photo of the lads under fire.

The Warrior Commander got on the radio and in short order there was artillery landing in the tree line we'd been engaged from. After about an hour, we mounted up. I thought we were going back to the oil facility. I didn't believe that we were heading back into town, especially not in our un-armoured 'Bread Van', but back in we went.

We turned right just before our stop point where we'd been rocketed, drove parallel to the barracks, and met up with some other Black Watch in Warriors and some Royal Engineer Armour.

The brief was that the BW had over-run this barracks earlier and found three ammunition stores. They had requested support to destroy the ammunition and deny this to the enemy – as a matter of priority.

I was briefed that they were told no one was available, and they were ordered to leave the barracks as they were engaged with the enemy for control of the site. When I turned up for the 51mm, I think a decision was made to deploy to target, to complete this mission; the Black Watch troops were instructed to re-take the barracks.

On arrival at the scene, there was a line of troops on a sand berm (a raised ridge) supported by Warriors.

On being given the brief by an Engineer on scene, I informed him that this sounded like a Combat Engineer task, and SO3 EOD would be pissed if I just ran in and did it. (I also didn't want to poach a job.) So I gave them the SO3's call-sign and requested he refer up for instructions.

The BW were at pains to stress that their position here was tenuous at best, and their problems of having to take, retake and hold this barracks against enemy fire until the ammunition was destroyed. I asked that they humour me and send the radio call. The importance being the RPG's stockpile that we had already experienced.

The answer came back.

"The Boss says get to it."

In hindsight, I don't know if that was SO3 EOD or the Black Watch Boss or the Commander in the vehicle.

It didn't matter I would have done it anyway.

I took one lad, Jaffa, with me, and we went through the infantry position and into the Barracks, supported by a small number of infantry who led me to the first bunker. The infantry IC with us was asking how long, and I said I needed to see first. Inside the bunker was floor to ceiling munitions on a scale I had never seen for demolitions before. It was the only time I remember hesitating in Iraq.

"Ten minutes and I'll have this rigged. Will that be a problem?"

"No problem," he said. "You need ten minutes – we'll give you that. But get a shift on – this place is crawling with them."

Jaffa and I laid a lazy line of det-cord linked to small charges. I needed to move some of the ammunition so I could use the explosive filling within to our advantage. There was no real way to clear it for booby traps, so we used torches and did the best we could and took a guess. It wasn't neat but it was the best I could do. I had Jaffa sort the fuse (which was American). We laid the det-cord out of the door and attached it to the American detonators, safety fuse and firing device that I'd been given by the US Marine Corp EOD prior to our parting. There is no safe way we could have fired off this much explosives on the cable and electric detonators.

The BW Sergeant came in and said, "Did you see them? Did you see them?"

I hadn't, but an RPG team had run past the door of our bunker and fired an RPG at the troops on the berm.

We ran to the next bunker, leaving the firing device on the floor near the first bunker; we'd covered the fuse coming out of the bunker in sand. The second bunker was just the same, floor to ceiling with ammunition. We started the same procedure: I gave Jaffa the fuse to lay out the door. The Sgt came and pushed Jaffa inside the building and told him to stay there. I told him to get outside and lay the fuse. He went back out.

The Sgt pushed him back in, and in a voice that you use to speak to small children he said, "I said stay. There is an Arab in the next building shooting at you when you go out the door. I can't shoot him while I'm looking after you. Stay here, got it?"

We stayed.

I took a photo of my handiwork. A few seconds later the Sgt came in, grinned and said, "Got him. You can carry on now."

We continued, and Jaffa laid the det-cord outside as we had done at the last bunker.

We ran, fast, to the third bunker and the wheels fell off. This bunker wasn't ammunition but weapons. I made a quick plan to pile them all in the same room, lay some charges down the centre and stack mortar rounds on top of the charges. Again not ideal, not in any books, but it'd ruin the weapons, denying them to the enemy.

On completion of this third bunker, I ran back out to head to the first and start the fuses. The longest was five minutes, the shortest three minutes. I met the Sgt pelting full speed in the other direction.

"Leg it, ATO!" he shouted. "The enemy have overrun the barracks."

"What about the fuses?" I asked. "I've pulled them."

"When?"

"I don't know. I've been a bit busy running and shooting."

He told me to get back to the berm: he would see to the last fuse. Him and his lads fought the oncoming enemy and gave us the chance to escape. I grabbed what explosives I had left, then headed off with Jaffa. As we left, I saw a belt-fed grenade launcher we'd missed in the armoury buildings, so threw that over my shoulder, too.

There were RPGs bursting around us as we ran, and although I don't really remember much of the shooting that went on, I do distinctly remember the RPG that exploded just above my head, close enough that my ears were ringing. Col informed me that he lost count of the RPG rounds fired during the battle, and that the enemy were everywhere in the barracks with rounds constantly striking the buildings we were in.

We made it back.

The Sgt and his lads followed us close behind. He told us to head off and that he and his snipers would engage the enemy to keep the RPG teams heads down as we left. The enemy overran the barracks and the fuses burned down. My parting words were to not wait any longer than three minutes. We made it out of the town and I stopped to watch, not convinced that what we had done would even work.

The explosions occurred.

I subsequently found out from the Black Watch snipers that they were still fully engaged when the first bunker, (approximately 10 tons of explosives) functioned. Fortunately, it was on the far side of the barrack and the Black Watch guys escaped injury. The enemy pouring into the barracks were not so lucky.

In his words, "It did give the fuckers something else to worry about," and allowed the BW to disengage and make their retreat.

The second and third bunkers followed suit.

We reported the contact, the ambush in town and the stiff resistance through Brigade. However, this information didn't stop the Engineers sending one of their teams into the town that afternoon in two Land Rovers. The Land Rovers were engaged and disabled by the RPG teams. Two lads managed to escape by jumping a wall and hijacking a vehicle from an Iraqi. They made it a short distance out of town and found a Challenger tank whose team they briefed on the ambush. The tank crews were not able to proceed into town and the other two members of the patrol were captured.

Si Cullingworth* and his driver were paraded through town by the Ba'ath, lined up and executed. Their bodies were dumped in a shallow grave at the edge of town.

Editor's note: we contacted the family of Si Cullingworth for permission before including this. We were unable to reach the family of his driver, so have not included his name here, out of respect.

CHAPTER 12

IRAQ MEMORIES

THIS CHAPTER WAS WRITTEN and sent to Troll by his friend and former colleague, Chris Meadows.

REPRINTED WITH PERMISSION.

WE WERE OUT CHATTING TONIGHT WITH THE TEAM HERE IN LIBYA. A friend of mine told the American he saw me draw my pistol on an officer in Iraq, I honestly don't remember it, but he was certain I did. As the night has drawn on, I'm wondering if I have a vague memory of it. Barking how some stuff fades from your consciousness.

This tour was my first deployed operation as an ammunition technician. However, I was to be conducting a role that I had previous experience in as an IEDD No2. The only uncertainty was who I would be working with. Luckily for me, it was with the infamous Troll Bell, who I had met and worked with in Northern Ireland.

So, I knew what standards were expected of me as the No2. Those standards were going to be very high, but having made the grade before, I was positive I could do the same again. Although Troll sets high standards, they were not anything he wouldn't have done himself, or had done already. It was also going to be a good opportunity for me to learn some new skills as an ammunition technician from someone who if he didn't know it, then it wasn't worth knowing.

Prior to the deployment, I was invited to Troll's house for a night of eating, drinking and just good old fashioned chewing the fat. Inevitably, we ended up playing HALO on the Xbox just to complete our pre-deployment training. I'm not sure how soon after Troll deployed, but what I do remember – and is my biggest moan of the tour – is the fact that I deployed too late to be the No2 on the team to go across the border into Iraq with the US Marines.

Eventually, I flew out to theatre to meet up with the section, and spent a number of weeks being the No2 of one of the oldest SSgt's the trade has, known as Chinny. After a slow and uneventful trip through Iraq, we made it to an airfield known as Shaiba Airbase. This was located only a few kilometres from Basra and the frontline, but also the point where I met up with a very tired looking and dishevelled Troll. He smelt worse than an open grave after having spent many days in full NBC rig attached to the US Marine Corps. It was still a happy moment for me because at that point I knew that I at last was going to see and do something exciting to tell my kids – what I achieved in the war.

After a short period of chatting, it was straight into it, driving to the far side of the airbase for Brigade orders. On arrival at HQ, Troll jumped out of the vehicle and headed into one of the tents whilst I remained outside. It had just started to get dark.

The next time I saw Troll, it was pitch black. He asked me to head back to our admin area to retrieve something (I have no memory what it was). Now this sounds like a simple task, which in normal circumstances it would have been. But I had no familiarity of the airfield, it was dark, and all white light was banned, for obvious reasons. I did, however, have a set of NVGs, but no way of attaching them to my head or helmet. Troll gave me a set of basic instructions to get myself back onto the main runway, then all I had to do was stay on that until I saw the last aircraft shelter on the right hand side: simples.

You could not be further from the truth – trying to drive one-handed whilst holding a set of NVGs in the other is no easy task, especially when trying to avoid Challenger tanks that are screaming around the area at top speed.

I eventually found my way onto the main runway and thought, that has got to be the worst of it. As I progressed, I was counting the hangars which I could clearly see with the NVGs.

Then all of a sudden, I was blinded by white light which obscured everything in the eyepiece. Thinking that my final memory was going to be being hit by a 120mm smoothbore barrel in the head, I jumped on the brakes. After about a minute of just sitting there expecting something to happen, I continued driving, eventually finding what I was looking for. The return journey went a lot smoother but I did get a look of where the fuck have you been? by Troll.

The remainder of the night was spent trying to sleep in the back of the truck next to the wheelbarrow.

The next morning, we were awoken by the biggest alarm clock the British Army could offer – the AS90 bombing the shit out of the Iraqi Army in Basra. After a quick field wash and briefing from Troll on the day's events, we made our way off the airbase and onto a main route heading in the direction of Basra. The tasking was to conduct enemy denial demolitions a couple of kilometres outside of the city. En route, we met up with a section of Royal Engineers who were there to assist but not conduct demolitions.

The ammunition storage site consisted of several buildings that were positioned near the outside perimeter with the centre part of the site just bare desert floor. You could see evidence all around the area of panic, as ammunition and explosives had been scattered everywhere and empty packages strewn to the four winds. This panic must have started the minute the coalition forces came into Iraq.

The first job was to do a walk around of the whole site to see how big a task lay ahead of us. It soon become clear that this was going to be the mother of all demolition tasks. For Troll, it was just another day in paradise – the chance to create havoc and mayhem the only way he knows, through the medium of explosives.

The RE lads were in their element after Troll had briefed them, because they got to dig three holes using their CET. When I say 'holes', they were approximately 10m x 6m with a slope going down to the bottom which was 4m in depth. They dug these hole in the middle of the building containing the ammunition.

The next task was to move all the ammunition and explosives into the holes. Again, this is where the RE became useful as they humped and dumped everything under our. It seemed that Troll and I had the easy task of placing the ammunition in the holes to ensure that it was laid out in the correct manner, but it soon turned out that we had the shit end of the stick because after a few hours, the holes started to fill up with water, something that we hadn't anticipated. It didn't take long for the water to cover the top layer of ammunition in each of the pits, so from that moment onwards, you had no idea what you were treading on.

We finished loading the pits just before nightfall, but still had some of the buildings to set up as part of the demolition. This would have to wait until the following day.

The next day, the dems pits were completely submerged which meant another day in the stinking water laying out the ordnance. Several of the buildings contained a large quantity of small arms ammunition which required either demolition using explosives (and we didn't have enough), so it was decided to set fire to burn the SAA instead. Also due to the lack of PE4, we needed a helping hand with the explosive train. The only way to achieve this was to use the 155mm artillery shells. This required the removal of the plugs screwed in the fuze-well to be removed. Not a very technical task but there was a lot of TNT exudation around the plugs. The one thing I remember from my basic course was how sensitive these crystals become, and in normal circumstances the removal of the plugs by hand would be a big no-no. But, this wasn't normal circumstances, so Troll and I set about removing the plugs with an 8-inch adjustable spanner and a hammer.

The dem was set up and good to go by midday. The means of initiation was to be safety fuze. The only experience I had, up to this point, was on my basic AT course. Having just done the course, I remember having to do a test burn, then time the walk to the safety point, then double the time for safety reasons. Again, following Troll's experience, we kind of guessed the length required as we were going to be driving to the safe area to watch the results of our work.

Troll told the RE lads to drive approximately 800m away from us. Once there, Troll briefed me up on what the plan was for lighting the safety fuze. He was going to light the furthest one, then as he walked past, I would light the next. We would continue this leapfrog method until we were both in the vehicle to drive to where the Engineers were positioned.

This plan was working well until I was by the last pit waiting for Troll to pass me so I could light it. Then, I lost sight of him.

Knowing the timings were tight, I looked around the immediate area to try and see where he had gone. My first thought was, *how long do I look for him?* knowing that I was in the middle of approximately 40 tons of explosives that were primed and lit ready to go bang.

What seemed like an eternity – which was more likely about 10 seconds – I heard the vehicle's horn. As I turned around, I could see the bearded face of Troll laughing his cock off at me. I quickly lit the last fuze and ran to the vehicle.

For anyone who has never had the pleasure of working with Troll, these are the kind of jokes he likes to play on people. Although funny afterwards, they aren't so funny at the time. That said, I think it's Troll's way of saying he likes you, not the other way round.

Luckily, the vehicle engine was running, so it was a quick getaway.

We reached the area where the engineers were waiting, got out of the vehicle and looked toward the area of the demolition. A minute later there were several large explosions in quick succession, and a lot of smoke and dust thrown into the air, followed by the shockwave travelling across the desert floor. Now, this was obviously a good sign that things had gone to plan. However, what wasn't part of the plan was rupturing the large oil pipeline. This immediately caught fire, pushing a ball of flame 100m into the air, reminiscent of the First Gulf War when Saddam set fire to the oil heads in Kuwait. I suppose you could say we achieved his aim.

With no experience of fighting oil fires of this size, there was only one thing that could be done – send the CET to the area of ruptured pipeline to bulldoze sand over it. Yes, it would extinguish the flames, but not prevent oil pumping into the ground. Not our problem.

The plan from there was to return to the airbase then come back the following day to take a look at our work.

On return to Shaiba, we were met with a very sad and glum looking Geordie. I remember him taking Troll to one side to break the bad news that Chris Muir had been killed.

Troll was very good friends with Chris, having worked with him at the Felix Center. I think this hit Troll very hard, but knowing that he still had a job to do, managed to concentrate with the task in hand.

His time to grieve would come at a later date.

The next few weeks saw the section living and working together. Living conditions were good considering we were in the middle of an invasion. The section pulled together, robbing kit when we came across it, or speaking to old friends to ask them for anything going spare.

We would also have section mealtimes; we would take it in turns to see what recipes we could make out of compo rations, and put together a menu. The one that always springs to mind is the time we come across some 5lt containers of ghee cooking oil. Gaz, who was Reg's No2 and I thought it would be nice to have chips.

After sourcing some potatoes, we got straight to work. First off, we got metal wash bowls and filled them with the oil. At the time, we had a small quantity of jet stoves which we thought would heat up the oil enough to turn make chips. Whilst the oil was heating up, we peeled and cut the potatoes.

Unfortunately, the oil never did reach a high enough temperature, so after about 20 mins and the section moaning at us they were hungry, the chips got served, slightly undercooked. I suppose you could say raw, and tasting of nothing but the ghee oil.

Work for the section consisted of the usual EOD taskings, mostly CMD tasks as there was a lot of UXO lying around.

One such task saw Troll running through the desert naked with only a Draganov rifle to cover his shame.

We also set about clearing AFV's and tanks of ammunition. This would normally be a relatively straight forward task. Find tank, enter tank, remove ammunition, then dem ammunition. However, due to the type of ammunition used by our own tanks, there was a hazard from the presence of DU (depleted uranium). We had instruments to measure the level of DU inside the vehicles, but what we lacked was the PPE to protect ourselves once inside. All we had was about half a dozen paper masks, which in normal circumstances would be fine, but when you have to keep using the same mask over and over, it kind of defeats the object of wearing it, but we cracked on with what we had.

On return from Iraq we all went to the medical centre to have DU tests. I remember it being a long time before the results came back. The results said that our background levels were higher than normal but of no concern. I have my doubts about that response, but will never be able to prove it until I die of lung cancer.

One of the everlasting memories of clearing tanks still remains in my possession – that being the Russian tank crew hat that became known as the 'Twat of the Week' hat. Each night after the section O group, each person had to nominate somebody who that day had either said or done something which made them look like a twat. Names were written down on paper then placed into a bowl. Whoever had the most votes won the coveted prize of the hat. They had to wear the hat wherever they went.

My only other recollection of the tour was the IED task in Basra which eventually saw the recovery of several suicide vests.

I can't remember much detail of the build-up to the task, apart from having an armoured escort to the ICP location. The start of the task was a little confusing for the team as the incident commander gave a description of a vehicle which was parked next to the house. I deployed the wheelbarrow following the directions given to me and got sight of the vehicle through the cameras. But then I was told that the vehicle I was looking at wasn't the correct one, even though it was the only car there and it was definitely the right house. By this point, the decision was made by Troll that the vehicle posed a threat regardless, so in went the maxi candles to clear the car. A remote search revealed nothing of any significant threat. This left only the house. Now, normally this would require me to drive the wheelbarrow to the ground floor, and then carefully manoeuvre around all the rooms looking for anything suspicious.

But this wasn't going to be a normal run of the mill clearance. The ground floor had many rooms, all furnished – relatively nice furnishings, considering this was Iraq.

To remotely clear the rooms using the wheelbarrow to a standard that lowered the threat significantly would have taken a very long time, which meant the cordon would be in static locations for however long it would take. Not good for them as there was still a very big threat from the Iraqi military.

Again, this is where working for Troll, there's never a dull moment.

The fastest way to achieve the clearance was to use maxi candles. I think we used two maxi candles per room. This still took most of the day, due to the design of the house which made wheelbarrow driving difficult, especially using the fibre optic cable. Going forward is easy enough, it's reversing out that is the difficult part.

After dropping off the maxis in each room, it still had to be cleared. Then the wheelbarrow had to be brought back to the ICP to have more maxi candles fitted, plus the odd battery change. It all adds time to the task. But I did achieve it (more luck than skill).

Eventually, it was time for Troll to suit up and go and have a look for himself. All the relevant ECM was deployed and he left the ICP. After several manuals, Troll called an end to the task due to the fading light. We would return the next day to finish off. However he did manage to recover several suicide vests for exploitation.

As the light was fading rapidly the team kit was thrown onto the van to be sorted out back at the airbase.

Then the normal routine kicked in with the whole team. Troll's first task was to back-brief Geordie, as he was the section Warrant Officer, and also conduct exploitation of the recovered vests. My job was to ensure that all of the EOD equipment was serviceable and ready to go. This meant stripping down the wheelbarrow, recharging all batteries and replacing any of the consumables that had ran out or were running low. Whilst doing this, I was also there to assist Troll.

At this point, I think it's worth mentioning that as a No2 you don't really appreciate how mentally and physically draining it is for the No1 operator. But once I passed my course and had done a few tasks, I definitely did appreciate it.

After working on the equipment, I'd just sat down to have something to eat and drink, and for the first time in about 12 hours to actually relax.

The next thing, Troll has asked me to fetch some item of equipment off the van to finish the report. I don't think I said anything out loud, but I must have given some look of disgust: *why can't you get it yourself?* Anyway, I retrieved what he wanted then sat back down again. After a number of hours, Troll and I were chatting when he apologised for asking me to go and get the equipment. As mentioned earlier, I now appreciate how hard it is for a No1 operator. As a team, we were all exhausted from the day's events, and being part of an EOD team requires all members to dig deep and help each other 24 hours a day, seven days a week, for eternity.

Smokers' mound was introduced to try and keep a bit of normality within the section. As the clue is in the title, it doesn't require much explaining.

Every night after the O group, certain members of the section would make their way to the top of a sand berm and light up a cigar, which when the fighting was going on, made for some interesting viewing as you could watch all the artillery being fired into Basra. It was a good time to let down your hair and talk to each, other putting the world to rights. After some weeks of doing this, even the non-smokers would retire to the mound to chat and have a few puffs.

By Christian Meadows

CHAPTER 13

AFTER IRAQ

CHRIS HAD BEEN KILLED, Si and his driver murdered. I'd nearly been killed, and the risks taken day after day must have had an effect.

The war was over and the chain of command wanted to downsize the numbers of troops. I desperately wanted to stay with my Unit. I'd been moved internally once to support another team, but I had kicked off so much they moved me back.

It was likely that being an add-on, one of the 50 technicians moved in to make up the numbers in an undermanned Unit, I would be sent home. The School of Ammo wasn't prepared to stand the gap in their manning anymore, so regardless of my need to be amongst those I had fought beside, I was sent home.

Much later, when I attended the TrIM (Trauma Incident Management) course, they recommend that soldiers involved in traumatic action aren't moved for at least six months. I do not apologise for not coping with the change.

I came home and had post-tour leave. But being away from work meant no one understood you; at least at work there might be some frame of reference. I was clearly not dealing with my return, but beyond drinking a bit in the evenings, I couldn't put my finger on it.

Leave was over too soon, and I had to return to being an instructor at The Wing (Felix Centre), teaching Northern Ireland bomb disposal.

Prior to going to Iraq, we were asked to create a pre-Northern Ireland selection course. Pass rates were low, so a means to increase this was sought.

We designed the course based on Northern Ireland skills and knowledge. The bureaucrats in the training and development cell didn't like our plan; they said it favoured soldiers who had previously attended the NI course.

Far be it for me to say that they were more likely to pass, and that a soldier who failed the NI course, who was subsequently beaten in the pre-select by a first time soldier who had studied and come above him, could have no complaint, and that the man who studied his craft might also be a bonus on the course.

I disagreed with their order that we must assess the students on the basic level of EOD as they had received training in this. This assessment was done on their six monthly validations while serving in the Regiment.

I ignored their instructions.

We tested the soldiers on their Northern Ireland knowledge and capability. The students' feedback also showed they preferred it this way; even if they failed, they felt they had learnt something. But not those who endured the official version.

On my return from Iraq, this pre-select course was my first task. I would normally have ignored any instruction to 'do UK' but I didn't have the fight in me. I didn't believe we should be teaching soldiers to fight in NI if we were going to send them to Iraq. I didn't believe in a chain of command that so carelessly sent their men to their deaths. I assessed a friend called 'Scouse' on that first day, and although I asked the questions and wrote down the marks from his responses, I felt numb, removed.

I said, "That's just not good enough."

Scouse thought I was talking about his performance.

I told him, "No, not you, me."

He asked, "Are you alright, mate?" and at that point, I knew I wasn't. I went back to the office and asked for help.

Initially, the Captain in there who knew me, asked me what was wrong.

I could only reply, "I don't know. I just can't do this anymore."

With hindsight, I clearly needed to be moved back to 821 EOD Squadron, to be amongst those who knew what I had been through.

Every day I came into work and saw my best friend's empty desk.

One friend said, "Come on, Troll, some of us had to face up to losing Chris every day while you were out there swanning about."

Through gritted teeth, with clenched fists, I replied that I didn't think what I had done in Iraq was swanning about.

I asked to be moved but was told by the CO (the Lieutenant Colonel) that I was his best instructor. I was his also first NI- and Iraq-qualified instructor. He was going to sell courses to the world: I wasn't moving.

The Army School of Ammunition sold bomb disposal training to augment its military budget. We were the second highest income generator behind Sandhurst (the Royal Military Academy for training officers in the British Army).

It impacted on our ability to train our own soldiers, and the effort to be that good an instructor meant that the posting was unbelievably hard work. This, on top of the fact that you were selected for instructing, usually happened as you came home from a successful tour. Operationally, it meant soldiers got the most up-to-date training, but from a mental health point of view, well, let's just say you can't afford to have too many cracks and be posted there.

Because of the course loading, we finished one course on Friday and started the next one the following Monday – there was little down time. I struggled to get on promotion courses and saw others loaded instead of me, all the time being told by my officers that I was too good an instructor to release. Worst of all, they cancelled our physical training (PT). I had been a fit soldier when I arrived, but we would usually only get onto one PT session out of every 10. That's one PT lesson every five weeks. It was a real issue for me as I knew my posting was only three years; then I had to go back to the real army. What state would I be in if I couldn't get to do PT? Officer's answer? Do it in your own time. We worked between 60-80 hours a week as it was.

The hours were so long that my friends with children, who had just spent months away from their families, didn't get to see their children from Sunday night to Saturday morning.

Again, I asked my officers to help, and said if they wouldn't, I'd have no choice but to seek medical help.

They said I wasn't getting moved.

I went to the doctor. He listened and said he would approach the CO. Again, the answer was no. What I was unaware of at this time was the CO was using his position in the school to feed approaches from overseas military to a civilian EOD company of which he was a shadow director.

I went back to the doctor. He offered me a week off – which was pointless, as being away from work was worse than being at work. I refused the leave but again asked him to help. I needed to get moved away from all the things that were upsetting me so much.

Nothing changed.

I went back to work and although I felt very ropey, I got through the first day. On the second day, it started again – people expecting me to be back to my old self. Something set me off, a thoughtless comment by one of the officer's. I exploded.

"Have you made any plans to move me yet?"

"No," he replied.

"Well fucking make some. I don't work here anymore."

He threatened me with the army legal system.

"You'll get charged."

I said I'd welcome the opportunity to display this unit's criminal neglect in a forum outside our trade.

Jim, one of my fellow Staff Sergeants, told me to go back to the Mess. I walked out of the office.

That night, I was told I was being moved out of the IEDD (Bomb disposal) wing and down to CMD Wing (Conventional Munitions Disposal). The first thing here is that at IEDD wing we train with plasticine and some EOD weapons. CMD wing uses all live explosives. I'll not accept that the officers in the school had any serious worries about my mental state.

I felt a bit better. I was away from a lot of my triggers, but I was told the move wasn't permanent.

Over the course of three weeks, it got worse. I was making do, but I still needed help. I went back to the doctor; I begged him to help me. He said he couldn't help further, but he could refer me to the DCMH (Department of Community Mental Health – military centres dedicated to treating serving personnel with health problems). I took the offer.

The DCMH said, "You've been sent here because you are having some problems about Iraq."

We talked about it and I said I wasn't sleeping, was drinking too much, not getting enough physical training. He said that I seemed to have a good handle on the tour and was aware of my problems. My plan to drink less and phys more was correct. What was the problem?

"My Unit won't let me do phys."

He couldn't believe it. They wouldn't allocate me the 3 x 40 minute lessons that army regulations said I must have every week? One hundred and twenty minutes where they would just have to make do without the "CO's best instructor".

The DCMH nurse put his recommendation to the CO to move me. It was again refused.

The nurse told me the only option was to go in front of a DCMH psychologist, but that might harm my career.

I said, "What career?"

If I didn't get moved, I wouldn't survive to have a career.

An order was sent by DCMH to submit form FMed-8. The CO filled in this paperwork, refused to allow me to see what he'd written, which didn't help my mental state, but I did subsequently access it. He said I was faking it: a troublemaker, and I was only using the medical system to procure a posting. Clearly, the actions of a caring and professional manager. I think he was a self-interested unprofessional who cared not one jot for his soldiers, and was only interested in how much fame he could amass in order to promote his civilian business interests.

The paperwork is submitted anyway. I go in front of the doctor. It's a risk; he doesn't have to decide I would be best served by being moved. The ASofA was now stating that because I was unwell, I couldn't and shouldn't be moved because of Army guidelines. It seems to have escaped them that the regulation was meant to keep me in 821 Sqn – the people I had been with in Iraq. The doctor agreed. I wasn't being helped by being kept at the school. I should be moved.

He recommended that I was sent back to the 821 Squadron, 11 EOD Regiment. Meanwhile, I carried on working in CMD wing. I tried to kick-start my phys regime, but depression was holding me back. I was still drinking too much in the evening, trying to numb my emotions and forget.

On Monday, the officer in CMD asked if I'd heard anything about my move. I replied that I hadn't, but I was quite happy here, so no rush. He said he'd go ask the CO. He returned at lunch time and said that the reason I hadn't been moved was because the school hadn't received any paperwork from the medical chain.

I got straight on the phone to the DCMH.

DCHM informed me that they'd sent the doctor's report eight weeks ago. The school had acknowledged receipt and had even written back to object to the instruction to send me to an Operational Unit – 11 EOD. Their position was, if I was injured, I shouldn't go to a Unit like 11 EOD because of the responsibilities i.e. using explosives.

Wasn't I doing that now? I believe they were trying to obstruct me. The CO had made it personal and there was no way I was getting what I had asked for, what I needed. The DCMH said they had written back four weeks previously, and had also faxed the same reply. They were aware that my move was taking an excessive amount of time and didn't want any more delay. The delay was entirely down to the CO.

On Tuesday, I'm grabbed by Seamus, the new officer in charge of the IEDD Wing. He takes me to an empty classroom and asks me why I'm not back up at the Wing, teaching. I tell him I don't think I can do that anymore; I think I need to go back to 11 Regt as I don't think I can teach.

"What's wrong with you? If there is something wrong with you, you can't be posted; you'll have to stay here until you're fixed."

I tell him that the doctors have said I should be posted. He tells me that if the doctors force the issue, any posting I get will be a punishment posting. The school will make sure I can only go to a depot posting which will be a killer for an active soldier like me. He bullies me on the issue for about 30 minutes and my head shuts down. I can't find words to answer him, so my mouth just opens and closes like a fish. My position doesn't change.

I finally find the words to say, "Sir, I can't answer your questions any more. I've nothing to say."

In hindsight, he may have been trying to do the equivalent of a slap around the face and 'pull yourself together, young man', but it was a poor choice and didn't help me.

On Wednesday, the CMD officer said, "Good news, Staff" (short for staff sergeant). "The CO has said you will return to the IEDD Wing, and if your condition has not improved, you will be moved at the end of the school year."

Which is months away. Why was I not being moved now? Why did there need to be a delay? He had no plans to move me. I just couldn't take any more.

After lunch, I returned to the school, the main building where I had undertaken my basic AT training. It was a square building with an open quad in the middle, benches, and a fish pond. I sat on the bench and broke down in tears. I had decided there was only one thing for it, and that action would mean the end of my career. That fucking man: all he had to do was move me, to care that one of his soldiers needed help. But he didn't. He wanted me to make him famous, to advertise his position at the school, and make both the school and his private business money. I'm going to kill him.

I don't have a rifle, or a pistol, so I've got a chit to sign out a shovel from the stores up the corridor. I visualise how I will walk past the adjutant in his office and into the CO's office. He deserves to die and the army will be a better place for it. I'll lose my job, I'll go to jail. Well it can't be worse than this. I'm just upset that I'm going to lose my job. I can't take it anymore.

I'm interrupted by the girl from the library, "Are you okay?"

"No."

"Do you want a handkerchief?"

I take it, and she asks me to stay there. She runs off and comes back with Crads, a good friend of mine, and the Warrant Officer in the CMD office. He takes me to an empty classroom and it takes him four hours to get me calm enough to stop crying and talk. I tell him I'm going to kill the CO. He knows I mean it.

He takes me to the School SAT's office and tells me to repeat my story. I say that I refuse to accept that I can't be moved. I refuse to believe the CO. He agrees, he says there is no reason why I can't be moved and he tells me to go to the Mess and leave it with him.

I'm moved two days later to a post in 11 EOD Regt, back to an operational existence, a means to feel worthwhile. I ask for anywhere north of the country. I get Tidworth in Wiltshire. Ah well, I'm used to the Army posting system.

The lads at Tidworth make me very welcome. I apologise a lot. My confidence has been destroyed. I don't think I can recover from the kicking I've had from the school. I'm hoping that my guess that this is what I need will be right.

I'm summoned to see the OC, Major H— QGM, for an interview. I'm a Senior NCO, so I expect a bit of a respectful conversation. You don't talk to your Seniors like you do a private soldier: he has earned rank and with it comes some respect.

"I don't like you," he says. "If I had my way you'd not be here, but the CO has over-ruled me. I don't care how good you were at IEDD; here I expect you to do paperwork and prove yourself in the ammunition arena."

I reply that I have no problem with the paperwork. I came top of my trade course.

"Well, I still don't want you in my Unit."

Great.

I return to Tidworth. I tell those who ask what the OC said. The general opinion is he's a 'clunge'. The Warrant Officer, who is leaving the army, tries to make me feel better and says, "Ignore him. He's a typical officer. Got his medal for fucking up in NI." It doesn't help.

I volunteer to be on duty. This goes down well with the lads there. The regiment is always undermanned, so someone who is prepared to go on duty lots is always going to be popular.

I also started running around Salisbury plain. Stereo on (might have been an iPod by then), on my own, running on the chalk tracks, the fresh air, the sun. I'd often pass others, clearly soldiers, out doing their own training run. You'd nod in passing, and I started to feel like my old self. Two weeks later, I was beginning to wonder what all the fuss was about. It made me sad that such a small amount of effort would have been required to help me at the school.

I was summoned back to the School to receive my report from the CO. It appears I wasn't his best instructor anymore. My report was damning: even my operational insert slip, the report that would have come from my time in Iraq which was supposed to be included in my CR, was missing, not referenced. It didn't help my condition, and I slip back. I concentrate on Tidworth.

My new Captain encouraged me to write a complaint. I resist. He argues that he has seen my report and it's not just. I'm all for forgetting it; everyone knows soldiers' complaints are rarely upheld. He convinces me with the idea that if not for myself, I should complain about my treatment so others in my condition won't be treated the same.

I write it up and send it.

I then have my 'incident' in Plymouth (and the 12 months waiting to go to trial).

The response to my complaint comes back. It includes every false accusation of wrong-doing made against me at the School; it references my 'Incident' as justification for their actions, and says the School and the CO did everything in their power to look after me. The CO of the Regiment talks to me about it. He says that their reference to the arrest in Plymouth possibly crosses a legal boundary. He asks me what I want to do? I tell him I want to go back to work.

A SHORT TIME LATER I HEARD FROM A FRIEND AT THE SCHOOL (HE'S NOW dead), that the CO had been forced to resign. His 'civilian business interests' had come to light, so he was offered a choice. He chose to resign. Obviously it wouldn't do for a proper officer to be sacked. In my head, I hope that in some small way the fuss I made helped bring the spotlight onto him and that his bosses saw him for what he was and pushed his departure.

But I doubt it.

CHAPTER 14

THE INCIDENT, 2005

I WOKE IN THE CELLS.

It wasn't the first time, but it had been a fairly long time since I'd been a young dickhead who got himself a night in the cells to sober up, then released without charge in the morning, with a stern word from the duty copper. (These days you get a token £80 fine for such things.)

But, I couldn't remember anything about the night before and had no idea how I got here. I sat up and felt dizzy, but didn't feel hungover. I was parched and could do with a drink. I pressed the alarm button and when the door opens I ask for some water. I down it and sit uncomfortably waiting to see what happens.

I get brought out into interview and I'm told that I've been arrested for aggravated burglary and an assault. What the fuck? That can't be right. However it's far more serious than, *you were asleep in the hedge and we brought you here to sober up*, so when offered a solicitor, you're damn right I want one.

I go back to the cells and wait for him to arrive. I tell him I can't remember anything past 9pm. One minute I felt fine – the next is blank and I wake up here.

He says, "Sounds like you've been spiked. There's a lot of it in Plymouth."

We ask the police to take a blood and urine sample. They refuse and say I'm being interviewed first.

The interview is unpleasant and the copper says, "Come on, mate, we've all been there. A few beers down town and a scrap with the civvies..."

I replied, "That's not me."

"I'm an ex-Marine, mate. I know the score, we all do it."

He goes on.

"Not me. I'm not that sort of soldier. My solicitor thinks I was spiked."

"Spiking's a myth, buddy. It never happens."

The tosser kept trying to 'friend me up' and to get me to admit my guilt. I subsequently discovered Devon and Cornwall police had come bottom of the arrest and conviction table so viewed me, as a soldier, an easy conviction to get regardless of whether I was guilty or not. Not letting me have a sample taken also helped their cause.

Fuckers.

The sum of it is this: I was knocking on a door in a block of flats saying, "Let me in, I'm back."

It sounds like I thought I was back in the Sgts Mess. I was down there running training for the Navy, so I understand I might have been confused and thought I was somewhere else while drugged.

The occupant of the flat comes out and we end up fighting. (His claim is I attacked him when he opened the door.) In hindsight, I think he may have come out and told me to clear off or be quiet, but in the absence of any memory, I have no choice but to accept his version of events. I won the fight though, and then went to sleep on the carpet until the police arrived and woke me.

Another struggle which I was clearly always going to lose, and then I got my proper accommodation for the night.

Eventually, after a lengthy interview, I get seen by the duty doctor for my bloods and samples to be taken. He sees the bruises on my wrists and says he thinks the cuffs must have been on bloody tight to do that. I roll my shirt sleeve up for the needle and my arm is covered in strike marks from the police baton. He stops taking blood and tells me to take my shirt off. I'm covered in bruises. He tells me that he will take photos for my complaint. I tell him I don't want to make a complaint. He says I should, because the amount of injuries I have is over the top.

I say to him, "If what they say is true, that I pushed my way into some bloke's house and had a fight, drugged or not, fighting with the police when they got there, then I got what I fucking deserved. I'm not making a complaint about the coppers; they were just doing their job."

The doc replied, "We don't get many like you in here."

The process continues and I eventually get released on bail. My mate picks me up. He's a 24 stone rugby player, and after we discuss the night, he says he can't remember it either and that's never happened to him in 25 years of drinking. He's pretty sure we were spiked, too.

The blood test comes back negative for drugs and I only have a tiny trace of alcohol which, when extrapolated back to 11pm, means I had drunk no more than six or seven pints. I'm not being funny, but I can handle that much, especially as it was over at least five hours.)

If I get a criminal conviction for this incident, my chain of command have told me that I will lose my job.

In the year between the arrest and the trial that was coming, I investigated every aspect of the incident. I had spent some time under the Department of Community Mental Health (DCMH) following Iraq. I went back to them to ask if I'd had a flashback. I'd heard of them and wondered if I'd thought I was fighting Iraqis or some shit. DCMH said they thought it unlikely and that it sounded like I'd been spiked. Really? I thought that was a myth. I even saw some TV programme like *CSI* or something and the actor says, "It's well documented that GHB mixed with alcohol can make you violent but saps your strength."

So, we go back and forwards to Plymouth, attending court to discuss if I'm being prosecuted. The chain of command keeps asking if I've 'been done' yet.

As this is going on, I continue on bomb disposal duties. While I'm down at the target, I often think I wish I had been killed in Iraq like my best friend; I'd be better off dead than putting up with this shit. I'm working with explosives all the while, and it would probably be quick and painless. One of the main things that stopped me was I couldn't think of a way to do it where the investigation wouldn't conclude that I had in some way fucked up. I'm not going out with people thinking I made a mistake, that's just not on.

The county courts say that the offence is too serious for them to deal with so I'm passed on to Crown Court.

The London 7/7 bombings occur, 7th July 2005.

When the second lot of bombings occur our team gets called into London. We're at Wellington barracks. We go for a coffee and one of the lads has the Sun newspaper. It has a story that the Regiment with bomb disposal have been deployed to London. How the fuck did they get that? We only arrived yesterday evening. The end of the issue sees us 'stacked up' (black kit and balaclavas with respirators at our sides), in a hallway in a block of flats of one of the failed bombers. (It was around this time the Brazilian John Charles de Menezes was shot on a Tube train in London.)

The police are going to make entry into the flat. If it goes noisy, we're on.

The team leader is so excited, he says, "This is going to be fucking mega. We're all going to be on TV, lads, just like the fucking embassy."

He means the Iranian embassy in 1980.

The police make entry and the fucker surrenders.

Oh well, back to camp.

A week later my final pre-court case is due. (After this, it's just the court case proper with a jury and everything.)

My barrister says I have a sound defence which would mean I wasn't guilty, but it all depends on the jury. He cheerily says not to worry as if I'm found guilty then we'd have good grounds for an appeal as the police prevented me from getting samples taken until long after the drugs would have left my system, blah blah. It means nothing to me as I've still lost my fucking job by that point, and the only think keeping me alive is doing my job.

I'm supposed to have a supporting officer from my Regiment to come and offer a character reference. The one allocated to me has a career interview so can't make it. A replacement is sought, but they all refuse. Not one single officer in my chain of command is prepared to come and offer me their support.

My Senior Ammunition Technician steps in and comes to look after me. I can't do his performance justice in print, but he types up a character reference, and instead of giving it to the prosecution like I thought he would, he gives it to the defence barrister. There is some conversation during this time where the prosecution tells him that despite the claims that I'm not guilty, I'll only get a slap on the wrist as it's my first offence, kind of hinting that I should just take it on the chin and do him (and myself) a favour. SAT replies that he doesn't care about the sentence, just if I'm guilty or not. The army will view it in a dim light as it's a violent offence. I'll get punished, it'll affect my career. And, as he knows me, I won't live with the stain on my character and will probably resign.

He finishes with, "And after, that he'll probably go to the Press. I would if I was him."

The Prosecution says, "What do you mean, the Press?"

The SAT says, laughing, "Oh, mate, you have no idea who you've got in the dock in there, do you?"

So this character reference ... the Defence gets it, reads it, then tells the Judge,

"Your Honour, during the trial I wish to make reference to Mr. Bell's employment. The nature of this employment is such that I wish to retire to chambers so that we can discuss this prior to any decision on trial."

This basically means they throw everyone else out of court, and it's just them, the Judge, me and the guard. The Judge reads it. He looks up and then says to the Prosecution, "Have you read this?"

He replies, "Yes, Your Honour, I have just been given a copy."

The Judge says, "...and does this information change your position?"

Prosecution replies, "Yes, Your Honour. We think it would not be in the public interest to proceed in this matter."

The case gets dropped. Nothing to do with right and wrong – just gets dropped. Un-fucking-believable. Couldn't you bastards have just accepted I was spiked in the first place?

The SAT's letter said something along the lines of (again I don't think I can do it justice)...

"This soldier is currently on attachment to the UK Special Forces. His specialisation and skill-set forms the core of a critical UK national defence capability. He's one of three individuals, but currently the only operational one available to the UK arena (with the others deployed overseas). He has, unknown to him at this time, been awarded a Queen's Gallantry Medal and will shortly be attending the Palace to receive this from the Queen. He has also been selected for promotion to Warrant Officer, a promotion which will most surely be forfeit if he's convicted. He has been written up for numerous other awards for service in Iraq where he defused suicide vests and radio controlled devices under fire, and Northern Ireland where he defused mortars and a half-ton land mine. Last week, he formed part of the SAS teams in London, responding to the recent attempted suicide bombings."

He finished by saying, personally, he didn't care one way or another if I was convicted; he just needed to know sooner rather than later because replacing me any time in the next six months would be near impossible, and would leave the UK less well defended that would be preferred.

FUCK ME, THAT WAS CRINGE-WORTHY TO READ AGAIN. BUT IN CASE you're wondering, I did pay for the repair to the door...

THE QUEEN'S GALLANTRY MEDAL

The Queen's Gallantry Medal (QGM) is a United Kingdom decoration awarded for exemplary acts of bravery by civilians, and by members of the Armed Forces 'not in the face of the enemy', where the services were not so outstanding as to merit the George Cross or the George Medal, but above the level required for the Queen's Commendation for Bravery.

THE LONDON GAZETTE

The following Army Soldiers have been awarded the Meritorious Service Medal

WO1 D. Appleby, RA, 24884943

WO1 A. F. Bamford, AGC(SPS), 24729076

WO2 S. J. Barrie, R Signals, 24853310

WO2 J. J. Bell, QGM, RLC, 24856074

WO2 M. Bell, REME, 24804471

WO2 G. C. Bentley, RA, 24878783

Sgt P. H. Bentley, LD, 24856413

Sgt A. Beveridge, Scots DG, 24586470

Bell, Justin John; Staff Sergeant; Royal Logistic Corps; Southampton WWI mortar; 2005/09/09disposal

"For his bravery in disposing of First World War high explosive mortars at Southampton on 22nd September 2004."

I'm not really that short.
HRH Prince Charles was standing on a box.

CHAPTER 15

ALPHA TROOP

ALPHA SHOULD HAVE BEEN the best Unit in our trade.

The Unit was established after a bomb threat to the QE2 cruise liner when it was midway to the USA, and the SF & EOD had to parachute in.

I mean, who wouldn't want to be the bomb disposal guy in an SAS team? Only a succession of self-interested weapons-grade fuckwits would be able to fuck that up, right?

As Chris was often heard to say,

"How can we soar with the Eagles when we're working with turkeys?"

This is just one example...

Alpha Troop was a little known group within the EOD Regiment, tasked with providing IEDD support to the SBS. They had secondary supporting roles to the SAS and Police TFUs [Tactical Firearms Unit].

The Unit should be co-located at Poole next to the SBS, or Hereford with the SAS but no. Despite numerous Commanding Officers assuring the Troop they will move them once in post, the black kit is just too shiny to let go. The urge to grandstand in front of visitors that you are in command of the unit is too tempting, and so the Troop is located at the EOD HQ in Didcot ... with fuck-all facilities and a bunch of RLC officers convinced they should interfere in the running of the Unit.

Even so, it still has the potential to be a good job, but the numbers of operational tasks are low, the numbers in the unit are low (12), the NTM (non-tactical movement) was correspondingly three hours, positively sloth-like compared to the main line IEDD units, but still 21 hours faster than anything the Wedge would field (their fastest EOD units were all on 24 hours' notice to move).

The Alpha Troop task was a mixed blessing.

The Units we supported are serious about their craft and good to work with. Sadly, with too few ATs possessing the right IEDD knowledge, the right physical attributes and the desire to serve in the Troop, the manning often comprised volunteers with only one of the three attributes, and tales of the Troop's mistakes travelled far further than any successes. The commander of the Unit was always a lottery – the current incumbent started off well enough, deferent to the knowledge of his Seniors and keen to learn, but sadly it all too soon became about him and his ego.

Capt J (of the CMD course) had submitted himself to the P Company course and passed. However, the parachuting 'Jumps' phase was cancelled and so he couldn't jump or receive Para pay, a subject of much merriment amongst the troops. It also proved to be a blessing because he couldn't lead missions if he couldn't lead the team out of the plane. On land, however, he was free to get in the troops' way. He decided that the Troop would go hill walking on Snowden, in itself not a bad team building activity ... if only he hadn't been such a knob about it.

Taking the whole Troop out of position happens often – exercises result in at least half the Troop stuck on some ship or oil rig, rooting out some fictitious terrorist group and their bombs. In these cases, there is always the helo support for the exercise to whisk a team into position if a real task comes in.

Capt J had decreed that the whole Troop deploy to Snowdon, not because he wanted to bond the team. No, it was all about needing 12 troops so he could get himself an outdoor-pursuits badge. Why couldn't he just canvass for volunteers? Luckily, I was scheduled to go to Hereford for training that week, but this was cancelled once the Snowdon party had deployed. The Troop was nice and calm that week, and I was even able to make tea and toast in the Sgts Mess at 10am.

I was on my second slice when the Ops WO, Phil, saw me and made mention that there may be an Alpha Troop task in the offing. We'd not long deployed to London in response to the suicide bombings, so two tasks in a year would be a turn up. Phil did mention that he'd notified Capt J of the possible task at 07:00 – strange how the commander didn't think to notify all of the team, ie. me.

Thirty minutes later, Phil finds me, and while he's not flapping, it's clear that someone has fucked up.

"That fucking knobhead has taken the Troop up onto the hills," Phil says.

So, instead of responding to the possible task, Capt J was only interested in his hill walking badge and was currently three hours from his van, walking up Snowdown. That's okay though because once back to the van he would have his Ops Kit and technically be on duty, wouldn't he? Only if he took the Ops Kit with him? Who the fuck drives 3.5 hours away from his Ops kit on a three-hour duty?

Phil started planning deployment with what we have on camp – handy that the unit's based at HQ – aware that I was his only Alpha Troop operator in range, with kit. I spied Mark, one of the Bleeps, strolling past. Odd, since I thought all the Troop had been spammed for walking. I asked him what he was doing and then explained he took leave rather than spend a week with Capt J. Fair enough.

"You up for a task?" I ask him.

"Can I put on the blue lights?"

"Yes."

He sprinted to the garage laughing and mumbling, "I love working with you, Troll."

I accompanied Phil to the Ops Room where the Ops Officer was desperately trying to justify Capt Jenkinson being out of position, without his ops kits and, instead of responding to his task, away on the mountains. My initial thoughts were that there could be no justification, but there you go. Some officers and their 'moral compunction' leads them to side with other officers rather than with values and standards.

More importantly, while Phil and I problem-solved the task, the CO, Andy, was on leave. Pity, as he was a good guy and would have signed off on our plan straight away. His second in command took (too much) convincing. Phil, being former Alpha Troop, would deploy as Silver Commander; I would be team leader ... and ... in a fit of bluff, we convinced the 2i/c that Moxy, who was a former Paratrooper, now in Charlie Troop, was actually posted to Alpha Troop on paper, and more importantly, had undertaken our training. Had he fuck!

As a last desperate attempt to dig Capt J out of his hole, the Ops Officer said the captain should follow on once he got down from the mountain. On the phone, I advised him to use the Police to get him to task location.

We had our permission to deploy, and for the second time in a month, an unmarked Mercedes Sprinter headed out of the HQ garages – destination, that well-known terrorist heartland ... Barry.

Phil got to briefing us more fully, mostly so Moxy and Mark were in the loop. An Asian woman had approached the front desk at Barry police station in Wales, and informed the desk Sgt that her boyfriend intended to become a suicide bomber and planned to target the Labour Party Conference being held in Brighton. He could be forgiven for his somewhat sceptical response. However, her next action was to plonk a brown paper sack onto the counter.

"This is the stuff he's using to make his explosives with."

That got his attention.

From this start point, the Police had his name (IB), age and address. We advised on cordon and evacuation distances from the non-descript two-bed semi-detached. Courtesy of my previous tenure at Hereford Troop, I had the Forth Road Bridge phone number handy and I requested them to open a lane for us. It's a little thing, but it means immediate access across the bridge rather than being mired in traffic queuing for the pay stations. Mark nodded his approval as I indicated Lane 1 would be open for us on the left when we got there.

While I was sorting the bridge, ensuring we knew where the police station was and that our route would not drive us anywhere near the target's location, Phil was teaching Moxy how to deploy and fire the Alpha-krait, the Troop's specialist high-explosive disposable disruptor. It's a good job the Alpha-krait is almost idiot proof, designed to be used in high stress environment. The operation requires a two-stage process to fire, at the end of 10m of shock tube.

At this, Moxy's head came up: 10m, not the usual 100m? And the realisation that should a device function during disruption on an assault task, the operator would be lucky to survive. I reminded him of Phil's instruction to emphasise the, "seek appropriate cover" part of the deployment instructions.

One training day, on an abandoned ship provided by the Navy (conveniently located near Poole – nowhere near our HQ), I'd placed an Alpha-krait charge against a training IED which was attached to a bulkhead door. The empty ship was almost devoid of any cover and I wedged myself (mostly) into a changing room locker. I don't remember which of my bosses coined the phrase, "Thinking backwards from the accident...", but it of often comes to mind.

The REME lad who helped build the devices for the training had no understanding of the Troop's actions or how we train. He would have been mortified should he ever have been told.

"Standby! Standby!" I called, pushing the plunger on my firing device.

We substituted our usual call of 'Standby Firing' to be in line with the SF calls.

The assault team stacked up behind me expect the explosion on the second standby, and through our pre-mission brief, they know my immediate action following the disruption is to confirm it's safe for them to proceed. Many is the time that the team batters you to the side as they aggressively prosecute their mission, and once the team leader yanked me out of the way by my helmet. I wore that indignity with pride.

The explosives in the training IED were inert, the explosives in the Alpha-krait were not. The flash-though of the shock-tube, almost imperceptible to the eye, initiated the detonator and a charge of CE stemming. This propels a water charge through the fibreglass container to disrupt the device. The safety distance for the charge is 10m, but I have on very good authority that you can survive the worst of it at 1.5m. Today, with having to loop behind the lockers, we were about 6m. The charge sounded larger than it was, amplified by the hollowness of the empty rooms. Bits of fibreglass from the krait and bits of plastic from the IED were propelled around the room – so was the 'shrapnel' included by the REME lad.

"IEDs have shrapnel in them right?"

A score of 6-inch nails pinged off every surface as ships are mostly metal, and a good handful of the nails pierced staccato style through the locker wall in front of my face. Even the SBS team leader was taken aback with the EOD team's 'realism in training' display.

I finished Moxy off with the quip, "We're not in Kansas anymore, Dorothy."

I was brought back to reality, and almost deprived of my consciousness, by Mark transiting the bridge turnstiles. Used to Hereford drivers who knew the turnstiles had ramps, I'd forgotten that bit of the briefing. I spotted it just as we hit at about 80mph. The van took off, we all took off, and the live high-explosive disruptor found itself momentarily weightless in front of three ATOs who may have lost some of their cool and calm demeanour.

That is until Phil snatched it from the air and said, "Lesson's over, you can work out the rest on task."

The rest of the trip to the police station was short and uneventful. The briefing to come was something else.

At Barry, the briefing room was too small.

JUSTIN J. BELL QGM

The South Wales TFU, the team we would be going in with, are already there. So was every other licensed firearms officer available to the Force (there are shockingly fewer than you'd imagine), the fire brigade, the ambulance service, and a handful of hangers on and suits surrounding the Superintendent as he made his way to the head of the table to commence his briefing.

The room was full to bursting.

Before he started, he leaned into the middle of the table and placed a Dictaphone on the table, his briefing commenced from a script he'd brought with him. I thought he'd done well to type up his orders in the 90minutes it had taken to get there. It quickly became apparent that his notes were not his orders, but guidance on what terminology he was to use. Throughout the briefing, he was careful to use the mandated terminology of the "deadly and determined individual" and his "potential device". This and numerous other mealy-mouthed political double-speak meant that the plan, as it was, came across as confused and lacking direction.

The TFU as a team were reasonably happy that we were going to make entry to the suspect's house and secure anyone in there. The plan to ring the target with Armed Response Cars and to evacuate houses out of sight of the target's view was greeted less happily. Eventually one of the armed officers puts his hand up and asks the Superintendent for some clarity.

"Look, Guv, are we talking about a suicide bomber?"

The Super visibly stiffened in his collar.

"We're looking at this individual being deadly and determined."

The armed officer inwardly groaning tried again.

"Do we think he has a bomb?"

The 'B' word caused another involuntary spasm to cross the Super's face.

"We have indicators that the target aims to complete a device, but as yet we don't know what state any device would be in."

Given the two answers he'd already received, the armed officer got full points for fielding his last question.

"Guv, if this guy comes out of the house and comes towards me, what do I do?"

The Super replied, "You will have to make a dynamic risk assessment."

I wasn't the only one open-mouthed at that statement. You're asking Officers, armed officers to face a suicide bomber with no direction from on high, and a clear indication that the decision on the ground will be left to those officers, and that decision has no support from on high. This

commander has sewn the seed of doubt into the trigger finger of his troops –
absolutely criminal.

At this point, a burly chap pushes his way through the crowded end of
the room, reaches the briefing table and leans his weight on to it via two
clenched fists.

"I'm Dave J. I'm the head of South Wales firearms training. You can
take it from me that this individual represents a suicide bomber; you are to
treat him as if he has an explosive device ... and you can take it from me that
that if you think your life is at risk, the Superintendent's instruction that
you should exercise dynamic risk assessment equates to you shooting him in
the head."

The rank and file of armed officers breathed a sigh of relief and the
Superintendent snatched his Dictaphone from the desk.

From that point, things started to feel more like a real operation.

The TFU requested two Operators to join the entry team and one
Operator to assist the armed cordon. Moxy volunteered to man the cordon
which left Phil and I to man the entry team. Mark sourced the police
comms guys, and confirmed that his ECM would not affect their comms
and identified where he was going to site himself for the assault. Then the
batphone buzzed.

"Captain J speaking. We're on our way, now on the M5, can you hold
on for us to get there?"

"What the fuck are you doing on the M5?"

Rather than request a lift from the local police who will know the best
route from Snowdon to Barry, he's opted to jump into a beat up Charlie
Troop Land Rover and drive all across the top side of Wales to reach the
motorways. That will add at least two more hours to his journey. Yeah right,
we'll be waiting for you to turn up. Besides, Phil is a size match for his
fireproof overalls and he's already wearing them. I'd like to place the
insanity of his plan (and obviously make a joke about offers of help and
maps) firmly on Capt J's shoulders, but embarrassingly, he's got the Alpha
Troop Warrant Officer driving him.

The insanity didn't stop there. As Moxy prepared to deploy with the
armed cordon, and Phil and I started rehearsals with the TFU: first the 721
Squadron Duty Officer, (Barry is in their Operational patch); then the 721
Squadron SAT; and then the 821 Squadron Duty Officer (Alpha Troop is
under 821 Sqn). The three of them start arguing over which of them was in
charge. The police were suitably embarrassed and it became a real
distraction. I encouraged the police to action the assault as soon as possible.

Phil and I are now on police comms, our earphones filling up with units checking in or reporting their positions. Moxy is in a police car deploying to the armed cordon. The police are evacuating the surrounding houses to the target house by accessing the blindside of the houses, and as we mounted the TFU vehicles, the three Duty Officers were arguing over which of them was in charge.

Sunset is upon us, and Moxy and his armed colleague establish themselves next to the corner of a house with a view down the road just off the line of sight to the target house. The TFU have de-bussed and we're heading to our Start Point behind the house next door to the target which has keeps us out of line-of-sight to the target. Calls are coming as the cordon is securing up, and armed officers are sliding into concealed positions or behind their cars.

The sun has set and it's dark enough to make the assault. The TFU are in line of march, seconds from issuing the Standby-Standby call, when a shadowy figure walks across the back garden of the target. The team freezes as the unknown makes its way out of the garden and then to the rear of the neighbour's house where we're crouched in the darkness.

As he approaches, the TFU I can see is one of our Duty Officers. I've no idea what he thinks he's doing down here and he's risked compromising the mission. I stare open-mouthed at him while Phil looks at me and gestures to ignore it. We turn to the TFU and are about to move.

"STOP! STOP! STOP! I have a possible Bravo 1 exiting Charlie 1."

One of the call-signs watching the front of the house has spotted movement. IB was on the move...

"Has he seen that fucking eejit prancing around his lawn?" hissed Phil.

The TFU commander halted the team as we waited to see what the suspect did.

Unsighted to the drama at the back of the house, Moxy and his armed officer were about to have their own.

"He's coming towards us," Andy said.

Andy was 27, married and had a baby daughter. Moxy said he found this out in the 2.9 seconds since IB had come into view.

IB was wearing a big coat but strolling along the path like he hadn't got a care in the world. Andy, on the other hand, was asking Moxy rapid fire questions and at the other end of the scale.

"What do I do?"

"Wait until he reaches that lamppost (about 30m away) then challenge him," Moxy offered.

"What if..." Andy trailed off and the realisation dawned.

"STOP! ARMED POLICE! SHOW ME YOUR HANDS!"

Andy drew down on IB with a steady hand and a less steady voice.

IB looked up and saw the two officers over the other side of the Police car and slowly ceased his motion to stand still.

"What do I do now?"

Moxy said the atmosphere was tense. Andy had his sights trained on IB's head and wasn't taking his eyes off him for an instant.

Instead, Moxy directed that he strip and moved to one side to observe, making sure not to obstruct Andy's aim. Once IB was down to his Y-fronts, Moxy approached and cuffed him. Andy visibly relaxed at this point.

"STANDBY. STANDBY."

The TFU decided enough was enough. With no details as to whether there were others in the locale, and at the sound of the challenge coming from over the other side, it was time go. It hadn't helped that the Duty Officer had stood behind the team with an un-earphoned radio, broadcasting the net without the sense or shame to snatch the speaker to his chest and fuck off. The unprofessional dick was compromising our assault. The TFU were correct, it was time to go.

Mark, who'd been quietly jamming comms behind the squad, made his move into the back garden, chose a shadowy alcove to set up shop, monitored his kit and the rear aspect of the property. The TFU, having chosen the rear window for access, stacked up. The rear TFU Officer indicated that I should pick up the 'Wham-ram', and all of a sudden I'm from the back of the bus to lead element. The windows are broken by the 'Hooly-bar' and I target the window supports. It seems to be taking ages, but in reality it's seconds. The TFU makes entry and Phil and I follow.

There isn't a delicate way to manoeuvre an armed response team and a couple of bomb disposal though a window, so it was every man for himself. The room smelled warm and lived-in, but there wasn't anything on show that warranted delaying.

The TFU make access into the hall and came face to face with an occupant clearly seeking the source of the breaking glass and crashing noises. TFU waste no breath issuing instructions, but instead wrestled him to the ground. Phil did a pat down search but he was clear. The rest of the house was devoid of people. The kitchen was obviously a bomb-making facility but the individuals were nowhere near having a complete device, and in minutes it was over. Phil and I confirmed that there were no glaring issues preventing us handing over to a conventional EOD team to complete the search, confirmed we had enough to complete our report, and made our way out the same way we came in.

With suspects in custody, we claimed a souvenir for the Det walls and stripped off our assault gear. There is always a bit of a lull in the mood once a task is complete: lists of tasks to be done once back at base to ensure we're mission ready, reports and stores requests, all the mundane shite that needs to be done in the background. We'd recently sacked our storeman for being a big time-wasting walt and thoughts of hastening his replacement were interrupted by the Batphone buzzing in my pocket.

"Capt J here, we've just paid to go over the Forth Road Bridge and the flipping Land Rover has broken down. Can you come and get us?"

Phil took the phone off me.

"We ain't the AA," and switched the phone off.

PART IV - AFGHANISTAN

CHAPTER 16
WISWO, 2006

WITH MY MOVE to Alpha Troop and a posting to the HQ, the chain of command has a clear view of my work is very happy with my performance.

It's a marked difference from the usual listening-to-rumours crowd. My selection for promotion to Warrant Officer is still a bit of a surprise. I'm not even wearing it on my arm before they have plans for me to deploy on tour in acting rank. This will be my first tour since Iraq. My nerves are immediately raw and I'm pensive: will I be okay with this?

Having completed high threat EOD tours, I'm now on the roster for a WIS tour – Weapons Intelligence Section – responsible for the investigation and reporting of all terrorist related incidents. This means IED attacks, successful or more preferably neutralised by someone carrying out my former work. As the Warrant Officer running the detachment, I'm christened WISWO: it reminds me of a magician.

If I thought we were making a difference as an EOD team, the WIS detachment was to show me the bigger picture. But it was going to be a struggle to get there. My pre-tour preparation starts with, The bear went over the mountain: Soviet Combat Tactics in Afghanistan, a 1988 book about the Soviet occupation and the Mujahedeen attacks against them.

Despite the names being translated from Afghan to Russian and then to American, it was still possible to link names to places we would be going to in Afghanistan. The road named 611 is mentioned throughout the book for being a favourite to attack, and it's certainly going to be used again against the British forces. None of what is to follow should have been a surprise to any of our military planners.

And yet it appears that the lessons long known are still being ignored at soldiers' expense.

The soldiers were part of a patrol travelling along Route 611 between Forward Operating Base Ouellette and Patrol Base Lashkar Gah Durai in the Nahr-e Saraj district when their vehicle was struck by an improvised explosive device.

I'm scheduled to go to Kabul for six months, which is nice, working for the British Embassy. The post is long-established, and the accommodation is sizable and inside brick buildings. The office is co-located with the intelligence cell, so the flow of information is good and the vehicle is an armoured civilian 4 x 4. Handy for the other Embassy role which is 'agency' liaison – for the purposes of buying back the Blowpipe surface-to-air missiles that we didn't gift to the Mujahedeen. It's not as front line as other work, but I'm content that it's a good job, so I start getting ready.

I've been single since the problems post-Iraq ended my relationship with my long term girlfriend. I've hopped from bed to bed and despite being happy with the current girl, I know there is no longevity in it. She gets me to promise to write to her.

After scheduling the pre-deployment training through any Unit you can find who is deploying, (you're going as an individual, so no one is set up to support you), I started on my technical build up. I contact our technical chain of command to schedule the deployment briefs and sign the required documentation. I get given a date the week before I'm due to fly. I remember thinking that it was a bit tight. The day before I give them a call to ensure that all is as it should be, and get an astonished officer on the phone saying, "Has no one told you?"

"Erm, obviously not. Told me what?"

"Well, firstly there is no one available to brief you, but more importantly, your deployment has changed. The UK has decided to invade Helmand. The current small force there is being expanded to a brigade-sized deployment expected to be 5000-6000 troops, and included in this will be a weapons intelligence role. The chances are Helmand is expected to be more 'kinetic', despite some prat in government suggesting we will return from Helmand without firing a shot. Because of this expected hostile environment, the decision has been made to send someone else to Kabul. As this will have the effect of freeing you up to deploy to Helmand. Lastly, as the new post has not been established we have six bergens and cases of equipment you need to take with you. I won't be here but we'll get a driver to come and deliver them to you. That okay?'

"I'm obviously chuffed," (sarcasm).

And hang up.

The only good news is that I got to choose my own guns as a perk of the job, so I had already visited Fort Halstead to go on what I'd like to refer to as a shopping trolley dash. Although the choice and temptation was huge, I eventually selected a Demarco rifle and Sig pistol so the ammunition would be the same as other UK troops. I've had time to zero (set my sights), qualify with the weapons and have them all checked prior to deployment. There were a lot of people who historically never did this despite the legal requirement to do, so I wanted to be above board. The briefing and documentation required was never delivered; our technical chain of command all had far more important things to be doing than ensure a new detachment was properly directed. The 600kg of equipment made it though.

The trip out was as expected, an admin fest of biblical proportions.

One of the Alpha Troop lads dropped me off at Brize Norton; he offers to help me with my kit, and we fully load two baggage trolleys up with the detachment equipment, my kit and weapons. We approach the 'crab-air' desk (RAF Movers). I'm not being stereotypical, but the lad has a glowing future as a traffic warden. Firstly, he says that we both have too much baggage to take to Afghan; he's under the impression we're both flying. I explain his error and that all eight bags and boxes are mine. This devolves into an argument and eventually he puts on his best traffic warden's face and says, "No way, chum. There is no way I'm letting you on a plane with all that."

"I'm setting up a new location so, it all has to go. If you can't manage that, then get your boss out here."

He's beginning to annoy me.

He makes a phone call to get his boss on the scene and I suggest we book in my personal kit and weapons, as the queue grows behind me. He agrees.

I pass over my weapons' case, take off the padlocks and he opens it. His demeanour changes, when he sees the Demarco rifle instead of an SA80, having a non-standard weapons he thinks I'm one of 'them': he's presumed I'm a member of a Special Forces unit, and it looks like he's now happy to send all the kit.

I don't like bluffing my case, but I'm bored of this game, so I do nothing to change his opinion. If it gets the bags onto the plane, that's all that matters. His boss turns up and Traffic Warden says it's all sorted. The kit goes on the plane. It's not lost on me that there is no way there will be anything set up to get this kit moved once I get to Helmand, but that's tomorrow's problem.

The RAF Tristar plane, affectionately called 'Timmy flight', is as cramped as cattle class on a commercial plane, but the seats are just that little bit more uncomfortable; threadbare in places, they show the age of the RAF's tiny fleet of transport aircraft: (three for passengers, and six multi-role). I try and sleep as best I can, but the flight is noisier than a commercial flight, so I manage very little during the next eight hours. These planes are relics, and I'm constantly surprised when they make it wherever they are flying in once piece, a testament to the skill and efforts of the RAF ground crew who get my absolute gratitude and respect.

I'm not really asleep, I just have my eyes shut. The intercom sparks up and the pilot says we're shortly going to land. Some reach up into the overheads to collect their protective gear; I already have mine at my seat. As one, the entire flight dons helmet and body armour for the landing.

Kabul is sticky and hot: above 400C. We exit and go through the rigmarole of booking into theatre. Despite being ID-checked and listed getting onto the flight at Brize Norton, you have to go through the exact same procedure getting off at the destination. I assume the computer systems aren't linked, otherwise the only explanation is that they suspect people get out of the plane halfway.

I have found my pallet of equipment, and as I'm wondering what to do with it, I see my fellow WISWO friend, Andy, coming through the crowd. He's been waiting for me, and his driver is parked outside. My struggle into theatre takes on a much smoother passage.

I have a connecting flight to Kandahar in a couple of days on the 3am flight. It's better to fly at night because the cold air is denser, and obviously the dark helps protect us from enemy fire. Between then and now, Andy has planned an induction all of his own, mostly involving meeting the forensic scientists I'll be sending my evidence to, and any other persons of interest (aka Special Forces, Intelligence Officials and the CIA types) around Kabul.

The nature of the work calls for us to carry our weapons in a 'ready' state. Andy said the post in Kabul was issued a card from the Brigadier authorising it, so it made sense to get me a copy. I didn't really think anyone would notice let alone care, but you never know. I spend the night in Andy's palace. The WISWO set-up in Kabul is palatial: his room has a double bed, carpet, fridge, TV and video. He even has a second room with four beds for guests – my room for now. Andy gives me some ammunition for my pistol for tomorrow; he has no spare for the rifle, although in the morning he lends me one of his magazines for the journey.

The next day, we're out in his air-conditioned, armoured 4 x 4 heading towards the US air base at Bagram. I watch the scenery as we drive through the city. I can't believe I'm driving through a country that the Russians invaded. Fascinated by the war during my time at college, UK news channels portrayed a bloody and beaten Soviet army exiting Afghanistan. It was still going on at the time I joined the Army.

As I went through training, I certainly didn't think we'd be here 16 years later.

The city faded into countryside and wide open spaces, mountains ringed the entire skyline – off in the distance many were snow-capped. If you'd asked me at the time, I would probably say it was beautiful.

I was still staring out of the window when the comms issued us a stop command. We pulled over and Andy called HQ on his secure phone. There was a suicide bomb threat on Bagram. We pull to the side of the road, not off the tarmac because of the risk of mines. Andy said this often happened, and we'd give it an hour or so then decide if we were carrying on or canning the trip and heading back to Kabul. About an hour later, we get the call and set off again towards Bagram. Andy says that a suicide car bomb had been used against a German patrol coming out of Bagram. As we drive on, my daydreaming has finished, I'm scanning the scant number of vehicles approaching, observing the verges of the road and eyeing up every pedestrian we pass. It would be fair to say that 24 hours after arriving I'm fully 'on mission'.

When my time with Andy is over – too quickly – he drops me off at the airport at midnight. My flight to Kandahar on a Hercules is more comfortable than the Timmy, and only takes a little over an hour. My equipment has all made it, too. My predecessor, Buster, meets me on arrival.

I'm fooled by the cool early morning temperature. During the day, the temperature rises above 50oC. I'm truly in the furnace now.

Buster has a plan to load the detachment equipment onto the EOD trucks which are making their way from Kandahar into Helmand. I don't see an alternative and I'm glad to be rid of the majority of my cargo and no longer humping nearly a ton of equipment around with me. Back to just the normal 120kg.

Buster has been covering two jobs while out here: SAT overseeing the arrival of the EOD teams, and WISWO reporting on tasks. He says he has only done six WIS reports in his time – work must be slow. He tells me that until the replacement SAT arrives, I will be covering both jobs, as well. He also says that between the two of us, we should consider job-sharing as transportation is a massive issue. He'll leave the decision up to us. The last thing he tells me is that my Royal Military Police (RMP) Cpl who will provide the police element of any investigation is already at Lashkar Gah.

Now all I need to do is get there.

While I'm in Kandahar, I attempt to meet my boss, a Major in the Intelligence Corps. He's just leaving his desk for a meeting when I get there. He points to one of his clerks and tells me to brief him. I also meet the two Intelligence Corps analysts who are attached to my section. I'm given the choice of taking one or both of them with me. I figure that leaving one in Kandahar will give me the means to communicate with the Intelligence Cell here better, and I can always call him forwards later if I need him.

I tell them my decision and they toss a coin for who goes where. Cpl K is staying in Kandahar and Cpl M is coming with me. Nearly a week into theatre, I'm now on a Chinook helicopter flying to Camp Bastion, the main British base in Helmand. I don't realise it at the time, but we virtually fly over Lashkar Gah to get there.

Of all the helicopters we fly in, I have a longstanding love of Chinooks. I think this stems from my time in Ireland where we'd wait for a pick up, soaked through to the skin – as it would obviously be raining – and the Chinook would arrive. I'd drive my EOD buggy to the rear of the aircraft then wait for everyone else to embark before I'd drive up the ramp. The brief wait behind the aircraft under the rotor downwash and behind the engines would virtually dry me out.

Even out here with the raging temperature, the Chinook is comfortable with the doors open and the air rushing through. Yeah, it was safe to say I loved Chinooks.

I arrive to be told, literally the second I get off the helicopter, that the EOD trucks are no longer coming here but will be going to Forward

Operating Base (FOB) Price about 20 miles away from Camp Bastion. Damn.

The next day I don't get to fly. The RAF are having a 'No-fly' day.

It's not that they can't fly, but they want a day to conduct training, catch up on maintenance and rest the pilots. (An officer returned from this tour and submitted a letter to the press calling the RAF *utterly, utterly useless*; I understand his frustration). Instead of flying, I'm stuck at Bastion. The collection of tents are surrounded by a giant sand berm. They're in stark contrast to the runway which was expertly built by the Royal Engineers. There's a former Russian airfield at the edge of Lashkar Gah, but the decision was made to base in the desert instead of clearing the mines and explosive hazards left by the Russians. The locals don't use the location because it's well known to be populated by a type of fly that lays its eggs in the eyes.

In the distance, you can see the traffic travelling along the road built by the Russians. Something about the image seems to make this place all the more grim, like the only civilisation around is just out of reach.

I have time to visit the Ammunition Depot, partly to show my face and see who's about, and partly on the scrounge for ammunition and explosives. If this tour is anything like Iraq, both will be inadequately supplied

When I go into the offices I see Chris M. He was on my team for Op Certain Death (as he called it), in Northern Ireland; and, luckily for him, he was on Op Certain Death II in Iraq. He says he's pleased to see me and even more pleased not to be on my team. He does like me – he just thinks I'm too much of a magnet to be around often. I blame him as the magnet, so we can be mutually happy.

I ask him if we can go and have a look in his RAG shed. The Returned Ammunition Group is a holding area for stock being returned by Units leaving theatre. Most likely there's nothing wrong with it, and I can inspect it myself to guarantee it's safe to use. I also know you never get enough, so it makes sense to supply yourself when you can.

Chris rolls his eyes but gets the keys. I'm allowed a free hand and stock up on ammunition for my weapons, some smoke and HE grenades, and some parachute flares. He tells me that I've had enough and kicks me out. I offer to help with the paperwork – and smile at him. He's on message and just tells me to take it, he'll sort it out. I love being an Ammo Tech.

On day nine of my tour, my flight to Lashkar Gah happens. I'm keen to get on with my work out here and have wasted the first week because we've got nowhere near enough helicopters.

The WIS Detachment is going to be co-located with one of the two EOD teams we have in theatre. This is good news, because historically, and certainly in my experience, EOD Dets are usually able to carve themselves a good bit of real estate and comfort wherever they are based. I remember inviting troops into the Detachments in Ireland, and they considered where we lived to be palaces compared to their conditions. The requirement to store EOD vans and explosives usually lends itself to getting a big building to start with; the need for a speedy response means you tend to live next to the vans, and whereas one group of soldiers will hand over to another group from a different Regiment, we hand over to our friends within our own trade. As a result, people tend to like to improve their Detachments – comfortable seats and beds are sourced, TVs get installed and so on...

The EOD team has been here for six weeks. I find them out and see that they have ... nothing. Well, four camp beds and a corner of a tent.

Their vehicles are parked outside; all their charging equipment (for keeping torches, robots and X-ray equipment running) is strung out around the tent with extension leads all over. It's carnage and looks like it's a fire waiting to happen, but I'm not about to become a health and safety Nazi just yet. Morale is low, there is a fair amount of apathy, and the team have not had a single task since getting here.

Boredom I can understand; laziness, unprofessionalism and giving in to inertia I can't: I'll get back to that.

I drop my kit, leave them to it and head off to find my empire. I discover I'm based in the HQ, a large double-sided tent. The first side is split between admin clerks and the Operations Room; the second half is split between the Intelligence and the Command staff. I'm with the Intelligence Section. I have a desk, a bog standard army six-foot table and folding chair. There is a mobile phone on the table with a yellow Post-it note. It's labelled WISWO, with the number on it. That is it – that is the Weapons Intelligence Section.

My equipment will augment this situation, but currently it's on its way to a completely different base in the back of another EOD team's vans.

I have my work cut out.

There is no sign of my RMP. I meet the Chief of Staff (CoS), a major from the Army Air Corps. My first impression is that he's a good bloke. He seems professional, keen and onside. He also informs me that I have my first task tomorrow – to go and investigate a suicide bombing in town that happened two days ago. The EOD team had attempted to deploy and been refused permission by the Afghan authorities. It's taken two days to convince them of the benefits of a professional investigation, and that it's the point of deploying forces that we would work together. It's another no-fly day so I'm not going to make it up to FOB Price anytime soon to collect my own equipment, so I go back to the EOD Detachment and ask if they will take me out. They instantly brighten up at the prospect of getting out of camp. That was an easy fix.

This isn't my first fatal incident, nor is it the first significant report I will write. It's not even my first brush with suicide vests having neutralised them in Iraq. However, my it's first suicide bomb explosion. I warn the teams about the dangers of biological contamination, the need for gloves and masks to avoid breathing in potentially contaminated blood particles. (A tip I got from the UK fire brigade who had one of their officers catch Hepatitis from a bloody scene.)

We're up early and the WIS team, the ATO team, and a Royal Engineer Search Team (REST) deployed to the Land Registry Office. The REST team was made up of eight soldiers led by a Corporal – the Army's specialists in finding stuff. They search areas of high risk, those likely to contain IEDs or where IEDs have functioned. They're a welcome addition. We have been given an interpreter from the pool on camp.

On reaching the scene, we get him to work questioning the local police. The target of the suicide bomber was Abdul, a hated local government legislator. His son had recently been arrested for kidnapping and sexually abusing a local boy. Abdul had arranged for the child's return and facilitated his son's release. This, along with constant complaints about corruption, made him an unpopular local figure. He'd been killed along with three others. I say three others – only two of the bodies were able to be recovered, the third was still missing.

The building was a mess: twisted pieces of rebar and concrete blocks were strewn outwards, the roof had fallen in and the glass from all the shattered windows was everywhere. The Afghan police and an ambulance were still in attendance. Despite refusing our assistance when the device was detonated, now they have agreed to us deploying. They are hoping we will be able to find the last body for them.

By the time we reach the building, the scene had long been cleared of bodies, and numerous people in local garb are wandering around. The bomb has blown out an external wall and this has caused the slab concrete roof to collapse, under which was the body of a local woman, so we were told. Our mission was to collect evidence of the device. Specifically, I had been briefed to try and biologically identify the suicide bomber. This information would be transmitted back to the UK to form part of a wider intelligence gathering exercise, and lastly and most importantly, we needed to do this without becoming the target of such a device ourselves.

The team very quickly get used to the plan. On arrival, we'd use some of the troops for security; the remainder would deploy with large forensic bags and gloves. They'd search the scene picking up anything that looked even remotely related to the incident, bag it and load it into the vehicle. Anything dodgy would elicit a call to WISWO (or ATO) for a second opinion. As quickly as could be managed, the scene would be stripped clear, photos taken and the priority information secured: each member of the team working in isolation but knowing the whole picture would become clearer at the debrief back at camp.

I was impressed by the REST, professional searchers they may have already been, but they went further. While I was preoccupied with looking for 'a bit of the bomber' they went from room to room collecting evidence. They were meticulous and, after this first task, if they were available any time I deployed, I would request their presence.

It's not hard to see where the device functioned – the hole in the internal wall with the debris blown outwards from inside the building is a fairly good indicator. While my interpreter is questioning one of the witnesses, his face covered with a scarf to conceal his identity, I see blood splatter on the wall radiating out in a fan. This is clearly from the bomber: if I had any forensic kit, I would be able to swab the blood for a definite DNA 'hit'. It's on my ever growing things-to-do list. I will have to do this a different way. I pull a piece of the plaster off the wall and put it into a bag on its own.

Within 10 minutes, we're finished. Everyone bundles back into the vehicles. The rear of one of the Snatch Land Rovers is now also full of clear plastic bags containing bomb scene detritus. We return to the base over the rutted dirt tracks. There is little tarmac in town and what there is doesn't head to our camp.

Weapons are unloaded, I thank the guys for their help, and we take the bags to my luxurious desk. It's obvious this isn't going to fit.

So I look around the HQ tent. There, in the middle, is the conference table made with a large map on it. It's called the Bird Table and is used by the brigade senior staff for meetings and such like. I get the guys to cover it in plastic from a large roll we have; we then empty the bags out onto the conference table and, with our forensic gloves on, start sifting through it. There is large pile burnt clothing, tiny bits of wire, an ever growing number of ball bearings, and finally there is a pile of flesh and bone, bits of scalp and a very clear ear, scorched by the explosion where it was in close proximity. It all stinks – it stinks bad, and before too long people are starting to notice. We go through the evidence and sort it into relevant piles, the clothing, the rubbish and the other stuff. Before long we're starting to identify pieces of the device and these are segregated into forensic bags. I knock off the WIS team and start my report.

My desk is close to the bird table so I can keep an eye on the evidence. I still don't have any of the WIS equipment, so against regulations, I use my personal laptop. As I'm typing, one of the young Lieutenants comes through the office, he pauses by the table and has a good look. I guess he hasn't worked out what it is because he then picks one of the pieces up for a closer look. He chooses a bit of 'the other dead person' pile and as soon as his fingers feel the texture, the realisation sinks in. He shrieks and drops it, looks around and sees me watching him. He curses me like it's my fault and walks out.

The report is fairly simple: when the IED has gone bang there is only so much to talk about that is relevant to the counter-IED battle. I guess it can be fairly dehumanising to ignore the tragedy of the incident, and the main text of the report just identifies those parts of the device we have found and speculates on the likely make up. Amongst the fragments I'm sure formed part of the device is a square of black plastic Velcro. I speculate that this was used to secure the bomb to the body. I don't know it yet, but the attention to detail is going to pay off.

The report is complete. All that remains is to transmit the DNA evidence back to the UK agencies. In consultation, it's decided to send the piece of plaster and a small fragment of skull and scalp home. I seal it in a biometrics bag then into an RMP evidence bag. Finally, I fill in an appropriate evidence log sheet and set out to find the RAF.

I explain my plan. This has to go back to the UK; I have spoken to the SO 15 agency representative and his phone number is on the evidence log sheet. If I can get one of the transiting helicopter crew to sign for it, they can transfer it to one of the homewards bound Timmy flights. Once in the UK, if they phone the number, a courier will come and collect it, signing for it, giving it a sealed chain of evidence from theatre to home. Realistically, the evidential value is limited, but it's the correct procedure.

The RAF refuse.

"It's not our job."

Ohyoufuckinguselessidletwats!

I arrange to camouflage it in a normal envelope and send it via our Intelligence cell back in the UK. Evidentially, it's spent, but for the DNA profile, I've achieved my aim. A few days later, it has made it back to the laboratory. The message of its impending arrival has not been passed on by the officer I spoke to. The lab assistant who unpacked it, used to receiving cotton swabs, wasn't expecting this grim bit of reality. A message makes its way back out to me, and in typical army fashion, what starts off as a small piece of bone and skin soon results in me receiving calls from mates asking if it's true I sent the lab a whole head.

Fast forward a couple of weeks and I have found my RMP. He was hiding in the RMP post on camp. It makes sense really – where else would a police officer hide except a police station? I have also found my way up to FOB Price. The command there had no idea we were scheduled to deploy the section to them. There isn't much space for us but they will see what they can do.

I have taken Cpl M, the Int Corps guy, with me and together we hump the equipment back to Lash. I've spent the last two weeks getting to know the Brigade staff, introducing myself and getting out on the local patrols to get the lie of the land. Initially, the Section Commander is a bit hesitant about my request to accompany him, but I assure him I won't get in his way. I do as I'm told, keep my mouth shut and eyes open. I do my best to behave like one of the squad. After the first patrol, he pays me a nice compliment and says with a bit of effort I could make a half decent rifleman in his squad. He also lets me go back out with him again.

In my meetings with the heads of sheds in the HQ, I have emphasised the need to move the section out of the HQ. The biological issues of bringing suicide bomber pieces back to a public area represent a health hazard, and there are other actions which are best carried out beyond the sight of the rank and file. They understand, but currently there is nowhere for us to go. I've got my eyes on two unclaimed porta-cabins in the corner of camp. The Quarter Master (QM) – the officer responsible for stores – says I can't have them as they belong to the SBS – who are no longer coming to Lash.

I don't understand his reluctance to help, but sometimes there is only so far you can push an issue against the chain of command before it causes you more trouble than it's worth. We still need vehicles, ECM equipment, radios, accommodation, a dedicated working area, a proper explosive store and a list of equipment that would fill a book in order to be properly working. The administration of fighting these issues fills my days and it's always a relief when some real work comes in. Unfortunately real work usually consists of people trying to kill us or each other.

The first request for support from DHU – one of the Intelligence Units we also support as WIS – has come in. They have a possible bomb they'd like us to have a look at. I tell the WIS lads I'll be working this evening and warn the ATO team in veiled terms that I might have some work for them shortly. I don't yet know which part of a bomb they think they have – it might be the explosive part. I only tell the ATO – it's procedure to keep the circle of those in the know to the minimum.

I have a small kit of hand tools I always carry with me, and I add some light scales forensic equipment and head over. The guy in charge is called Rick. He invites me to sit opposite him at his desk. We have a conversation about my skill set and where I can support his Unit. We then get onto the task at hand and I start asking him some background questions: where has this come from, who handed it in and what has he said about it?

Rick isn't very forthcoming with information but I'm not offended. It's not unexpected, and understandable with the world these guys work in. The Intelligence world is often this way for good reason. Secrets aren't kept by spreading them around, but the safety aspect of an ATO's work is often based on finding out the whole picture, so initially our meeting consists of me asking questions and getting the reply, "I'd rather not explain that."

I explain, that in order to work safely, I need to know some information about the items' background. I change tack and start asking for some negative confirmation: "Can you tell me it definitely isn't this?"

This goes down better. Mainly, I need to know that it hasn't turned up under suspicious circumstances. We have already had a rocket handed into an American camp, ostensibly by a 'concerned citizen' who wanted to remove dangerous ammunition from where his children were playing. The rocket was taken and put into the UXO explosive store, on top of other UXO (rockets and bombs already handed in). Later it's found that the rocket is a 'Trojan' – an IED camouflaged to look like something else, and it has a radio controlled bomb inside. The intention being to blow the camp up from the inside. Luckily, the device fails – had it functioned on top of all the other ammunition, the camp would have been devastated. It's with incidents like this in mind that we continue our conversation until we get to a position where I'm happy that whatever is I'll be looking at is safe.

I tell Rick that I'm ready to go and look at what has been handed in, expecting to go to some sandbag enclosure safely away from the accommodation and living area. Instead, he indicates the item wrapped in the plastic bag that has sat on his desk between us. I roll my eyes.

It's the Afghan way, everyone eventually comes to accept this out here. I ask him for somewhere to work.

Before moving it, I pull on some forensic gloves from my pocket, pick up the whole thing gingerly and follow him to a desk in an adjoining room. I haven't had the chance to X-ray it and see what's inside, so the risk is based wholly on the fact that someone else has moved it to get it here. This isn't the normal standard for EOD work.

Rick introduces me to Gaz, his second in command, and heads back to his office. Systematically, I photograph and unwrap the item in stages. It's not a quick procedure and probably takes me a long 15 minutes – it seem longer while I'm concentrating. Finally, its secrets lay bare: it's a radio control unit for an IED. As I'm taking details, Rick has come back in and I hear him whisper to Gaz, "How's he doing?"

Gaz replies, "He's all over it boss."

I'm keen to make a good first impression and smile as I work.

While it's fully open, I brief Rick on its capabilities and use. It's going to go back together the way it came out, but Rick asks me to stop it working.

He says, "Can you make that not work?"

I tell him that I can neutralise it – job done!

I close it up, seal it, wrap the thing back inside its carrier bag. At every stage, I check my handiwork against the photographs I took as I unwrapped it: my OCD being put to the best use.

I'm utilising a skill set I gained training with a similar Unit.

There is a hushed conversation behind me. It appears I have more than impressed them. I'm asked about my background and who taught me to work. I repay their initial reticence to tell me anything in kind and say that I can't tell them. I grin and say that all ATOs get taught to do this. They're not upset. They know the game is played this way far better than I do. They have another hushed conversation, and the decision is made. They explain the nature of their world and again and ask me to explain how far I can go in assisting them.

TROLL: I WILL SAY NOW THAT IN WRITING THIS, I HAVE DELIBERATELY *changed details to preserve operational security.*

CHAPTER 17

AFGHANISTAN, 2006

ONE OF THE NGOs (non-government organisations) 4 x 4s has been attacked by suicide bomb.

The vehicle has been disabled, but no one was injured inside the vehicle. Some of the nearby Afghans had caught some of the blast, but no one had died. We rushed out of camp with the Quick Reaction Force (QFR) who went to secure the scene. We know not to get in their way, and the team scuttles over the scene under and around them.

It's clear to me that this was another pedestrian suicide attack. The explosion is too small for it to be anything else, and there are certainly no remains of a vehicle. The WIS team have almost finished the search; everything has gone into the bags including a pair of black sandals followed by a pair of lower legs, when Kit calls me over.

He's found the head.

A suicide bomb carried on the upper body will often do this. The neck is a weak point, so sometimes it'll just pop off. For some reason, Kit's not okay with it, so I roll it into a bag, and we jump back into the Snatch Land Rovers and head back in. On the bumpy ride back to camp, I give some thought to sending the whole head to the Agency in the UK. After all, I've already been accused of it – I might as well go two for two.

It's been a couple of weeks since the last attack but the routine is the same: Bird Table in the HQ and lay out all the collected material. We know that all the biological material is 'his', the bomber, but none is any more suitable to send home than the previous attempt. I still don't have any biometric kit for taking swabs. We sift through the pieces of clothing: parts of striped suit trousers, a dark jacket and purple rags, maybe bits of a turban? Lastly we find a two inch square of black Velcro. I bag the body parts to be taken to the medical centre for disposal/incineration. Some may object to this, but I don't think a suicide bomber warrants a funeral. I tell the guys to hold onto the head, and I will process it after I have been to the Med Centre.

I deliver my cargo, then sit down for a chat, although I'm clearly on the scrounge. I ask if they have anything I can substitute for DNA swabs to send back to the UK. While we're discussing the legalities and suitability of some of the medical stores, I notice that they have a fridge. They tell me that the QM has received 40, but only gave them one of the two they need. One for water for heat casualties, and one for drugs. I'm somewhat annoyed.

I get back to the WIS detachment (table in the corner), and finish processing the cadaver with my improvised swabs. I need to make a phone call to make sure the Agency will be happy with my improvisation, so in the meantime, we need to store the head. I double bag it, seal it, and clean with alcohol wipes, so it's biologically safe, and then look around for the new WIS fridge. The nearest fridge to me is the Colonel's water fridge. That'll do.

I open the fridge which is already stocked with water. The little bottles with the light filtering through them look like a vision of crystal loveliness, but the drawer at the bottom is empty. It's a bit of a squeeze, but he fits.

I go back to my desk and start my report. Again, it's not going to be lengthy but we can now begin to draw some data on the timings between attacks and targets etc. I'm watching the fridge out of the corner of my eye; it's only a matter of time.

Sure enough, the boss comes out of his office and opens his fridge. He takes a bottle and shuts the door. I wonder if I have escaped detection, but he pauses. Obviously, if you're used to seeing a pure clear white fridge with only the reflected colours of the fridge light, a bloody mess in a bag might be noticeable.

He opens the door again, pulls out the crisper drawer and shouts, "WISWO!"

I make a hasty arrival from my desk.

"Yes, sir?"

"What is that?"

I lean around him and look.

"It's the head of a suicide bomber, sir."

"I can see that. What the chuff is it doing in my crisper drawer?"

He doesn't seem too angry with me yet, so I chance my arm.

"Come on, sir. We all know you don't put fresh meat at the top of the fridge."

This will go one way or the other; luckily for me, he's got a sense of humour, and after I give him a proper explanation, I go on to talk about the 40 fridges. It's not that I'm so annoyed that the WIS didn't get allocated one, I'm more enraged that the HQ has 12, the QMs has three, the gym two, but the medical centre still only gets one.

The Colonel looks at me.

"So this is your way of asking me to speak to the QM?"

I have no idea if this will facilitate the detachment finally getting some equipment support, but it's worth a shot.

Later, I heard that although the Colonel had a sense of humour with me, that part of him wasn't in evidence when he spoke to the QM who got a royal roasting for making the WIS detachment store body parts in his fridge.

Following this exchange, the QM came to me and had a whinge about "the mother of all bollockings" he'd just received. I don't know if he was looking for sympathy, but after his obstructive performance when I'd asked him for help, all that came out of my mouth was, "Well stop being shit then!"

How to win friends and influence people? Maybe, but he was never going to help, regardless.

SSGT LEE RIDGEWAY

This is the letter written by Troll in an attempt to have SSgt Lee Ridgeway's brave actions recognized.

Dear Sir,

   SSgt Lee Ridgeway

   Please forgive me, but after too long I have decided I must seek your assistance with a matter which I can no longer leave unresolved.

   You were my CoS during a tour in Afghanistan in 2006 and your professionalism enabled the WIS capability, for which I'm beyond grateful for. I was inspired by your leadership, and enabled by the 'top cover' you gave me, which with my inability to follow the rules, I surely needed. It's with my belief in your nature I wish to relay the conduct of a soldier, SSgt Lee Ridgeway, who during our tour went without recognition.

   SSgt Lee Ridgeway deployed as one of two ATOs to run the first EOD teams into Afghanistan. He was a young SNCO, fairly quickly promoted, even by Ammunition Technician standards, and this was to be his first High Threat tour as an EOD No1. His training for tour, conducted at the Army School of Ammunition Felix Centre, was unfortunately, solely based on Northern Ireland and woefully inadequate as preparation for EOD Operations in Afghanistan.

   On or around 24th August 2006, the 3 Para battle group conducted Op Atomi in the town of Musa Qal'eh. During the operation SSgt Ridgeway and his team neutralised 2 x IEDs. Following this Operation, I failed to seek correct recognition for his actions during this incident and I wish to expand on the circumstances of this action to you.

SSgt Ridgeway was supervised by a WO1 M— who was mandated to provide experienced over-watch to his EOD teams should they be deployed on a significant task which Op Atomi would qualify as. WO1 M—, at the beginning of his tour, identified to myself that he felt himself not physically fit to cope with the rigours of this tour. Between us, we agreed that I would deploy in his stead to provide the experienced over-watch and advice that a young operator should have. Op Atomi was one of the first tasks (if not the first, he will know) that SSgt Ridgeway deployed on, and due to issues surrounding helicopter support there was no airframe available to enable me to deploy. *As a result SSgt Ridgeway deployed on a major operation with no EOD supervision.*

Earlier in the month, an IED attack had killed three of our soldiers in Musa Qal'eh, when a patrol from the HCR suffered an IED strike on a Spartan AFV. I'm sure you remember this incident. In the response to this, a Royal Engineer call-sign was deployed to the scene to destroy the Spartan by demolition, and a Scimitar which had been immobilised in the attack. The Operator who responded, only destroyed the Scimitar and collected the IED evidence from the scene with no safety procedures. He recovered a motorcycle battery and 15 metres of command wire from the scene, picking up these items up by hand. I suspect from subsequent evidence he was observed by the enemy doing this. His failure to destroy the remains of the Spartan almost certainly influenced the devices that SSgt Ridgeway disposed of on the 24th.

The Royal Engineer in his report identified that he had recovered the evidence by use of a hook and line. Under questioning by myself, he later admitted he had not used equipment but had collected the evidence by hand. His actions and false report, if not discovered, represented a serious lapse in professional judgement which effectively increased the threat to all other operators in theatre at that time. I assessed that the device used in the attack likely consisted of multiple stacked anti-tank mines with 15 metres of command wire. (WISREP RC(S) 06/016 refers).

During Op Atomi, the two devices recovered by SSgt Ridgeway were also command wire IEDs constructed in general terms of a single anti-tank mine and 7.5 metres of wire. I believe that an original device of 2 x mines and 15 metres of wire was divided to create 2 IEDs in response to the success of the previous incident. The enemy was able to observe the success of their attack and that their main charge was over-matched to their target and as such, increase their war fighting ability by splitting 1 IED into 2. This link to a previous incident and the dangerous precedent created by the render safe actions of the attending Royal Engineer are both factors I consider relevant to the actions of SSgt Ridgway.

Sir, I'm unaware if you have served in Northern Ireland, but from experience I can tell you that a simple Command Wire IED would require at least 3 hours to be dealt with under NI procedures in a high threat non-contact environment. From the start of Op Atomi the UK forces were under contact from small arms and RPG fire. (RE Post Operational Report UK/056 refers).

The following is anecdotal between myself, SSgt Ridgeway and others. Simply, SSgt Ridgeway cleared two command wire IEDs within 30 minutes while under enemy fire.

Following the incident and as information became known to me, I approached SSgt Ridgeway's Senior Ammunition Technician WO1 (SSM) M— and suggested that Lee should be recognised for his actions. WO1 M— indicated that he would not submit a recommendation for an award for SSgt Ridgeway. When I questioned as to why, his response was that he (M—) had not received any recognition from his own tour as an EOD Operator. I didn't realise that I could submit a recommendation for someone in a separate chain of command and I have been saddened to this day that in some kind of misguided loyalty to a brother Warrant Officer I didn't 'tread on his toes' and submit the recommendation myself.

I believe the following are most relevant:

a. SSgt Ridgeway's prior training in no way prepared him for conduct of this Operation. In his position as an Operator, he should have expected a senior EOD Operator to be in attendance for guidance and supervision during such a task as per NI guidelines/history.

b. The Operation was conducted without the supervision of a senior EOD operator and as such SSgt Ridgeway had to interpret his SOPs, modify them to fit his task, an action that should have been conducted by way of referral to a Senior EOD commander which didn't happen.

c. SSgt Ridgeway had to break SOPs in order to carry out his task as rapidly as possible in order to achieve the mission and reduce the danger to supporting troops. Any break in SOPs mandatorily requires permission from a higher command as such actions carry an inherent increase in risk.

d. The previous activity in the area significantly raised the risk to SSgt Ridgeway during his task, my assessment is that both the successful attack at the beginning of August and this attack have similarities which can't be ignored. Though no booby trap was encountered, the previous conduct of other EOD at the previous incident represented a danger that was likely but fortunately didn't manifest itself.

e.The Operation was conducted under fire, with SSgt Ridgeway having to return fire whilst at the IED.

In summary, a young EOD Operator, inexperienced at working at this level, who should have been given a far greater level of supervision, performed a task demonstrating conduct far above his station. His supervising Warrant Officer refused to recommend him due to a poor personal bias. I failed to endorse him due to a combination of naiveté and misguided loyalty.

Subsequently, SSgt Ridgeway deployed to Northern Ireland as a WO2 in support of SRR. A post that historically has attracted a high percentage of recommendations amongst its supporting ATOs. I solicited WO2 Ridgeways OC with a request that in order to address a previous failing, should any action by WO2 Ridgeway be in any way close to the level deemed suitable for a recommendation, his previously unrecognised action be considered and reflected accordingly. I'm sure you understand the nature of the environment I indicate here.

Sadly, I observe no recommendation has been successful for this soldier.

I have spoken to numerous others regards this issue and it has been identified to me that the amount of time elapsed since this incident will have an unsurpassable bearing to those who would examine any subsequent recommendation. It's my belief that there is no statute of limitations on the recognition of an honourable action. It's entirely my fault that this issue wasn't suitably recognised at the time.

Sir, it's with the above story that I approach you. I know from my time serving under you that you were an excellent and honourable officer. I appreciate that the amount of time passed may be a crippling factor in any submission, but I ask you kindly, please submit a recommendation for SSgt Ridgeway, by ATO standards such action would be worthy of an award.

It may not be my place to suggest he should at least be considered for an MC as I know far lesser acts have received this award. I feel if his limited experience and lack of senior support was recognised, I could easily justify a higher award (CGC). Should it come to nothing, I would be content that his actions had most importantly been submitted for recognition. I know the value of such a submission without award and the effect such subsequent knowledge has on an individual who may or may not have suffered a lasting effect from his work in dangerous climes.

It's my hope that you will consider supporting this action.

Respectfully Yours,

Justin Bell QGM

CHAPTER 18

THE QM

THE EOD TEAM had a Playstation in the accommodation, or an X-box, I don't remember which. A TV and a homemade bookcase with a few random paperbacks completes the recreation facility amongst the sand and the dust swirling around the corner of the tent. There is very little out here for the troops' downtime. The Estonian EOD team next door are better supported than the UK mission; they have a giant TV, a fridge and some stereo thing that is in use most nights. It's embarrassing.

The WIS Detachment is just about ready to start. The QM is a broken man and the CoS (I told you I had a good feeling about him) has totally supported us. He helped because of the fridge incident and the anti-tank mine incident, and possibly because the Brigade staff were growing nauseous every time we brought home the remains of a suicide bomber. I'd like to think it was all happening because I was a professional in a professional army, but it wasn't. We'd just broken those who were obstacles – with a little help from friends.

The QM has finally agreed that we can claim a piece of camp for ourselves. He has offered us a strip of land against the perimeter wall in the far corner. I know he's doing it to be awkward, but it suits my purposes just fine. The move is imminent when I get a visit from Gaz. He's the OC of the Unit, the guys I have been helping with 'stuff'. (I know it's all a bit cryptic but it'll come together, trust me.)

Anyway, I've done work for Gaz a couple of times and he has already got the measure of me, which is why he came in my direction.

"We've got an emergency. You know our detachment is next to the SIS (MI6) compound? Well, that QM bloke is planning to put the LECs next to us."

LECs are the locally employed civilians. At best, they could observe and spy on any of the work going on around their location, at worst ... well, you get the picture. I've never agreed with the UK policy of employing LECs. The UK does it to engender good will from the locals, but I just think the risk outweighs the reward. I've already caught one pacing – walking in a straight line counting – measuring the inside layout of the camp for a rocket or mortar attack. They also do it to save money, as importing the workers from elsewhere costs, and we couldn't or wouldn't fly them out and back regularly. Sticking the LECs next to these two locations is a balloon's idea.

Gaz asks, what are the chances that we could put the WIS detachment next to them before the LECs move in. Currently, most of camp is open ground, so if we're going to get away with anything, now is the time.

"Leave it with me. I'll find some regulations meaning we can't be next to the perimeter fence."

"Good man," he replies, and off he trots.

I have a quick scan through A&ERs (Ammunition and Explosive Regulations), the AT's bible. (It has since replaced it with some poorly written joint service rubbish.) The WIS detachment, by definition, will handle and store explosives. I have already got one ISO container for explosive storage, but it's buried under gravel next to the heli-pad. I don't know what genius put it there, but if we have an accident, it would turn itself into the world's best anti-helicopter shotgun; so, I need some local storage as well.

I've managed to secure three or four ISO containers to help with the new Detachment. The CoS has allocated me one of the two SBS porta-cabins, and I have my eye on the other one. I've made friends with the Royal Engineer Foreman of Works (FoW) who has some spare Hesco Bastion – a brilliant invention, like giant steel reinforced sandbags that are used to create protective walls. These will have the effect of providing some security and protection for the Section, but will also protect those inside the camp from our activities.

It's all ready to go, and was due to be put into the far corner of the camp. I look up the regulations for safety distances relating to explosives and civilian dwellings. Suitably armed, I head off to see the Chief of Staff.

The CoS is totally onside, as ever, and agrees that we shouldn't put the troops' accommodation or local population at risk. The only suitable place left is nearer the middle of camp, and I point to the spot on the map earmarked for the LECs. He agrees and asks if I will go and let the QM know. I grin.

"Not a problem, sir."

I wander into the QM's open-plan brick built affair. It's possibly the best accommodation on camp. It would have been taken by the HQ, except it wasn't big enough. The offices are cool, as numerous electric fans waft slowly back and forwards; their quiet hum is rather therapeutic as I walk over to the QM's room in the corner.

When I met the QM, (he's an ex-ranker like me), I had hoped to gain some Sergeant Major to former Sergeant Major advantage. When he turned out to be such an unhelpful type, I'd have to settle for ordinary professionalism on my part, if not on his. Before long, I just wished the bloke would do his job. He was always part of the problem, never part of the solution. If he'd exhibited even the slighted bit of courtesy, I wouldn't have made it one of my missions to destroy him, refrigerator by refrigerator.

"Sir, a quick word. I know you said we could have this small strip of land in the corner, but I've just realised that the IQD between our explosive store, the troops' tented accommodation and the civvies on the other side of the wall mean we can't put the detachment there."

He already looks a bit hesitant, then replies, "That's the only bit of camp I can spare you. What's an IQD?"

'It's the Inter-quantity distance; it's a legal requirement for explosive storage, and if you breach it by putting the Section over there, we could get ourselves into trouble."

I know I'm making it sound like his responsibility, the danger being that he might not care. He's about to open his mouth again, so before he has processed it and made his decision, I follow with, "I've already spoken to the CoS and he's decided that I should put the detachment here."

Seeing that he has already been outranked by my use of the CoS, the QM loses a bit of self-control.

"Just do whatever the fuck you want. You're going to anyway; you don't need to come back and tell me anything just do whatever you want. I don't care."

We quickly find an Afghan with an industrial-sized fork lift. He picks up the cabin and moves it. The second cabin is only going to gather dust being stored where it is until someone claims it – it might as well gather dust stored next to the first in my compound. So that gets lifted, too.

The IOS containers are moved in and used to form a wall, and the promised Hesco Bastion fencing is unpacked and dragged to make the edge of the compound. It's not filled yet, so the cloth bags inside the wire frames blow in the wind, but it stakes our claim and starts to shield us from view.

We've gone from a desk to a compound in a matter of hours. Not bad for a day's work. Now we just need vehicles, ECM, communications, computers and the office sorting, showers, toilets, and a workshop.

The Detachment now had 'real estate'.

Over the coming weeks, the Section would all do their part in establishing the location to provide a professional environment. On days where we had no operational tasks, the team would all turn their hand to any of tasks needed: digging trenches to run power cables, scrubbing and cleaning the second porta-cabin for use as a 'clean room' and photography studio, finding the plant equipment (digger) to fill the Hesco-Bastion.

REST again proved their generous professionalism and built a low sandbag wall to contain a 'Mines lane' and a 'UXO Park'. The mines lane was for practising the drill for extracting yourself from a mine field (of which there are plenty in Afghanistan), and the UXO park, complete with a razor wire fence, to display inert items of ammunition and explosives found in the area. I have never seen a group of people put such dedication into filling and placing sandbags. The REST are often overlooked and on the whole unappreciated, but not by me. Truly, in every dealing I had with them I was a grateful recipient.

A shady deal with an American contractor saw one of the ISO containers wood lined and fitted out as a workshop with lights, power points and even an air conditioner. They also built us a wooden doorway at the edge of the Hesco, so we finally had a secure location to ply our trade. Despite an offer to co-locate, the EOD team No1 could not be enticed to join in.

I rewarded the team with a television I found. It belonged to the HQ, but was a spare for the briefing room. Prior to them needing it, I arranged a long-term loan for the price of a crate of coke – 24 cans.

The progress on the Detachment made some noticeable differences. We attracted some visitors with information, queries and requests. Initially, we had to trek over to the HQ if we wanted any form of computer, but that was a good excuse to go see the head sheds. Soon we were plumbed in and hi-tech – well, we had a laptop and a phone line. Most importantly, we had privacy.

THE EMPTY MINES HAVE FOLLOWED ME: ONE HAS BEEN PUT INTO THE UXO park – it looks a lonely and sad affair on the sand but I have no doubt more will follow; the other sits in my new office as I scratch my head about the pressing need to put it back into service.

We're lined up for dinner, the food here is something else. The chefs are from 16 Bde and the two senior NCOs in charge are miracle workers. When I say every meal was a banquet, I'm not kidding. It was beautiful, all garnished and laid out like the best hotels, only the plastic plates and diggers spoiled the fantasy. There was also pie and chips for those who were inclined.

The pie trays have been stacked up on top of the counter and I ask the chef if he will keep them for me. He looks at me in 'that way' and says sure.

I'm eating dinner and the idea comes to me. I finish, drop my plate into the rubbish bin and make my way out the back of the kitchen. Afghanistan is hot but this place is beyond furnace hot. I find the SSgt and I ask if he's up for doing me a favour.

"Can you or one of your boys make me something that looks like this?"

I pull a plastic bag out of my pocket and there is a small yellow/orange crystalline lump in it.

He and one of his Sgts has a look at it, and they discuss it being somewhere between a fudge and a toffee type affair. I tell them I want a fake cake to spoof one of my lads. They tell me to leave it with them. Later, I get a call and go to see their work: nothing less than geniuses. It's perfect, the look, the colour, the rigid hard nature. I'm in awe. I ask them what went into it and they rattle off some ingredients. They ask me how much I need. I reply between 20 and 30 lbs.

I get that look again, but a few hours later, one of them turns up at the detachment with a black bag full of cake mix. I can't thank him enough. We're almost ready to go.

CHAPTER 19

THE JOURNALIST

I HAD AN EPIPHANY IN AFGHANISTAN. I'm a little embarrassed that it took me so long to realise it, but I don't hate officers; I just hate unprofessional people. We can't be perfect all the time, but we can try to be professional as often and as much as we can. It makes me seem grumpy and I don't get wheeled out to meet visiting MPs much.

So I have no idea why my CO out in Afghan would send a greener than grass reporter to talk to me. She's on embed with the Americans on the other side of the valley.

"Charm offensive time," he said brightly.

"Not sure about the 'charm' bit," I muttered.

I don't think he heard me. He was going to wish he had.

The reporter is trying to look like she's seen it all, heard it all, just as tough as us. You know the type. You've probably seen them on the ten o'clock news, wearing their accessorised body armour. Well, not quite, but you get the picture.

We introduce ourselves, and she starts asking me about my 'career'. She's nice enough but 'naïve' hardly covers it. She wants to know about my work and how I learnt to do my job. I tell her about Northern Ireland.

"I had to check out the aftermath of a UVIED, a booby trap placed under a car. There was one fatality."

Those cold words don't cover the callous murder of a husband and father. The curse of my job is in the details.

"He was in the car, breaking and changing gear at the time."

She looks up and frowns.

"How do you know that?"

I'm immediately back at the scene, remembering everything about that day. I don't want to remember, but her questions have taken me down that road.

He was heading down hill into the town. It's obvious that on a hill going to a 'give way', he'd be breaking. It was this combined with the slope of the hill that caused the mercury tilt switch on the device to function. He'd driven from his home and the device didn't function until the hill, so it's likely that the switch wasn't set at a particularly sensitive angle. The mercury in the switch touched the two terminals and allowed electricity to flow; the electricity ignited the matchhead in the detonator and the spark of flame was transmitted to the explosive pellet, most likely lead azide or mercury fulminate. In an instant the flame becomes a detonation wave. It ruptures the thin aluminium case of the detonator and spreads to the pound of semtex. The explosive force gathers momentum and shatters the wooden box container of the under-car booby trap, held to the underside by two speaker magnets. The magnets are propelled upwards; the metal floor of the car ruptures and a hole is punched through the car as shards of metal now fly upwards through the driver's seat.

"He was changing gear. How do I know? Because... * "

Why did she have to ask me about NI? Now I'm back on a Northern Ireland street that is awash with blood, with the smell of it in my nostrils like it never left me.

"The explosion snapped the back of his seat; it threw him into the rear of the car and shattered all the windows.

"The car rolled forwards ... when a vehicle is blown up, the engine usually stalls and the vehicle stops almost immediately. He was in neutral, breaking and changing gear, like I said. This meant that the vehicle rolled forwards even though the engine had probably already stopped. You can see the explosion point at the give-way junction, the small crater in the tarmac, the pieces of the device scattered around and the circle of smashed glass from the windows.

"The driver's door buckled, flew outwards and broke off in the blast..."

I stop, remembering, seeing, but not talking any more. The journalist is pale.

I don't tell her about a nearby RUC man who saw the explosion. I don't tell her what he saw as he ran towards the car.

I do tell her that he wasn't even the target. His wife is a widow and his two daughters lost their father because he had the wrong name.

He's dead because terrorists are cunts, plain and simple.

* EDITOR'S NOTE: REDACTED AS PER TROLL'S INSTRUCTIONS - HE DID NOT *want to risk a member of the family reading this graphic description of what happened when the terrorist's bomb detonated.*

CHAPTER 20

RESCUING BOB

BOB WAS SUBSEQUENTLY RE-ARRESTED and was then sent to Pol-e-charki. He survived 38 days in captivity there.

Andy heard about it that morning and went off to the SF detachment and found the two biggest bastards he could find. They made Andy look small, they were that big. He got a fleece jacket and some good boots, they travelled to Pol-e-charki and went in to see the prison governor. Andy hands over the jacket and boots, the governor is very grateful. Andy says,

"These are for you, and if anything happens to the 'round eye' in your nick, these are the two guys who are going to come and kill you."

Bob was moved into solitary confinement that day.

While he was in there, the CIA visited. They lined all the prisoners up and went along them looking for individuals. Apparently, they were quite surprised when they saw Bob in amongst them. Bob was paired up in the solitary cell with a failed Pakistani suicide bomber. After both having a night sleeping with their eyes open, they agreed a truce and spent their time talking about cricket, so I'm told.

He was released and there were rumours he was trying to sue the UN, but then as he probably did try and kill the guy, maybe it's best left to lie.

EDITOR'S NOTE: TROLL BECAME VERY ILL AS WE RUSHED TO FINISH HIS memoirs and the job was never completed, but what follows is the story of how they came to be published in this book.

CHAPTER 21

LATER, AFTER

IN 2013, I was contacted by a friend at *Felix Fund: the UK Bomb Disposal Charity*. The charity had only been founded two years previously and was basically run by one member of staff and some volunteers.

My friend asked me if I'd be interested in responding to a request for technical information from a writer who was planning a film script based around an ATO.

I was cautious and polite, but curious as to what a civvy would know about the Trade.

Below are the email exchanges that began with commenting on a film script (that eventually became a stage play), to an unexpected friendship.

PART V - AN UNLIKELY FRIENDSHIP

CHAPTER 22

JANUARY 2013

16 JANUARY

TROLL

Dear Jane,

I was passed your screenplay by Holly. I have read it once and added some comments for your consideration. Initially, I struggled with some concepts of it, but I then understood some of what you were portraying in your character.

I have included a small related incident that occurred to me in case it can be of use to you.

I am interested where you got your idea from, as it seems very similar to a friend of mine in a lot of ways?

Towards the end, I have played devil's advocate a little and protested some of your position. I have done this only to offer you my views and it is not meant in any negative way towards your creation.

Please feel free to get in touch if you have any questions.

17 JANUARY

. . .

JHB

Hi Troll,

Thanks so much, so much for commenting.

I'll work in all your ideas, which will make a much better read. Just what it needed. Excellent. Comments on the things I'd got wrong, made me laugh, too. Nope, I wasn't trying to make anyone look like an idiot – well, just me.

Your supermarket scene will work in perfectly and I'd really like to use that if it's okay with you.

I'm not sure I can say where the idea came from. I was out walking with my dog when the story came to me (that happens a lot), and I just had some of the images playing in my head like a film. Then I turned to the internet and read accounts of people out in Afghanistan and also the work of bomb disposal teams in different places. There were some really useful film clips on YouTube, too.

If it seems at all like a friend of yours – although I don't know if you were referring to a particular scene or Alex's personality – then that's a huge compliment – and I'll take that!

I have a friend who's an ex-police sergeant who checked that side of things for me, and a woman who's a psychologist read through and commented, as well, but you're the first hands-on person who's seen it.

I said to Holly that the chances of this getting made were slim to none but I felt I had to try. Your input helps a lot. Thank you.

If you have the time, could I ask you to re-read it when I've put in the changes? I'd very happily add you to the acknowledgements, anonymously, if you prefer. Up to you.

After that, the next stage will be to send it to my agent, and then she'll pass it to the production company and see what happens next. (Probably nothing, but never say never.)

Thanks again,

TROLL

I'm happy to re-read for you. Just so you're aware, my company (a small company of friends), has supported previous EOD productions and one has just returned from providing SME input to a BBC production.

JHB

I haven't asked anyone else to read the ms.

The only other military person I was considering asking to take a look is an Australian, Major General John Cantwell, because his book, *Exit Wounds* is all about PTSD. Also, he's based in Queensland where my agent is. I haven't approached him yet, so if you have any concerns about that, please do let me know.

I've made the changes you suggested (damn, they work well). They're all in red, but I'm assuming you're not colour-blind...!

Summary of changes:

* ok to use your nickname in the acknowledgments?

* Alex is now treated in the med room at the police station

* could you have a look at the call sign used in scene 39, please?

* Sir is 'boss' and first names are used. No knobs.

* Did you want me to change the phrase 'the fuse is stuck in here'?

* have added correct procedure in scenes 66 and 69, and call sign (scene 69)

* DSO changed to OBE

* have added your supermarket scene - thank you

* have added detail about your colleague who carried on working with one hand; I have rewritten the scene so Alex says his hands shake all the time, that's why he can't continue with his work

* I have taken out him smoking dope; instead his (ex-) wife has an issue with him drinking

* have included correct pension info

* self-harming: I have clarified that he did this a couple of times as a kid, then stopped. He has started again since being discharged.

And some other, minor changes, all in red.

Huh, so the BBC are already working on a similar story? I'm pleased and pissed off in equal amounts. Well, I'll just carry on with this and see how it goes. Never say never.

Thanks so much for all your help. It's very much appreciated.

TROLL

I have no issues with who you show your work to, you created it, it is for you to decide how much or how little influence you wish to invite into changing it. I am aware of the book *Exit Wounds*, and I have an interest in PTSD etc. You may have noticed a veteran of the Falklands war 30 years ago recently took his own life which made the news briefly.

I am okay with you not using my nickname. I don't need acknowledgement, but feel free to reference Ammunition Technicians, as they need all the help they can get.

Relax about the BBC, their project was (as I was told) a modern day *MASH* comedy type based around a Brimstone team in Helmand. So nothing like your work. I referenced it just to highlight that our company is involved in providing subject matter expert support. I don't know how old you are (or which girls watch war movies), but they changed the ending in *Rambo*. In the film, Stallone smashes the town up etc but in the book he gets shot by the Sherriff, and the book was meant to highlight the tragedy of men returning from Vietnam and being unable to adjust.

My friend was one of my team back in 2000. He grew up, made Warrant Officer and when I met him at a royal visit, I could tell he was in need of help. I went to my friend and boss telling him so. They subsequently medically discharged him which is criminal in my opinion, but then I guess I have to count myself lucky not to have suffered the same fate.

I will re-read the work and pay attention to your changes and get back to you.

18 January

TROLL

A couple of adjustments but mostly just your radio procedure. I have singled out your rocket attack but I don't think I have explained myself very well. Let me know if you'd like more detail.

JHB

Thanks, Troll. I've put 'Ammunition Technicians' in the Acknowledgements line.

The BBC project sounds interesting. I wonder when that will see the light of day. I always enjoyed the original *MASH* and the way it could move from laughter to tears and back so quickly. But my all-time favourite moment must be when Hawkeye shot his jeep, just before returning to the US.

I didn't know that the ending to *Rambo* had been changed – although

I'm not surprised either, I guess. I always enjoyed that film, although not the sequels so much. I thought the first one packed an emotional punch that was lacking later on.

The cost of war is something I've come back to a few times in different ways, both in my children's books, and in my foray into adult romance (probably not your cup of tea, although you never know). But the discharge of your friend – that sort of injustice, that hidden cost of war – colours several of my books. If you're interested, *Hero: A War Dog's Tail* touches on the war in Afghanistan. It's a book for kids aged 8 to 10.

Thanks for taking the time to re-read the ms. I look forward to hearing from you.

JHB

Quick question: would you see a flash from a mortar as it's launched, or would it be somewhere they probably wouldn't see it at night? That's in scene 39 - I think I get what you were saying. Perhaps you could just look at that again.

The radio procedure in scenes 63 and 69, I've amended as instructed.

If anything else occurs to you at any point, please do say.

And I'll let you and Holly know if we make any progress with the ms. Don't hold your breath.

TROLL

Some research for you to have a look at...

I think these are worth having a look at, and might help you put yourself in the right place for your scene. I'd say the louder you can bear it, the better obviously. Ignore the 'flapping' American in one of them he's clearly a REMF.

This first clip shows Americans firing mortars. You'll note that the ammo is in protective covered area and is unpacked as they need it. The ammo is new and well made so that it's designed to give limited flame and smoke. Some nice covering fire going on and not a bad clip. You can see from one lad's reactions at the end, where he doesn't cover his ears, that it's very loud which is why you can always hear them further away than you can see them.

This clip is night firing, here you can see that there is a flash. If the enemy fired his mortars from within a couple of Km, then it might be possible to see a flash. However, in my experience, you always hear the thump. It's like a quiet *crump* in the distance and you know you have incoming, followed a few seconds (that last for a while) later.

This one is the attack alarm going off with some incoming mortars. The lightshow you see is an amazing piece of American kit, a radar guided chain gun designed for shooting down missiles attacking a ship, now used in the ground roll to destroy incoming mortars. Towards the end you see a flash where it gets one.

So hopefully you can get an idea of mortars and rockets from that, in my experience you hear mortars launch and land, you hear artillery and rockets coming in.

Incoming RPG, you can only hear the whistle briefly but if the rocket misses by more or is airborne past you (they go approx 950m) then it is very distinctive as it passes.

Afghan footage, RPG launch heard at 5:02 and the rocket explodes nearby at 5:05, the guy who lists the video identifies the airburst, but you can hear and know the launch once you know what you're hearing. Mortars are just the same.

Let me know if I can be of any more help.

20 JANUARY

JHB

Thanks for all of these. That American chain of light was amazing. Come a long way since tracer fire. I had no idea.

I've gone through all the others, too, (had to turn the sound down because I was scaring my dog). I liked the one where the English lads were being told to smile at the camera – yeah, because that would be my first thought with an explosion happening 40 feet away.

Hopefully that scene works now. So I'll send the ms on its way, launch it into the world, so to speak. If anything comes of it, I'll let you and Holly know.

Thanks for all your help. If you're ever in Penzance, I'd love to buy you a drink.

Take care,

. . .

TROLL

You're very welcome. Team Troll visits a friend who lives in Cotehele which isn't a million miles away. We're usually down Sep/Oct time. I'll drop you a line if you'd like to catch up and meet the family.

Best of luck.

31 JANUARY

JHB

I nearly deleted your Linkedin request, only working out at the last minute who you were. Yeah, I know, I'm not the brightest thing on 2 legs.

Hope you and Team Troll are well. Or should I call you Justin now?

TROLL

Yes the Linkedin thing... The dangers of clicking a button thinking 'what's the harm?' The intention was to select a few people who were already on LinkedIn, instead I think it's emailed everyone I have ever conversed with like some sort of damn virus. Oh well, all things for a reason – lots of people now won't lose touch.

Please refer to me as you feel suits. On a good day I'm Justin, when I'm grumpy I'm definitely Troll.

I'm off to see a preview of the BBC production [*Bluestone 42*] in a few days. Please let me know if you get a positive response on your production.

CHAPTER 23

FEBRUARY 2013

5 FEBRUARY

EMAIL SENT TO JHB FROM THE MOD PRESS OFFICE

I have been passed the email which you sent to Holly Davies at the Felix Fund. Our internal processes require Holly to let us know and thus the EOD chain of command passed it up to me in the MOD. As you will appreciate we do get actively involved in many factual documentaries but when it comes to dramas or films we do tend to steer clear. Firstly there are just too many dramas with a military angle to engage with properly and of course the drama writer does not need to take our advice, unlike a documentary maker who is obliged to deal more in facts. If we are seen to have advised the writer on the script then we are invariably considered to have been complicit with the final outcome regardless of whether the writer has accepted our advice or not – artistic licence can understandably get in the way of our preferences for accurate portrayal! Hence we usually steer clear.

PERSONNEL/ WELFARE ISSUES

Alex seemed to be at the extreme end of mental illness.

Alex's persona was not recognisable as a reasonable reflection of an EOD operator including one that was suffering PTSD.

Alex's analogies on diffusing a bomb are more 'fairy tale' than reality.

The storyline does not reflect the considerable work carried out on these human factors and the strong support mechanisms in place.

Every effort is made to retain those injured if feasible

EOD families who have suffered losses will be hurt by the portrayal of Alex

EQUIPMENT

The script casts negativity on our EOD equipment which over recent years has seen the UK EOD operator being provided with cutting edge equipment.

I AM SORRY IF THE BULLETS ABOVE ARE DISAPPOINTING FOR YOU BUT despite that, we would be very grateful if you would let us know if your screenplay is coming onto the screen and a date if possible. It allows us to provide advance notice to those who might need to be advised and also to prepare some lines for us to take, primarily with our internal audience.

JHB THAT'S EVERYTHING HE SAID. WHAT DO YOU THINK? PLEASE BE candid.

TROLL

I am not diplomatic, somewhat bitter about some things, but I will try and be brutally honest. I offer this for you to digest and decide what direction you wish to go. Please do not use any incident which identifies someone personally, but I offer it for you to decide how close your fiction is to the truth and if you wish to add or remove anything.

The MOD (and PRAVDA, I mean the BBC government propaganda department) will not want to show anything about the Army in a bad light. Current government cuts are not popular, the war in Afghan is not popular and they will want recruitment high and public opinion behind them when they start on the next adventure/invasion/small war. I will write my own experiences for you to pick the bones out of.

I was one of 250 Technicians when I joined. A decision was made (by shit officers) to allow technicians to promote above Staff Sergeant without doing bomb disposal. In my mind that made me one of 125, as half the trade were (referred to by a lad who had his team blown up by a suicide bomber in Iraq as) *white feather war dodging bastards*. I will estimate the damage done to me and my friends for you to decide if the MODs position is correct.

I am aware of ATOs from the 1980s through to Afghanistan who have suffered varying degrees of mental illness. I am not aware of any up until Afghan who had been medically discharged. (Maybe two, although not directly as a result of bomb disposal duties.) However, in recent years, I have met a small number (amongst the small number of us) who were stuffing more than previously seen. I am 41, I saw the end of the PIRA campaign, the start of the Dissident IRA campaign and Iraq and Afghanistan. My era had it easier than earlier generations. The IRA were difficult and dangerous. The younger generation don't all see this but the last time the IRA tried to specifically kill an ATO was Oct 2009 (or 10, I'd have to check). For the first 10 years of my career, there was NO mental health care except if you requested it through the Medical centre, but there was huge stigma to this. Then the trade tried Critical Incident Stress Debriefing (CISD). I was told by the Department of Community Mental Health (DCMH) Colchester that CISD was flawed and was binned. My team in NI got CISD'd after a fatal incident. The Warrant Officer (WO) who conducted it did not include me. I asked why not and he said 'records showed I had already seen loads of shit so if I went mad later I could blame the shit I'd already seen so no point debriefing me'. (Accurate as best I can remember.)

Then people decided (post Iraq and post my breakdown caused by my officer not just not looking after me in 2003 but actively bullying me for asking for help) that we were going to suffer mental health issues with Iraq veterans and Afghan on the horizon. I was sent on TRaumatic Incident Management (TRIM) course. The Royal Marines were leading with it, so I attended with them. I wrote a report saying it needed to be implemented immediately and was ignored. (Funny, when a commanding officer told me three years later another WO had recommended it and the regiment would now take it up.)

My last five years in the army, I had two years of horrendous bullying from an officer who made scathing references to my issues post-Iraq (the days returned from a bloody tour of Afghanistan), and I sought a posting immediately even though it damaged my career. From my escape, I spent my last three years propping myself up with the DCMH. Without this self-sought support, I would have been unable to finish my career.

I was not the worst ATO I knew of at this time. I had friends who were all going through the things I had grown used to. Some were not handling as well as I had been lucky enough to.

Are there ATOs who are on a self-destructive spiral? Absolutely. Do they ever get any leeway from command that their incidents are caused partly by their mental health and lack of care? Not that I ever saw.

I know dozens of ATOs who at some point or another resorted to excessive drink because of the job. I recently met a lad who said his discharge from the army for drug use was because of the job. (In my mind, he is a very small minority in the drugs compared to almost everyone else who is just an alcoholic.)

A quote from an officer, "I grew up in a hard drinking mining town and served with the Paras but I've never met a group of people who consistently drink so much."

My high threat course in five weeks took us from about 21 units a week social drinking, to well over that amount per day. My highest test score came the morning of the last week where I was baggage from a night on the drink. Not recognisable? The trade only survives because the mental health care is done in the bar. (This is not a reflection of those saintly types who never needed a drink.)

Yes, absolutely, your bomb disposal stuff was more Hollywood than fact. (I might have mentioned this and told you I did not intend to change it.) However, I am a staunch advocate of not showing anything real on TV. Firstly, if you do the job right, it's boring (exciting shit usually means you've fucked up or been out planned by the enemy). Secondly, Hollywood bomb disposal is what Joe Public wants to see.

The Hurt Locker: I read an interview where she said she was trying to display the mentality of the men who did the job. In that she did okay. The bomb disposal and the operational side was tragically shit. Sneaking down town, pulling wires, fire extinguisher on bombs, sniper rifles, etc all really, really shit. However, I loved it. When my friends ask if the job's like that, I grin and say, "Yes, exactly."

They know I'm lying but don't know which bits.

If you want to understand the real EOD stuff, I'll send you some actual tasks for you to look at. You can't use any of it, but I will let you read it.

I retired at the end of 2011 and there were no support mechanisms in place in 2008. I was bullied.

At some cost and risk to myself, I told the CO of the regiment and he replied, "Well, some people deserve to be bullied."

I can give you an independent witness to this time. I'm not just a whinger. The only support I received was self-sought.

Those retained have physical injuries – big names such as Pete Norton, Ken Bellringer and Col Whitworth (Open source names). The mentally damaged ones (I won't name) but if you look up 'soldier wins 100k in damages for PTSD'. He was one of ours, never looked after and medically discharged. He had to fight for damages, but if you read the article, you'll see how lucky he was to win anything. None of the others will ever have enough purchase to win what they deserve.

EOD FAMILIES WHO HAVE SUFFERED LOSSES WILL BE HURT BY THE portrayal of Alex.

jhb: This really bothers me the most. I wanted to show the problem, not make it worse. If this is true, I'd rather pull the ms now.

TROLL

I don't see this either. I suspect that guilty consciences have more to do with that quote. I'll talk about my thoughts about your work at the end. This comment seems more about imparting their will through making you guilty than about fact related to your work. All EOD families are hurt by loss at any reminder. Your work refers to the death of a team member. This will bring back terrible memories for those. If it is graphic in its portrayal, you will induce horror to those who have not thought about it in such terms. If you cut scene just prior, you induce the memory, but the individual will make it what's inside their head. If you watch *Our War* series, they have helmet cam footage of an IED strike, the bang followed by the enveloping cloud of dust is Afghanistan. Other theatres, you might see it coming down the road to you. See BBC footage of car bombs functioning.

Your work does include the death of a soldier, but the BBC felt it appropriate to show footage of two EOD soldiers who were captured in Iraq and subsequently executed as 'in the public interest', despite the fact that the widow of one of the soldiers begged them not to. I think you are on safer ground.

· · ·

THE SCRIPT CASTS NEGATIVITY ON OUR EOD EQUIPMENT WHICH OVER *recent years has seen the UK EOD operator being provided with cutting edge equipment.*

Jhb: I didn't think I'd shown shoddy equipment. Puzzled by this. Thoughts?

TROLL

Ha ha ha ha ha ha ha ha ha ha. I reference Ken Bellringer who gave a press statement to the effect kit was shit in Afghan and more recently the enforced procurement of a new EOD robot that is shit compared to its predecessor as 'the money for it has already been allocated'. Not a single technician wants the new robot. (I caveat this with the following: the old robot climbed stairs and was designed to fit between a standard door frames. The new one is wider and has rubber tyres instead of tracks. It's shit at getting upstairs, it's shit at getting through doors as it only fits if you ram it, and it's highly complex, impossible to self-fix, and just shit... However, if you are not planning on fighting the IRA in NI but instead planning on pulling roadside bombs out of ditches in yet another desert shit hole, well this might be the robot for you.)

Okay. Example: my friend was a quiet kid on my team in NI, hard-working, intelligent, just a nice guy. Go forwards six years, he's a rapidly promoted WO, he's done desert tours. We meet and he is hyper, has gone out and got some huge tattoos all over his arms and legs and spends our whole conversation talking about how he goes out looking for fights with civvies. He said he even drank water at the bar or sipped a pint so he knew he'd be sober enough to win, and flashed wallets full of cash about to try and tempt a mugging so he could 'smash them up'. I don't think your story is far of the mark, but I do think he was in the minority, just as the guy with the drugs was. But then with a pool of only 125 operators, how many examples do you need?

I said I would talk about your work. I read the first few lines and it made me angry. I felt you portrayed an ATO as being weak and giving into vices to cope. We don't do that. If you want to portray the masses, we die from the inside. Those around us suffer, and we often can't tell them why.

I did persevere. I left the unrealistic EOD [in the play] as I didn't want to portray any real procedure that will put soldiers' lives at risk. I hope you understand I do not dislike your work but was happy to help offer you some guidance. The official answer from MOD is nothing like that. The MOD is entirely self-interested, they are only interested in the political direction for government, keeping recruitment up and covering up all failings.

All of this used to be balanced out by the fact that in a trade of 250 we could get 'down time' Cyprus, Canada, depot tours etc. But because some oxygen thief decided half the trade could avoid EOD and just do ammo jobs, all the cushy downtime posts were filled by guys who could not do EOD, meaning the EOD lads could only stay on duty and do all the bomb disposal tours. I think Oz Schmidt's wife references this fact. Shit kit, reference Ken Bellringer. So fuck the MOD and their bullshit! (Told you I was bitter.)

Ok, rant over. Nearly...

I hope that helps give you perspective. I could fill a book with the tragedies I have seen. However, I don't regret my choices. I am sad my best friend died, but I am proud of him and glad he got to go out fighting.

It took me a long time to realise I don't hate officers. I have a small circle of them as friends but they are some of the best you will ever meet. I hate unprofessional people. A lot of my officers fit that bill.

A friend of mine gave his 22-year leaving speech: "I've learnt one thing in my time ... all officers are c*nts", and he sat down.

I understand why he said it, and it's sad that he never met the few like I did who gave me perspective. MOD is full of 'them'.

Let me know if I can fill in any more blanks for you.

JHB

Hi Troll,

Thank you. You've given me a lot to think about.

This is how I answered the PR guy:

Thank you for your email. I appreciate your candour and that of your colleague. I can only improve the draft ms with quality feedback, so thank you.

To address some specific points from your colleague:

Yes, there is a 'Hollywood' element to the representation of EOD's work: scenes have to be visual, although I did take examples from several helmetcam episodes that are widely available. However, I will rewrite, trying to achieve reasonable authenticity.

I have already been advised that there is every effort made to retain injured staff, and have rewritten accordingly.

I am particularly concerned that your colleague thinks the portrayal will hurt EOD families. Out of everything s/he said, this is my biggest worry. I wrote the ms wanting it to 'do good'. Clearly this was horribly naive. I suspect that any portrayal will upset those who have lived through it, but I wanted to show a survivor in Alex. It is a failing of the writing that this is not the case. I will redraft.

In summary, no, I'm not disappointed with the comments; I'm grateful that so much thought has gone into them, and I thank you both for your interest.

I understand that you do not have the time or resources to get involved with a fictional representation. Realistically, the chances of this being made are slim to none, but I will, of course, let you know should it progress further.

So, that's the diplomatic bit done.

One thing I said to him was from the heart: I do think I've been naive. I can rewrite and improve the draft ms, but if the idea is flawed, that's a bigger problem. I'll be chewing this over for a while.

I didn't want Alex to seem weak, just the opposite, so that definitely needs some work. I see him as a survivor who's just about able to function. I wanted to show his isolation, both deliberate and circumstantial. I would also like to use your comment, if I may, 'we die from the inside'. I think that's a very powerful statement. Let me know.

Yes, could you please send me some of the real tasks for me to look at. I won't replicate, simply use them to inform the ms.

I'll give the ms some more thought and look at the potential rewrites, but if it can't be fixed, I'll just pull it back from my agent.

Thank you for being so open and frank; I really appreciate that. Do you think I should pursue this or should I just put it to one side and chalk it up to (lack of) experience? If this a pretentious, potentially offensive piece of writing, I'd rather bin it. I'm not asking you to make that decision, just asking for one for more piece of bluntness. Please.

6 FEBRUARY

TROLL

A couple of thoughts from both me and my wife.

She said, as far as she's concerned, anything that brings the subjects into public focus is a good thing. Some may find the subject difficult to watch, others (MOD) will hate if you show their failings, but you do no harm to the families by showing the problems caused by their service. You're not hurting the families by promoting the fact they have problems. I think I see what you're trying to portray. I suspect I have a vast amount I could add, but that to do so compromises my position. I'm not against it, but we'd need to formalise our position if you felt the idea was worth pursuing.

JHB

Thank you so much, to you and your wife. I was worried I'd gone completely off track.

Yes, I'd very much like to work with you to make this a better ms. How do you want to do this? I could ask my agent to draw up some sort of non-disclosure agreement along with a formal partnership percentage/rights. Whatever you want. Or if you prefer to have a contract drawn up, that's fine, too.

As you know, my thoughts are that this is a long shot to get made, but if it does ... I'd want to do it right and I'd want it to make a difference.

I don't know where you live and, as you know, I'm in Penzance, but I go up to Surrey every 5 or 6 weeks as I have an elderly mother living in Godalming. I'll be there over Easter. I could easily meet you in London if that's doable for you, or pretty much anywhere around the M25. Otherwise we could use skype – email – phone – whatever you prefer.

TROLL

That's exactly how I see things. I would need to remain un-named primarily to avoid MOD witch hunt (over paranoid? Possibly. Comes with the job and a low opinion of officers) but secondly, as I really don't want my life under a microscope as it doesn't help conditions.

An agreement between us is fine, percentages I will leave to you. A lot of us work on agreements between friends so if we agree a low minimum, I'm happy for you to decide the amount at the end depending on how much work you've got out of me.

I'd then feel safe to tell you examples for you to convert to script. We could see how that pans out. I suspect that your production could increase in size though as the examples cover numerous theatres/postings/etc. However that's something I'd leave entirely in your hands.

· · ·

7 FEBRUARY

TROLL

I am down in London on 12th for a BBC screening. (In fact, they said I could invite guests, if you want to go to it I am not shy about kicking the arse out of their offer, let me know?)

I can also do skype if you wish.

Let me know if you need any more.

10 FEBRUARY

TROLL

I hope the book launch has gone well today. What was the book? If I have google'd (stalked) you correctly, you have produced a library of books for children already. I didn't realise how accomplished you were when Holly put you in touch.

I just thought some background might be appropriate. I kept diaries and notes piecemeal throughout my career and have always had the idea of writing in some shape or form in mind. However, I am often held back by the knowledge that the trade is best represented by those quiet dignified men who did the work and never made much of it.

I wrote poetry when I was younger, possibly as a means of getting some of the emotion out. This continued until 2003 when I wrote my last. Following Iraq, I was injured and asked for help. What I got was bullied, threatened and ultimately punished. I eventually wrote a complaint about my treatment, attempting draw attention to the issues. What returned was a character assassination causing me more damage which had to be processed and overcome. I saved my sanity but it cost me significantly in career terms and the scars I am left with make me over sensitive to some things. I suspect that this will come out in my writing so I'll apologise in advance.

I had a lucky career, luckily for me, a friend steered towards the end. Some become arrogant and self-interested. I was told that I'd had my fun and now was the time to pass on what I knew. My last three years helping young technicians learn they have all the choices about how they want to develop was very beneficial to me (and hopefully them). It was also during this time that I was on referral to the DCMH at Colchester. I am not as affected by my time as some, (I have all my arms and legs attached), but I've asked for help when needed. Now I'm out, that responsibility hangs on the shoulders of my wife. The support of the NHS is just not the same.

It is a combination of all of the above that results. I enjoy writing and getting things onto paper, it is sometimes helpful for me. A biography is unlikely though, as on a bad day, I could not cope with the exposure or slights. Some of the tales under a pseudo name to draw some attention to some of the issues seems a much better way to start.

When you are not snowed under, I hope we can thrash out some ideas. I'm happy to write in advance of any agreement, on trust, currently it is more a case of not wanting to send anything uninvited.

13 FEBRUARY

TROLL

This has all come in a bit of a jumble. I keep trying to write and explain it. It's just not happening at the moment so you're getting it as it came out. I have some more in mind, some of the rubbish treatment that happened, but to be honest with you, that is probably going to sound like one long moan.

You'll hear the phrase 'pick the bones out of it' often. I am also doing my best to tell you about some of the incidents. It makes me uncomfortable because we don't usually talk about it, but it's being offered for use/modification etc, I can't think of a better way to get it over. I'm guessing that it might lead to questions, you might want more of some stuff and less of others etc.

Lastly, I do have some images in mind from the poignant times in my life to offer, including some of my poetry, similar in that I used to write it and bin it, but I got asked to send it home in letters and thus ended up keeping some of them. Same deal here, once I send it, I can't get rid of it. I'll apologise in advance for when I change tense, style and go off on tangents, it happens.

So there you go.

I'll wait to see what you think?

Justin (Occasionally I'll refer to myself as Troll)

JHB

I'd be honoured to help you in any way I can.

A few years back I was able to help, in a minor way, a guy called Pen Farthing, who wrote One Dog at a Time and had recently set up the Nowzad Dogs charity.

He'd written large chunks of his ms, and I was able to give some comments and suggest an agent for him. He's done really well, and it was good to be able to contribute, however minutely. (And it was only a small contribution.)

So, yes, whatever help I can give. I think the idea of writing fiction is an excellent one. We can definitely thrash out some ideas. A series with an ATO as the quiet hero – now there's an idea.

I have a keen interest – from my limited perspective – of writing about war and the consequences of war. That probably sounds ridiculous when I have no direct experience. But I've also written a children's story set at the Battle of Trafalgar, and I wasn't there either. I live by my imagination, that's what I do. But doing the research is also important to me.

And, you're not the only one with an alias. About six months ago I started writing 'adult romance' or what my husband jokingly calls 'smut'. Well, it's probably not a joke – he won't actually read the books, he just knows what other people say about them, which is enough to put him off! My launch was for the second book in a two-book series. The hero of that story is a US Marine who is injured in Afghan, and his girlfriend helps him heal, mentally, emotionally and physically.

It's fiction – it's a romance – it has a happy ending. But I also tried to get as many facts right as possible.

I was helped by an American friend whose husband was in Iraq. I could email you the Word doc. Just if you're interested – you're not really my target market!

I really wish I could be there on Tuesday to meet you and be at the screening. I hope it goes well and that you find it an interesting experience. Please let me know.

Your ideas, emails, thoughts, suggestions are not uninvited. I promise that Lisa, myself and John are the only ones who know about you – and your real name. I have a good imagination but I can only guess what you've been through. I do understand why you should have a confidentiality agreement in writing from me. All I can say, until that's in place, I will still keep everything you tell me confidential. Promise.

If you're back home on Weds, we could talk further if you like.

Thank you for trusting me with this.

. . .

PS Do you have kids? Uf you do and they're between 8 and 11, I'd love to send you some of my little books.

Troll

I thought you captured some good bits of ATO in your ms. As I said, you reminded me of a friend. I stopped myself from telling you about the parts of my life that were similar as I didn't want to influence your product, just offer the bits that corrected military stuff that needed help.

I can't write a book, I write it and throw it away. I can't face it daily, I can't keep remembering it.

I couldn't take the exposure or the predictable character assassination. I am inconsistent, some days I talk about it and it does me some good and others I don't want to remember it. It took me 10 years to show anyone a poem, then I sent them out anonymously, then I showed some friends but then I shut them away again. I constantly change them fiddle with the wording as I read them and my position has changed a bit. If I wrote a book, I would do that exponentially and it would probably drive me mad(der).

A lot of my wounds were made worse by the treatment when I got back. Some things I still can't put into words. I'm happy to send you stuff. I don't know what to do with it, if it helps you create a fictional character with similar events that's fine by me.

Tentatively, if I wrote the stories do you think you could put them together? For me, I think it has to be changed, made into something fictitious based on fact rather than me trying to write it accurately.

Also, I kicked my own arse. I meant to warn you about the content. Sorry.

I have looked on the hard drive and found some other stuff. Just written to get it out of me, do you want to see it?

13 February

JHB

Where do I start?

Well, firstly I feel like a naive fool for thinking I could portray an ex-

ATO in my ms. What you've written is a thousand times more powerful. You paint pictures with your words – that's a real gift.

Trying to be clinical here, when what you've written has me reeling.

With your permission, I can use large chunks of what you've written to flesh out the story and to make it more realistic. I think, together, we could produce something very strong.

As for the character of Alex Hunter, I wanted to show somebody who deliberately goads people, so he seems unlikeable, because that's easier than people knowing that he's struggling. That was the intention. The 'real' person is revealed slowly through the psych's conversation. I can fix that. I have work to do...

But I keep coming back to the other idea of you writing your own fiction. I've thought about that quite a bit since you mentioned it. I liked it as an idea, but now I've seen how you write, I really think it's got great potential.

The story about 'Bob' turned from humour to horror and back again – it makes it powerful but you also have a very easy, readable style.

The question is: do you want to turn your memories into stories for other people to read?

Technically, a book for adults is going to be around 100,000 words. You've written 5k already. Yes, it'll need to be structured and to have all the usual story requirements: a beginning, a middle and an end. But you've got the essence there.

If the answer to my question is 'yes', then I can help you plan out a book. If you want to write just to get the words out, then I'll be happy to just read it and comment, if you like.

Thank you for sharing your words.

JHB

Yes, please send me whatever you have. There don't have to be any specific plans of how, when or if we work on a novel. As Americans say, it can be 'organic', or as we say, 'see what happens'.

Please don't worry about the content you send me. I don't want you to edit yourself before it gets to me – kind of defeats the object. I'm fine.

How old is your man-cub? Would any of my books suit? Sci-fi?

TROLL

Man cub is nearly two, and although your sci fi is a bit ahead of him, he's a smart kid and it won't be long.

Thank you very much, I love reading to him and he loves adventures.

I'm going to add some stuff to the things I have written and send it over. I'll worry about what we're going to do with it later.

JHB

Good morning,

Thank you for your last piece. Beautifully written, upsetting, moving.

I loved the poem. Great economy of words. Reminded me of some of Wilfred Owen's poetry, the less flowery ones. Have you ever read any of his?

I don't know if you'll want to go down the fiction route, but if you do, it could work a bit like this.

See what you think. Fine if you'd rather bin it. My text in yellow.

14 February

Troll

You're clearly a genius. It made me laugh and it gave me shivers. I can see it needs some work to get it right from my side, and I can see I'm going to have to do some serious work to make it less obvious, (or it's not going to be fiction). There is only one story about an ATO in jail in Kabul. I'll let future Troll worry about that side of it.

And I studied the war poets at college; my English instructor would be so proud.

I'll keep sending you the poems as I come to the incidents. Your weaving of introducing the reporter is pretty accurate. I used to use them in Afghan, and one of them was close to me and Gaz. There is humour to be had. I'll get around to it, so don't think it's going to be all doom and gloom.

I really like what you've done. I'm aware of problems getting stuff past MOD, slander etc. I've always argued that it's only slander if it's not true, not if you just can't prove it. I have photos of a lot of it.

Also I have no issue with removing the swearwords; some of them are in because that's what I actually said at the time, others are because while typing it, words fail me.

. . .

JHB

Thank you very much! I'm so glad you liked it, or can at least see the potential of it. I thought there was a lot of humour in it, and swinging from serious to laughter helps it to come alive.

There are probably lots of ways to make it less obvious (Kandahar for Kabul, WHO for UN) but people who know you will suspect. As long as that's all it is, and dressed up a little more as fiction, it should work.

I wouldn't edit out swearwords – it's part of the story. Doesn't bother me in the least.

Really happy. And you've read the war poets, too. Very happy!*

*EDITOR'S NOTE: TROLL ORIGINALLY PLANNED TO WRITE FICTION – A thriller based on his experiences. But the more he wrote, it was clear that sticking to the facts of what he experienced was the way his writing needed to go. Had he lived, I'm sure he would have written some cracking novels.

15 FEBRUARY

TROLL

The poem was written early on, sometime around 1991-93, far more has happened since.

Today's effort is on a lighter note. I am conscious it is too long but prior to a good edit you can have it in its raw form. There is no rush to read it.

Also I can't remember if I thanked you for your stories. Thank you, I look forwards to reading them to my boy.

JHB

There is redemption in this poem. I think that surprised me, but I'm very glad to read it.

This has very powerful imagery and really shows how a mind can be damaged. When you use the word 'weight', that really works well and you can feel the heaviness of his soul - or the memories that have been loaded onto it – and of his dreams. The last two lines are beautiful.

I've saved it. Thank you for sharing.

16 FEBRUARY

TROLL

Lots of good comments, I'll work on them and get back to you. There are times where I have avoided talking about things, sometimes because it seems to me it is dragging a point out, and others for other reasons. You seem to have spotted them all. I will fill in the details of those I can and let you decide what's worth using.

Has made me smile though.

You have raised the subject of my background. I have a bit of an issue with this, but a large part of that has to do with an article I read about military biographies where, 'I had a rough childhood' seems to be standard. I didn't have the worst childhood, and I don't want to seem like I am whingeing.

I have done some on it tonight, but it has been done with a plan in mind for some bits of it. There were some issues in my career which relate to my father, so I thought I'd start on it. While I remember, I also learnt to make IEDs and homemade explosives when I got my first shotgun.

17 FEBRUARY

TROLL

My time on the farm was brief but was my happiest time as a child. I never considered I was running away joining the army as all I can remember is wanting to join up.

Like your husband, I got my first shotgun at 12 and made my first homemade bomb at 12 and a bit.

I have written about the choice to be an ATO, but I will (as I write) probably cover some of the nuances that made me, me. I'm also very conscious that, at the moment, a lot of the writing is all about me, makes me cringe. I will cover some stuff about the real heroes in the trade and the people I am truly grateful to have met, know and have fought beside.

It's nice to know you shoot. I am hoping I can sort my fire arms certificate but at the moment it is low on my priority as I have a lot of other stuff to sort out. I will be heartbroken if after all the responsibility I had in the army the police refuse me a couple of rifles to go hunting with. Well done for out-shooting John, didn't happen to me much while I was in.

Your comments are perfect. Firstly, if you are viewing my work as a layman and have to ask questions, then I have not explained myself well enough. Secondly, a lot of what I write I often don't want to read again. Your notes mean I have to and it's probably good for me to have to re-read stuff. It's also very generous of you to do it and then say 'in case I ever want to publish'. The more I write the harder it is to back out. I appreciate the flicking between 'I' and 'we', it's partly to do with how I deal with things. A lot easier to think about the tough stuff when 'we' faced it as a team. I'm sorry, must be annoying for you, but don't think there is anything I write that you can't change, tell me to re-write or cut out because it's boring.

I've attached the notes and the recruitment stuff. While I remember, where you were looking for a nickname. Although Yogi did once christen me 'The Monk' but as 'Mad Monk' is squaddie for spunk, I don't like that much either.

I am also not sure I like my title. I think I just did it for ideas so don't think it's my lead.

I'll just keep plugging on. My business partner gave me the squadron war diary from Iraq so I'll have that to catch up on. He said he's all for writing too, so you might have trade.

My weekend was fine, my boy is great and most importantly my wife is happy (took her shopping). I hope you had a good weekend.

18 FEBRUARY

TROLL

This wasn't easy to write, it probably doesn't make interesting reading. But it's true.

I wanted to write it because the MOD told you they look after their soldiers.

Sorry if it all comes across as a whinge.

JHB

This is really shaping up well. You've got nearly 10k of good copy. That's 10% of a whole book, if you want it to be.

A few more comments and I've included some of your early stuff. See what you think.

21 FEBRUARY

TROLL

This is a work in progress, it is all coming out in a jumble as I jump from theatre to theatre. I think maybe I could do with some advice, but I'll wait until you've read this. If the whole tour pans out in this fashion, it's going to get quite long. I've stuck some pictures in just because. They don't have to be used.

JHB

I'll read this tonight and get back to you.

Have you had to work with any WW2 ordnance? When I lived in London, the DLR was often suspended because with all the building working in Docklands, uxbs were found fairly frequently. And I was thinking about the SS Montgomery in the Thames Estuary. Is that something that got talked about ever?

Might be an interesting contrast to make with overseas work. We had a controlled explosion here on the beach a couple of years back.

Just a thought.

Hope all is well with you and the team!

JHB

I was just thinking... it might be an idea to mention what you did during down time. I know you wrote poetry, but what else? What did other people do? Especially somewhere like Helmand which seemed pretty lacking in amenities. Also, that way, you could weave in excerpts of your poems if you wanted to.

TROLL

Up at 6-7, I worked to midnight had an hour in the gym then used the computers to send email then went to bed. I had a Sunday off once; it was two weeks before I came home.

I was a boring work obsessed nerd!

22 FEBRUARY

TROLL

I will explain about the downtime, Northern Ireland where the Dets were all set up we would happily while away the hours with books, TV, and computer games. Afghan (for me) the mission was such that if we weren't busy with work we were busy building stuff to make the guys who replaced us more comfortable. I did get the guys a TV, which I am writing about now.

JHB

Oh, okay. I'll cross out the paragraph that I put in about you starting a glee club. Pity.

25 FEBRUARY

TROLL

I've not managed any writing this weekend. Something else has dragged up my past, and I'm having to go through the character assassination that was my return from Iraq. It's making me nauseous going through their paperwork which cost me so much.

Ho hum, it'll pass, always does.

26 FEBRUARY

TROLL

Did my interview for Channel 4 News today, but sounds like I've been bumped off the running by more exciting news. No matter, was good for me to do it anyway.

I hope all is well with yourself.

27 FEBRUARY

TROLL

I was an anon source hidden in shadow because even now the MOD would make my life difficult.

The print one did get published; the film bit got side-lined by the balloon crash in Egypt. They say they may still run it, in my experience the news world on moves fast, so don't hold your breath.

Is that the definition of irony?

28 FEBRUARY

TROLL

I like that poem, and that it's from Vietnam that's pretty cool. I'm midway through a bit for you. It has holes in it as my mind becomes more staccato by the day. However a pause is always good.

TROLL

I am uncomfortable with all the me, me, me-angle to the writing, but I understand it's my memories, so it's going to start out like that. Also I am conscious that my tale is a little pedestrian. (To me anyway). So...

It jumps about a bit but I'll sort that and fill in some of the explanation about why we decided to do this. This is missing some details as we discussed but it's a start.

Let me know what you think. Also did you get my poem about Chris?

I have to stop now and go pick up the man-cub.

CHAPTER 24

MARCH 2013

4 MARCH

TROLL

All is well here, my boy is doing just fine, thanks. I am gearing up for some paying work. We are off overseas for a few weeks so my writing may slow down somewhat as I really have to concentrate for this stuff. I'll be back by the end of April though.

As for the palace, I do have pictures of the event, but no idea where, so you'll have to wait until they turn up.

As my intention is to highlight the nature of the work and the excellence of the team around me, I don't see any point in including them as part of the book. Far more interesting would be if you could get hold of the 'write-ups' – the actual documents that were submitted when people tried to nominate me for a medal.

I am told by a friend that she has seen a few of them, but she isn't very forthcoming in delivering them to me. Maybe one day I'll set you onto her.

Feel free to utilise any of my sayings.

15 MARCH

· · ·

Troll

Go have a look at the picture here [broken EOD wheelbarrow robot].

You'll observe a dead white whale. The white part at the side is where it's snapped a bit of itself off. The green robot is what we've paid millions to replace.

Feel free to send that twat at the MOD a question about the 'properly funded and perfect kit brigade' that he was waffling about.

JHB

Yes, I could do that. "I just happened to notice that this robot appears to be broken. Does that happen often?"

When are you off?

Troll

USA 23rd March. Libya 1st May :)

CHAPTER 25
APRIL 2013

22 APRIL

TROLL

Am back from States now and trying to gear up for Libya. I'm going to hate being away from my boy ... and my pregnant wife too, of course.

I attach some more NI stuff. I don't know if I sent you this part way through, but tonight I got to an appropriate point to stop. There is tons more to write about all the tours, but I guess the point is to get it all written first.

Please feel free to just read and return some notes, don't feel like you have to integrate it into the story as I have seen your skills and know you can. I just think with the shotgun way I am writing, I'll just create you more work than necessary and you might like to just jot your ideas down until I settle a bit more.

28 APRIL

TROLL

I don't know if this will read as well as other stuff, but in the interests of talking about more than just work...

Let me know what you think please.

Also have you watched any of *Bluestone 42?*

TROLL

I've only ever been to one concert. Helen took me (out of morbid curiosity, I think), but the artist was very good and as I felt she'd saved my life it was nice to see her in person.*

I liked Bluestone42, it had its good points and bad points but on balance more good than bad. More importantly, they're going to use us for the next creation. We've already been offering them truth about the increased likelihood of becoming transgender or transvestite in the trade, and how many get sacked for various reasons. I'm liking where they're thinking of taking it.

As for Libya, if I can access the Internet, I am all for communication. I fully intend to take my laptop and carry on writing in the time I'm not working. I've no issue about sending stuff, I'll just try and avoid anything controversial until I get back.

All is manic here, Libya will be a rest.

* EDITOR'S NOTE: THE BAND IS EVANESCENCE, AND THE SONG TROLL *refers to is entitled, 'Bring Me Back To Life'.*

30 APRIL

TROLL

That is very nice of you, and James loves books, so I am very grateful for the offer.

I hope all is going well for you. I passed the medical yesterday so should be going any day.

Take care

CHAPTER 26

MAY 2013

5 MAY

TROLL

The books arrived thank you very, very much. Funny, they arrived same day James got into trouble with Mummy as he'd torn a page out of her baby magazine. What can I send you in trade? It is not the done thing to get freebies in our lot.

25 MAY

TROLL

Obviously, I am behaving myself. I've only broken the company regulations on having guns, moving dangerous explosive articles and porn on the company computers so far. I have been writing, the NI stuff is now 11 thousand words and not yet to the good/bad stuff. Since your mail, I felt like a break and was inspired to write about a night out. It's a bit modified for the obvious reasons as you'll see. I haven't written it to go in the book, you were just interested in what a night out looked like.

We had to evacuate the compound the other night and come back to Tripoli because of a specific threat against us, so we're moving location and going to work somewhere else. It may mean I have time in Tripoli getting paid to write my book. I'll not complain.

As for *Later, After*, I am happy if my writing has given you any ideas and would be more than happy to help in any way that I can.

Home is okay. Helen is struggling, but the man-cub is fine and getting all his teeth, being snotty as a result and growing up while I am away, unfortunately.

Stay in touch,

JHB

I'm sorry to hear you're missing the two-legged beastie. Perhaps you could write him a story – something about the desert, perhaps? Just a thought. As for the snottiness, he's a male of the species. Didn't you read the handbook? Note: check small print at the back.

I'm sure Helen will tough it out. Not that I know her, but she married you, after all. As long as she recognises you when she gets back, that's a good start.

Thanks for saying you'll help with *Later, After*. I really want to get back to that and make it fly. It's inching its way to the top of the list now I've finished that literacy work for teachers. Well, we can argue who has the harder self-employed job. I think the fact you got evacuated means you're edging ahead. But I don't have an excuse not to be in Godalming, so I think it's neck and neck.

Keep your head down, keep safe, and if you can't keep out of trouble – don't get caught.

TROLL

I think the rules problem comes because I have a moral code. It comes first, and as such, I'll do what I think is the right thing no matter what rules or laws it breaks. I have a very strong sense of justice which tends to be at odds with a lot of people like MPs, lawyers, officers and so on. So no, I don't have a list of rules to go out and break – it just happens. When someone tells you that there might be some people coming for you, why would you not want a gun, and so on?

I have not written anything about the place yet, but at your prompt I've started a diary which I'll use for reference afterwards. I've looked up 'sociopath', have made my own notes on the subject and now await your offerings to return it. As for the porn, it's not a common thing, but we males are visual in nature. I can take it or leave it, but the start of a tour is the worst.

The writing, my intention is to finish NI, it's a good way to explain some of my later decisions and it needs to come out in order or it's going to cause me problems. Your idea to write James a story is a brilliant idea.

If things carry on the way they are here, I may have plenty of time on my hands for the next couple of weeks.

Take care

27 May

JHB

I just saw this in the paper today and thought it would make you laugh ... or something...

"I did some tests at Essex University with a guy who studies psychopaths. He found if I was two points higher on the scale I could go to court and plead criminal insanity if I murdered someone and go to Broadmoor." Andy McNabb

The article was in the Times2 for 27 May if you want to read the whole article. He says *Bravo Two Zero* is required reading at Quantico. LOL. Anyway, I liberated the cutting from a National Trust teashop and will save it in case you want it and can't find it online.

Take care, stay safe.

28 May

Troll

I'd be interested on the date from the article. I like Steve Mitchell although after reading Bravo Two Zero and some other accounts, I've not read much of his fictional work. My friend knows his ghost writer and while his stories are interesting, they now delve into James Bond territory designed to attract the younger generation, rather than useful facts that someone more serious might use. Much of his work has been discredited by others which may be sour grapes, but I'm surprised at his comment, because Quantico have enough of their own 'stars' from history. Maybe the fame has gone to his head.

I had a look at sociopaths, these are my findings:

10 signs for spotting a sociopath

#1) SOCIOPATHS ARE CHARMING.

Hmm, I'm not charismatic, I'm gruff and horrible and people sometimes don't want to approach me, but the people who sought guidance or direction did it in the work arena because I obsessively studied work so I don't think that's the same. I'm not sexy, am told I look manly though, hairy, smelly that kind of thing. No comment about sexual appetite and no weird fetishes that I know of.

#2) Sociopaths are more spontaneous and intense than other people.

I am sometimes spontaneous, other times boring for months on end. I am told I am a good and loyal friend, so I think I follow some social contracts. I don't take risks but control my fear when doing risky stuff at work. I am intense.

#3) Sociopaths are incapable of feeling shame, guilt or remorse.

I am hugely ashamed of every failing I have ever made. Unfortunately, my brain catalogues everything in order so it's unlikely I will ever be allowed to forget any of them. Fortunately, the feelings of shame do fade with time. I feel guilt and remorse, but no emotion could stop me from taking an action I felt necessary. What I do have is the ability to turn my emotions off to enable me to do some of my work – that comes with a penalty that all things must be accounted for at some point.

#4) Sociopaths invent outrageous lies about their experiences.

I don't wildly exaggerate. I will employ poetic licence if I think something is lost in the retelling. I usually have photos or witnesses to it all anyway. Their recounts are usually far worse than mine as I tend to downplay it more than them.

#5) Sociopaths seek to dominate others and win at all costs.

I have a strong will to win. I hate losing and if it's a fight, I really hate losing. However when I was a child, I was taught there is also value in losing, how it is not fun to win all the time and sometimes being a gracious loser is a sign of strength.

It is not common that I lie, but it has happened – no one is perfect. I have a couple of lies that I have used over the years, but I suspect these were to do with PTSD rather than anything else. Stories made up to explain how I was feeling, and done for a reason.

#6) Sociopaths tend to be highly intelligent, their high IQs often makes them dangerous.

I'm bright, I teach lots. I know I'm dangerous.

#7) Sociopaths are incapable of love and are entirely self-serving.

I feel love. My emotions may have been damaged, they have been hugely suppressed for years but I do feel.

#8) Sociopaths speak poetically. They are master wordsmiths.

I used to write poetry, I have not since 2003. I do not consider myself an expert storyteller.

#9) Sociopaths never apologise.

I apologise.

#10) Sociopaths are delusional and literally believe that what they say becomes truth merely because they say it!

There is a bit of this in me. See the lies made to explain a feeling, possibly I maintain the lie because I don't want to open the box and accept the alternative.

It certainly harms no one, but it does get so practised it seems the truth. Someone really good might get me to admit the truth, but it's never fully happened.

I don't think I fit the mould, merely have some traits in common. The line I usually follow is that when people say they could not kill. I propose the situation where someone is attempting to hurt their children and they usually say they would kill to protect. I don't see the difference – we all have it in us to kill.

Spent the day yesterday (not under arrest) but detained by the Libyan Security. I'd rather be watching *BGT* even though it's like brain death to me.

JHB

I'm deeply relieved that you failed the sociopath test. I was only teasing – hope it didn't offend you. btw, you are a good storyteller, so you do fit that part of the profile.

I'm glad your incarceration was temporary. *BGT* is on all week. You do the maths. A friend whose husband was with US intelligence in Iraq said they played *Dora the Explorer* non-stop to prisoners. I don't think she was joking when she told me that – maybe he was. But it sounds credible.

Take care.

No more run-ins with Libyan Security, please.

TROLL

I had an idea for James and was not going to send it until I had run the idea by you. My idea was to have a picture of James with his favourite monkey-teddy with James telling the teddy that 'daddy went on a plane' (one of his sayings). The monkey decides he wants to know where daddy is, but knowing monkeys are less common in the teddy world, he asks teddy bears to help. I then have various teddies on all sorts of transport looking, cars, trains, boats etc, Then they decide to look from on high so they can see further – balloons, planes, and a rocket so they can see the earth. Finally, they can see Libya and get a message sent (teddy on a camel, maybe), so message arrives, and Daddy knows James is missing him and promises to come home soon. Finish with a picture of daddy hugging mummy and James. James loves rockets, trains, and cars, and likes all the transport things – that was my thinking. I went for an idea that would allow me to google various types of teddies do the artwork.

What do you think?

JHB

I love it! It could be the secret teddy bear network, each passing on the 'super special secret message'! You could even do it in rhyme...

Daddy went on a plane
A boat, and a train.
But bears have a way of knowing.
We know where he went and the message he sent
We know where he's been, where he's going.

29 MAY
Troll

None of them rip the piss out of me, Jane. No one wants to start a war they know they'll lose.

And now I have my teeth into it, setting me a five line rhyme as a challenge, were we? I'm so much better with four, it makes much more sense to my simple OCD brain...

I can't change now, firstly I'm halfway through and secondly to change for any reason would be 'to break' or admit weakness and we're not allowed to do either.

Historically, I had a box of doughnuts delivered to my captain while he was in the field in Afghanistan via a Herc flight and a helicopter. Fresh mind, baked that morning.

My way of letting him know no one is beyond my saving or my reach ;)

29 MAY

JHB

Oh crap. You're only 3,000 miles away. Now I'm quite scared...

By the way, I saw a friend of mine today. She does some acting on the side, but her friend is a semi-pro. They're interested in me turning *Later, After* into a two-head, one act play, to take it around to festivals. If they did, we could get some leaflets from the Felix Fund for them to hand out ... I'm quite keen on the idea, but what do you think?

TROLL

Yes, I think when you said you wanted to raise profile of ex-military and their issues. It's a good idea.

No one is going to complain about advertising the Felix Fund, and I'm sure Holly would sort you out.

TROLL

I attach the story, it's only halfway done and I have switched style in some of it. I've also shrunk the pictures so it's easy to send. I think I've sent it for some advice, some bits read well and I like them, others I am not happy with and will change. I'm not sure that I am getting the 5 line bit at all?

Anyway, I took out the bit where the teddy bear was killed and now he's lying on the sand because he's helping daddy. You'll see it.

Please have a look. My plan is to mount the words nicely, tart the pictures up on the pages and send it home in a format that Helen can print off. I might get really excited about it all and do it in A5 form so she can make a booklet out of it but that's trivia.

You'll forgive me for sending it half done, but I'd like to see if I can get it to my liking before Sunday and we go back out into bandit country out here. I'd like it to make it home to my boy before I go.

31 May

TROLL

Thank you for your help, your advice, your changes. I don't have photoshop on my new PC so the pictures are not to my standard. I also have the original picture of the family hug on the way too, so I'm sure I'll change it over and over. But in the interests of getting something home to my boy, I have put it all together. It might be a little too busy to be perfect but I think James will like it. I've sent Helen two copies: one in story order, and one she can print if she likes.

Thanks again for suggesting it and your help.

TROLL

You really must take credit for the inspiration. It is not something I would ever have done for myself. There are many things included that James loves: he loves rockets, cars, planes and his monkey. There is a Mummy story about why monkeys are so prevalent, I don't know if I told you.

As for if I could do anymore? At this moment I don't think I am a contender, one decent story for my boy will do I guess. By the time Helen gets home and is ready to print this out for James, I will probably have found all the little mistakes that need correcting, so the idea of doing this multiple times... I'll go back to trying to push on with my career writing, I don't think I could take the pressure of actually having to produce something to order. I'm much happier when it just comes to me. Helen has seen the draft and it made her cry. It does make me wonder if she'll be able to get through it when she is reading it to James.

To give you an idea of how tragic this place is, while we have not been able to work back at Misdah because of the threat against ourselves, the locals have had two more fatalities in the place we were working, one in the minefield and one in the debris field. I know that one of these was a child.

Back to work Sunday, risks or no.

CHAPTER 27
JUNE 2013

5 JUNE

TROLL

The book went down very well. Helen was away for her brother's birthday when it arrived so she saw it on her phone. How she could read it is beyond me, but she said she loved it. She has told one of her friends I've written it, and her friend welled up too, so I've managed to make them cry.

While in my younger days I used to like travelling by train, these days I approach it as more an expedition into *Star Wars* bar territory. There is never any shortage of mutants and bandit-looking types on the trains, and I spend my time people watching while attempting a zen like trance to get me through the journey. The late trains and the frustration evident on the faces of those around me. I consider hugging my rucksack while reciting the Koran to see if the carriage empties? Really, I just watch people, their baggage and behaviour looking for threats same as I do every day.

So work is going slowly. We finished off in Mizdah and have started setting up the next place in Waddan. The clearance in Misdah saw me tasked with getting rid of the energetic recoveries, mostly rocket motors, artillery propellant and some TNT. We had no serviceable explosives so it all had to be improvised. I'm content with my safety even though the pit burnt to detonation and exploded rather than just burned as preferred. It is always a possibility. The guy in charge has changed his plan and has asked me to take over a project for him ... I'm only over here as a tech advisor but am not going to turn down the promotion. It will keep me in Libya, commuting to the site an hour away, so I'll have a little more freedom. I've taken to walking to the locations around our base now as I prefer the freedom over going everywhere by car. It comes with its own risks as they drive like lunatics over here. It is not uncommon to see them driving towards you on your side of a dual carriageway, and the saying when you see it is "Libya free" which just means there is no law out here.

There have been a lot of local arrests of terrorist group's bomb-making targeting the government infrastructure that does not appear to have made the news. We have seen an inject of government agencies over here like CTU staff from UK, so something is going on, but I've no sight of it.

I've tried to make progress on the NI story but at the moment things are conspiring to drag my memories towards the desert countries, and my memories are firmly about work in Iraq and Afghanistan. I've had some flashbacks and some emotional pulls to go back to my old work while out here. I miss being involved in operational work. Maybe when I get around to writing about it all, the reasons will show through.

I'm four weeks in, got another 10 to go, it's always slow going in. The last 3-4 weeks will zip by. I'll have another go at the NI stuff tonight. I amend my work when you comment but if there are any other questions you have, don't feel like you can't ask. I am not precious about it, I'll just say if I'm not ready to talk about something.

I think that's all the news. Oh, I took a video of the burn if you're interested?

TROLL

I've had to edit the video to make it small enough to send. The bit cut out shows me try to do the burn once and walk away (you don't run while doing demolitions). However, as we don't have professional kit to do the work with and because it needed a second attempt, I stand to make sure it works then peg it. You'll see, just don't think me unprofessional for running.

It worked as expected second time.

6 JUNE

. . .

TROLL

Walking from demolitions:

You plan the demolition so you don't have to run, if you use burning fuze, you walk from the pit to your safety point, time it, then double it for the fuze so you have twice as long to get there.

You walk so that you do not trip over and end up stuck/broken too close to the demolition.

If you have to run, you're probably not doing it correctly.

You look cool :)

We don't have professional kit because it is the commercial world who try to save money and it's Libya, they won't let you import anything like that so you have to buy it from them but then won't sell it. A very Arab mentality and I've seen it before.

I understand special effects, but it's chalk and cheese. There is no market for realistic looking effects, people want to see Hollywood, they want to see a big fiery explosion, not the dirty black puff 50 metres away that kills the lad standing next to you with an invisible bit of fragmentation travelling too fast to see. My business partner spent a lot of his time on the set of a military production battling to tone down the effects with the special effects guy.

I'm not Northern. I was born in Norfolk, went to boarding school and got rid of any accent. I then joined the military and we all take on a universal lilt. Can I imagine living anywhere else? Yes absolutely. Where I grew up, we rented a house on a 600 acre private estate where you saw no one all day and our nearest neighbour was half a mile away. I doubt I will ever be able to afford to go back there but I'm looking to move somewhere more rural (and maybe more southern as the weather is shit up north) but currently we are tied due to her work.

TROLL

It's not a rest day out here, we work to a Muslim week which means their day of rest is Friday. The US has pulled funding for the project (and the rug out from under the feet of my employers who have also not been paid by the US state department since December), because all the efforts have been towards starting a new project. The outlay has probably cost around 25k which is now all wasted. The new plan is for us to do some local assistance towards explosive safety but even that is not really enough work to be throwing 5 technical advisors onto. Saturday is classed as an admin day for us which is a bit of a no-man's land. Personally, with the limited work out here, I'd be inclined to garner some good will from the troops, admit that forces have conspired to leave us no work and give the guys a paid day off, but then I'm not the boss so we all sit in on Sunday twiddling our thumbs. Well, we did until I got bored yesterday and got my friend from the UN over at 10:30 and bailed out for the day.

When you're in a position like this on tour there is always something to be done. You square away your personal admin, your weapons are clean, get all your washing done, go to the gym. Then you'll look at the bigger picture and look to make your living accommodation more comfortable, same detail on your working area. Then you'll start thinking about what you can go relocate from those who don't deserve it (usually the FCO and government types who think they are important), and then organise some social life amongst the Units you work with. Out here it's all pointless and there is no gym. To try and keep us all busy, the boss keeps giving me powerpoint presentations to produce which might have some long term use but are probably pointless. It's not the ammunition safety work amongst all the destroyed ammunition depots that I came out here for.

The result is it is as bad for me if not worse than prison. A few years ago, I was so bad that I struggled on long journeys on my own. My head would ruminate over things and torture me, solved only by loud music and some 'advanced driving', probably some shouting/singing too. I'm a lot better these days, but I'm still no fan of long protracted periods of sensory deprivation, and the music has been getting a hammering while I've been stuck in my room doing boring computer work for the project. The nasty thing about the condition is that you fix one aspect of it (I used to have vivid flashes of crashing into oncoming trucks while driving) and it pops up again in another form. The flashes of trucks stopped (with a bit of help) and morphed into something far more horrible. The worst images of my past were brought back to me and overlaid into my new life. The violence of my past still comes back to haunt the peace of my family life and sometimes I think it tests my limits. I endure it and do not often talk about it, but after a period of time you need a night on the piss to go and get rid of it for a while.

If the next two months are as boring I imagine, I will look forwards to coming home and having a night on the drink. So in comparison to your good deed, day out at the beach, successful book launch and reviews, my time is somewhat less entertaining or rewarding (I am not complaining, only making the observation). I am making slow and steady progress through the slower part of my first NI tour but I know what is coming so I'm happy it's got purpose. I am happy to be writing, and sometimes the stuff that comes out makes me wonder what you think of a soldier's lot.

I've been thinking about the book for James. I have been speaking to the wife of one of my friends about her changing the pictures I sourced into illustrations so the whole book would be free from copyright. I've been thinking about how to make it less personal and perhaps try and appeal to those military families that have partners on tour with a view to it maybe being used to raise funds for a military charity? If I was to go that far. The alternate idea of not making it impersonal but sending out there as a story to be told to children about 'another family' who have someone away to help them understand where daddy is? I'm conscious that you said the children's book area was hugely competitive but as I'm not trying to break into the market, merely put the story out there I wondered what you thought? Especially before I committed my friend to start her artwork.

Let me know if there is anything else I can talk about that is entertaining for you. I'd hate to think you were bored by any of it and it's good to keep the monkeys active.

Troll

Tried a different tack on this, I'm not sure if I like it. I'm sure you'll let me know.

I've also dug out a poem about a soldier killed in 1991. I met his brother years later. We were both out there when his brother died. I think he was even cordon on a task I was on, the day they whisked him out of NI. He's since written a book about his brother and I have given him the name of the man who invented the bomb that killed him.

The doc told she believed I saw all the army as my family. She might have been right. I did and still do take every death very personally.

16 June

Troll

Many thanks for the Father's Day regards. It's fairly rubbish being away from my boy, and I think it's just starting to make an effect at home. Usually (the American trips), I'd be back by now; so he's now disengaging with

Mummy every time she talks about me. I'm hoping he gets over it quickly when I get back.

When we are trying to avoid noise, I have in the past put my waterproofs down the inside of my combat trousers. They don't rustle then, but I find it too hot, so just don't bother and get wet. If I had to lay for an ambush that might be the only time I'd think about it again. Skin is waterproof.

We do some really good 'capes' called ponchos that go over your head and keep all but your lower legs dry, maybe something like that would suit you?

How do you scotchguard a dog?

I'm sure you're finding writing your stories easier than I am mine. Not least that I could do with a decent English lesson on grammar and to unf*ck my spelling. I was schooled by my grandfather when I was tiny, he said I was reading newspapers and playing chess by the time I was four. I then went to school and back in the 70s they had some random new idea for reading. Only work I can remember was school was spelt 'scwl' so they made a mess and never fixed it, that's my excuse anyway.

Film wise, us lot watch anything, we watch the good stuff first, then when we've watched all them, we'll watch any other junk and then we'll re-watch the good stuff and talk along to it. I like watching films based on books I've read and to be honest my mainstay on my hard drive is David Attenborough, though I like a lot of the old black and white war time movies. It would be hard to pick a genre that I favour. I'm not against chick-flicks, I find horror pretty lame and boring. If you want to scare me show me a documentary on MPs corruption or tax law. I've enjoyed the Bourne films, they have a fun overlap into the whole James Bond/real life interface.

Live, I prefer opera over the ballet though I am not averse to either, I took H to see *Die Fledermaus* while we were in Budapest and she loved it too. I'm not much of a fan of 'camp' comedy. That lad with the specs who looks like the *Bo' Selecta!* bear does nothing for me. I'm a fan of equality though, 1.5% of the population should get 1.5% of the air time. It's going to be a fun trip when I have to meet up with all the 'lovies' when they film the second series of *Bluestone 42*.

Otherwise, the childishness continues, the funding that was cut by the state department which meant the project out here would end in August is back on. My business partner who is out here working for the UN grassed up the DA at an ambassadors meeting which seems to have put the cat amongst the pigeons back in the States, so we're funded until March next year.

The boss out here has complained about internet usage. It's not for me to suggest that shutting 10 blokes into a house, complaining that they are not working and expecting them to sit in their rooms during working hours might lead to increased internet usage... instead of admitting there is no work, sending lads to the beach to get them out of the house and treating everyone like a grown up might have been more productive in the long run. Either way I now log on, do email then log off at most once a day. I've stopped doing ammunition research for them, stopped doing the mapping and generally just dumbed down my work to moving the boxes they tell me to move. Tedious it is.

What else is worth knowing? One of our long term plans that I thought had gone the way of the dodo has exploded back into life. I start my MRes this September, and start teaching at the University next September... no pressure. But I now have to populate the MSTs for the lessons as soon as possible so that I can get them agreed and start putting the lessons together, plan the evening work and set out the criteria for marking their work. I guess I am going to get busy.

I'm making progress through NI, I have two moves left to cover. As ever, I have no idea if I am writing too much or not describing enough but I figure I can always cut bits out or go back and add colour if required. I'm sure this will not be the last time I re-write bits of it. Little to write about out here although some of our staff failed to show this week as they have been fighting their neighbours in their town over the weekend.

Hang the data usage, I'll send you the whole NI thing once it's done.

TROLL

I start my MRes in September as it's been on the cards, but the good news is the tuition fees are being paid for me. Although I'd be happier finishing the course then starting instructing, the University (Wolverhampton) needs to progress the plan we have, so as I technically qualify under their rules. Funny thing is, we've done the timetable, the MST is the detail to the plan that I have to fill in and we've realised that I will probably not be allowed to teach one of the lessons. One of those pesky security signatures you made while in, means that even if all I was doing is reading straight from Wikipedia I'd be in breach... Well, discussed it with my business partner and we think it'll be a university problem first. We might just have to get someone else to do that lesson.

I'll get first tour in NI cracked and send it over ASAP.

17 JUNE

TROLL

Hi Jane,

I was not going to send this until I got to the end of NI, I can kind of see where this is going and as I look at later tours and the risks increased I guess I can see some pattern to it. Not that it makes any difference does it?

Anyway, as I say I was going to wait but here it is anyway.

18 JUNE

TROLL

Hi Jane,

I'll reply to your mail another time, sorry.

I have written more on NI sorry, I have got to the last job and I will try to write it, but figured I would send it again as it is all part of the whole.

Damn thing is making my hands shake and I'm sweating.

19 JUNE

JHB

Stop any time, Justin. You're under no obligation. Write if you want to, if it's useful. If it makes it worse, just stop. Better still, write something completely different, a story for James, an email, a letter, anything. I have never found it possible to think about two separate things whilst writing.

Take care. Be safe.

TROLL

Hi Jane,

I did stop. I sent you 'man in frock'.*

My scars from my NI tour are old, I relieve stuff on a daily basis regardless of if I am writing about it or not so I've no issue about writing it down, what has surprised me is the emotion it brought back. Shouldn't have really should it.

I think when I have this into a story, I'll test it out on my sister or father?

Anyway, work out here is providing me ample opportunity to continue. I suspect I may go over some stories more than once if I write about a whole tour again.

* EDITOR'S NOTE: STORY REDACTED

22 JUNE

TROLL

I'm pleased I have finished my first NI tour. It got a bit difficult to try and make it entertaining at times but then it's also representative of the boredom of tour, too. I don't know really; it was just written as it happened, the petty fights, the booby trapping people for various reasons and the misery of the work. I've no doubt it will need polishing more than once before I am happy. I was quite young by soldier terms on that tour, 29/30, maybe I just felt young. As I have said many times when recounting my SATs opening shots, why would I want any confidence in my abilities taking over the most difficult job in the world?

As I have written, I've seen a link to my later behaviour and I wonder if this will come across. The second job on the railway broke me completely and a lot of the dangerous decisions came from the fact I was already dead in my own mind. I can't read what I have written without my eyes welling up even now.

You have made me laugh with my own writing when you have returned it, in the first times by the clever way you twisted and reformatted it, and later just by your comments in the margin. It is no wonder people run screaming from us at times.

It's close to Remembrance Day. I might see about coming this year but

H will have a new baby then. I also blow hot and cold on the day as it's tough emotionally sometimes.

Work's been shite, the personality clash is getting worse and more childish, and between me and another director from my company, the inside view is making us question the validity of supplying them any further workforce. I'd suggest some management tips, but I suspect that some people may be too set in their ways to change.

My son puked all over grandma this week...

I'd offer you more anecdotes, but it's just the usual squaddie whinges – we're never happy unless complaining, and it's when we go quiet the bosses should worry.

I'm not sure where to go from NI, maybe it's appropriate to start bolting the stories on in order? Maybe I'll just explain the gaps between tours and go through the next tour same as I did NI. I'll have a think. Either way it gets pretty horrible from here forwards.

I hope you have a good week, I'll try and not kill anyone this week.

30 JUNE

TROLL

Your timing is excellent as ever, stir crazy fended off for another night thanks to your mail and your efforts looking at my writing. I have realised that I want to talk about my team more, and also to talk more about the areas and background to help explain thoughts, but I also figure that this is something I can slot in here and there as I go back over the work. It's made me look at the other tours in a new light.

Anyway, I'll be having a look at your comments tonight, gratefully received and appreciated. Otherwise, as things have continued to be messy out here, I have happily shortened my tenure out here. July is Ramadan and little will get done out here. The boss wants to save money and I'll get a month's paid leave despite my temporary status. I'll lose a couple of thousand on the month's pay and half a month completely off the end, but the plus is I will be home by the end of the week. I'm not letting H know I'll be home until I am on motorway then will warn her off so she can let the boy know. I'm hoping that the extra time at home will buy me a leave pass for Remembrance weekend so I can be down in London for that at same time as you're doing your celebrity bit. If so, I'm likely to book a room for the night before as getting there on the day of the march is a pain in the backside and for the night of the march so I can have a drink before going home. If I get the pass and it fits with you guys it'd be good to see you for a drink.

You'll like my current work: it's a video lesson called 'suicide bomber slideshow'.

TROLL

As usual you have made me laugh and your comments have often highlighted areas where I either did not find the right words to express what I wanted, or (more often), I have reverted to full on squaddie speak, in which case I need to do you a list of translations. What has made me laugh most of all this time is your notes where you want to know the technical detail of things, specifically things that I have deliberately avoided putting in for security reasons. It's not that I wouldn't explain in person, but I'll have to re-word and explain carefully to avoid crossing any line that I'm not prepared to do. Again, it's no issue on a private text, but I'd not put something into print that would compromise the safety of my friends and those who follow me. You don't need to explain; I know you'd not either.

While the majority of the text has been general memories, I struggled to express myself clearly about the morning of the second job on the railway line. This is partly due to not writing down the full explanation of the technical problems and the holes in our procedures that the enemy could exploit, and also the problem of explaining just how young, scared and out of my depth I felt. Did you think this came across at all?

I know you've been busy so I don't want to take up your important time but I'm conscious I've written a lot about the same subject area, did it read ok, I plan to add better background detail to some to try and explain the decisions better but in 'insider' terms it's all nothing special and all of my friends did just the same if not more on their tours so to me it loses a lot in print.

Some of your questions like asking if I am ever spontaneous on task will get answered in later tours. My current position was that I was a very soft kid who had to grow up both at home and in work. I created an outer persona (Troll) to survive. There are varying views from people about how that worked out, but the two are fairly polarised.

Often I am tempted to answer the questions you ask in an e-mail rather than submit them to the story. I guess it depends on if you're asking because I need to explain for the story or if it generally has your interest.

Chris, the lad who was my No2 on the railway jobs (referred to them as Op Certain Death 1 & 2) was told he was to be my No2 for the Iraq war, he was late getting out there. The days he missed were the ones where Si and his driver were killed, and following catching up and joining the team, we did a load of work which I'll talk about in Iraq. He has subsequently re-traded to become an ATO himself and has toured in his turn as a boss in Afghanistan (decorated I think). We're still friends and I tell him he was the 'magnet' not me.

CHAPTER 28

JULY 2013

1 JULY

Troll

Thanks for such a long answer. I am, as you say, unsure of my writing and struggle to ever say I was any good at anything. A couple of notes while I am thinking out loud. The mention of the re-trading or changing jobs... when I was 24 I'd decided the trade sucked, told my CO the same and said I was not for hanging about with rubbish officers. He told me to go on a 'Selection Course' basically to the layman it's the SAS, but not: it's something similar. Of 240 I got to the last 13, had about a 50/50 chance of passing but decided I didn't want the job now I'd seen it all (too many people telling me what to do). So, I thanked them and came back to being an ATO (hardly anybody tells me what to do). I also found out that they had an ATO post inside their world, so I had plans to come back, get promoted, and go back as the ATO. That's what I did.

The other bleep went mad and ended up in Woolwich psychiatric ward. All of us who'd been his boss at some point pointed the finger, blaming each other for sending him mad. I've no idea if he sorted himself out, but on looking back, he was just one of those kids who was not ready for the army yet. If he did move on, then it was safer for him; if he came back in, I hope it was as a better candidate for the work. Better to find out early and survive, than find out later you're not up to it and have a drama.

The trip home is not 100% again, as this morning, I am told we're waiting for a decision from US. Also, I know he's tight on money, so he begrudges sending me home and paying me just as much as he begrudges keeping me out here, paying me more and having no work to give me... Madness.

As for Remembrance day... The term 'Leave Pass' is one I have adopted late in my time. Traditionally, it was referenced by single soldiers (living the life of Riley) talking to married soldiers who were now not as free to come and go as they please. My use is simply identifying I respect my wife and will ask if she minds me having the time away. We both have it fairly well balanced for giving each other a night out with mates. She does it far more often than I do.

As for company... I'm all up for it if you and John are up for meeting. I've not decided if I want to be in the march; it's likely not this year. I'm not ready for it, but I'm better in company now. I am over the worst bits rather than on my own. I can easily see it being even handed with you on your book signing one day and me and the march the next. Plenty of time for everything to change yet anyhow.

I will let Helen know when I am driving up the motorway, she will be excited I am home early and I will get the night before free with my business partner en-route home.

Have a good day, I'm off to play with mines.

Troll

Have you watched it? Does it change any thoughts you have regarding your work?

Gill, Chris's widow, has a video she keeps promising to send, of Chris and me drunk in her kitchen one night, with me applying a selection of make up to Chris. As I remember it, it was a great drunken night and was not long before Chris was killed. I've never seen it but imagine that a play about relationships between soldiers in the EOD world would trigger a few more memories.

Regards the railway tasks, in a sterile environment, mathematically, there was little else I could do. Would I change anything? Maybe. Maybe I'd tell the SAT to go fuck himself, and I'd carry out my RSP (render safe procedure) as I saw fit. These days I am a different person.

Operationally I can smash most before me, and even those who have gone to Afghan recently remember me as one of their instructors. And although they too have grown in confidence from their own performance, a lot are still scared by the photographic memory and database of EOD history I keep in my head. There will always be room for improvement; there are always things that could have been done better, and part of the great thing about our trade is that your mates will always be there to point it out to you. Would I change anything? No, the actions I chose made me what I am. Would I remove the hurt and trauma it caused, if I could do so without losing the good bits? Then, yes. I could do without the pain.

Ultimately, you cannot change a thing. I was lucky to survive. It has probably changed a lot inside me, but then I survived other events because of the way I changed after this one. I was never the same after NI, but then I was always a bit odd.

What advice would I give? Become a pilot!

If I was the SAT talking to a young Sergeant in that position, I would tell him we were all scared, (bugger, I have to add a bit to the NI story now). I've told young soldiers that I was scared and they cannot believe it of me. Hmm, also there was this one time in Iraq where I gave a speech to my team.

Anyway, at the time when Tim Collins was giving his 'Fight with honour' speech that made the papers, mine went something like this:

"Right lads, there is good news and there is bad. The bad news is that we are all going to die..." (on a long enough timeline, I suspect this to be fact) "...the good news is that this fucked up mission might just give some of us the chance to choose the how, and the where."

Lots of worried looking youngsters! Nowhere near as inspiring as Monsieur Collins, but in hindsight I still like mine.

The thought occurs to me... You should meet the guys.

There is a pub I'd recommend for Remembrance day, but it depends if you are staying in London on the Sunday night.

If I cannot make it, I'll send the details and you can go in undercover if you wish. However, the better arrangement is the AT Reunion which will be in Oxfordshire. We usually have a dedication at the memorial followed by a dinner and a chat in a hotel nearby. If you'd be interested, then I'll see if the stars align and sort something out for you and John. It might help you see a wider view of the trade? If it's a daft idea then just say so, I'll not mind. I've also probably got an 'in' to the IWM, and the VC/GC wing they have there has its share of EOD legends amongst it.

I've really got the bug about writing you know. There is tons more to come. I take it that trying to then put it in order and make sense of it is a mission in itself?

Sorry, random monkey moment over.

TROLL

Weird day here too, in a funny way. Thursday's flight is back on and they are effectively sacking me for no reason. I've learnt a valuable lesson about contractor work. Luckily, I am only out here for some savings and not paying the bills, the short termination will cost me 11k, but on other side, I've put about the same in the bank for very little work. I've saved others who might have needed the funds from being caught out. Because of the issues with my contract, it has also highlighted this for the permanent staff here who all now know that they are about to be given the same treatment and have no guarantee of future employment. I've obviously been duty bound to inform them of the risk and a mini-revolution has occurred. Most are now looking for other employers. All things for a reason.

As for *Later, After*, I still think it is an excellent idea which came from a very good intention. If it is lacking, out of the two of us, only you see it. Nothing you wrote is beyond the credible and indeed every incident has at least one guy I know who can fit the mold. I have only offered guidance where I thought you might like to represent the majority in order to represent the mainstream issues. There would equally be nothing wrong with singling out the isolated cases. We are all suffering it as individuals, after all. You say it needs work; I, in return, hope I help give you ideas. As I said to you from the start, many of the things you have portrayed remind me of either myself of others I know who have their issues. I'm sure you'll hit upon the right psychological hook to satisfy yourself, if you think it needs it. I felt it portrayed a friend of mine pretty accurately, to be honest. Certainly, many of the shrinks I have been in front of seemed keen to keep me under their services – the German one did sack me though.

One of the benefits of meeting more of us is that you'll see the same thing manifested in hundreds of different ways; you'll hear the stories about each other from different perspectives, some who were there, and others who heard about it and made the rest up. The AT reunion is a very informal affair. Last year, it was a curry in the Sgts Mess at Kineton where, after a dedication at the memorial, we all drifted in and ate in groups, no formal sitting down or speeches. As for turning up, many bring family and friends, so you'd be fine.

As for why you do it at the time, there are many reasons: training, fear of failure, not letting the team down, not letting the terrorists win, a preference for death than to fail or show weakness, peer pressure, and also just a general desire to shout 'fuck you!' at the terrorists by action or deed. I'm an ATO, I save lives, that's what I do. The problems started in earnest for me when the job description changed.

The video is an old trick used by a friend; the Americans are all up for 'Let the bodies hit the floor' video of fast planes and whooping idiots. We use the same music, start with street scenes where the idea is you'll be lucky to spot the suicide bomber coming, then give them the results with no punches pulled. The message at the end asks them if any of their smart bombs have the intellectual capability for hitting a target that the human brain has. Their smart bombs are not as smart as a suicide bomber can be. Now switch on for your tour because the enemy is watching and death awaits the unwary. Usually gets them silent. I have a much better AT trade one you'll like, I'll let you see that when I've finished it.

Lastly, my writing... If I had not taken up the offer to read your work, my story would likely have remained talked about and never written. I really cringe at the idea, but I have plans now, and if this goes to my family I will write an apology for doing the job and leaving them all at home to worry. I'd like it to lead to something being produced where the profits can go back to the AT trade; the lessons reminding the youngsters would also not be a bad thing. But I'm way ahead of myself there, just feeling that it's okay and might go somewhere one day, even to my son, is enough.

It is entirely down to you that it has come on so well. I have often struggled and you've given me every encouragement. It's very appreciated.

It's fucking rubbish out here tonight. Roll on Thursday.

2 JULY

TROLL

The Americans have been in touch, the funding is now back on. Luckily for me they have decided that they will only fund 4 not 5. This is good because it saved me having to tell the boss here not to bother and to put me on the plane just the same. I've spent enough time in the company of amateurs and besides that, the UN have given me a heads up that things might get noisy out here. That would not scare me off, but is just another reason to say enough. The boss nit-picked about $45 dollars for my last day here... In response to this I then dug into the regulations and found I have earned three days paid leave... That's cost him a lot more and made me smile.

As for the money, it was only going to sit in the bank for H for a new car in a couple of years, but it's not important. I've been offered six weeks in Moldova if I want it. I also managed to rally the whole workforce behind me yesterday, there was no real cause; I just felt like showing them how a proper leader works, and within minutes we were all over the road having lunch discussing how a real company works. Most are now aware that the company here has no loyalty to them and are seeking other employment. Do I cause mutinies? Er, yes.

I don't know the chap running the MSc, but as it is East Anglia-based, I may offer to be a test subject for them. As for why I do it, yes, I guess that's it. I've taken many risks to make that difference. When the doc told me I see the Army as my family, it also explained why I take each loss so personally.

Your imagination reminds me of me (you should probably worry), but I love the imagery of history. You're also fairly close to the mark with things, too. I was born in a thunderstorm.

My ancestors also came in on Spanish galleons. After the Armada had been spanked in the English Channel, it had to sail up and around the UK to get back to Spain, some of the ships were wrecked on the west coast of Scotland, and one of the survivors married a Scots girl. My grandfather has the family tree somewhere.

I've started packing. I can't wait to get on the plane, and although I could leave NOW as I've not a thing to do at work, the boss does not want to release me. I asked how early I could go, it's either this afternoon or tomorrow afternoon... Just symptomatic of a manger who is worrying about the pennies but letting the pounds run through his fingers. He relented and I get to go tomorrow. He's worried because the lad I'm staying with is the head of UN weapons mission out here and has massive influence over their contract. From the chat I had with him this morning, it appears that this fact has just dawned on him. Oh well, if they see it coming, it's not an ambush, is it?

I'll try and remember to copy the stuff I wrote about the railway, bits like that just fly past really.

Right, I'm off to scavenge for food. Have a good evening there.

. . .

TROLL

I am a Norfolk boy (Scots immigrant). I am well aware of Nelson and travelled all around where he grew up when I was a kid, regularly past his birthplace, and there are too many pubs called the Nelson to miss the link. He obviously said 'Kiss me, Hardy' despite the fact that in his death and as a man who has been seriously injured before, he will have looked back at his life and 'fate' would have been an apt observation. He had a couple of hours before he died suggesting a chest or stomach wound. Certainly, he would have survived by today's standards. He was lucky to have the chance to go out that way.

One of my friend's last words to me were 'I'll do it later'. I was almost killed that day and blamed myself for his ending for quite some time. It was also the first day I had what they call a 'confirmed kill'. I don't remember it in as much detail as the NI stuff, however this day, I had a lot more witnesses and I have started to ask them to write to me their recollections of the day. Once I have written my bit about it, I'll let you see their statements for a laugh at how random and different everyone remembers an incident in crisis.

Oh, I've been a good man and kept my head down, taken the lectures and pedantic mis-management in my stride. My coin is now spent and I've reverted to form. I'm no longer an employee and am now back to being the boss. End result, the boss here is now asking my mate Stu to make sure I don't 'do anything silly'... Waaay too late, fella, I've already done it.

Roll on tomorrow afternoon, and I can get out of here and have a day with my mate before home.

I talk to you about so many things in my life, my family know me but not much about my work, my mates know me at work but not much about the other bits of me. Now I think about it, you know quite a lot about both sides. How did that happen? Damn monkeys, that's how!

I've started tapping up my friends for Remembrance Day, too. Any excuse for a catch up. Chris is dead, so the real dirt can't surface. One of my youngsters might come though, so you can ask him what it's like to have me as a boss, if you want a laugh. He's a cocky kid, so he'll gob off and tell you what he thinks while keeping an eye on me. I hope he comes in. My current idea is to look for the pub next door to our traditional, see if that works.

When I am back in UK remind me to tell you about the other stuff out here.

Regards,
Justin (Mischief monkey)

10 JULY

TROLL
Home life is great.

TROLL
The stuff was fine, a few seconds on FCO to read the usual government standard but it did bring forth that I now rate the US site more than our own. Same decision but more detail about why, how very British to decide you don't need to know why, just obey. The whole idea of hers has me interested, and if I was not a responsible husband/father/etc it's something I'd love to be the manager for, the recce, the planning and so on. I'd also consider jogging a few lengths myself but I know what doing anything in that heat does. I did 5 hours in the EOD suit in Basrah at around 45 degrees, I drank 12 litres, every 3rd bottle was laced with hydrating salts and never peed; that tells you how much fluid leaks out of you when you're exerting yourself in heat. I defused 15 devices that day and obviously loved every moment of it.

Since I have come home I have been a different person, the weather is obviously helping as it's grim up north. I've done the gardens, built a fence panel to finish off the fence and stained the lot. I'm now starting on the garage and when that and the shed have been looked at my next big project is a toy house for James. I have a spot between the shed and garage and have the idea that I will hinge the roof so it can lift and be used for storing his outdoor toys too. I'm going to wire it for lights and see what else I can do that he'll like. I have a TV DVD player I won years ago at some Mess function. Maybe I'll put one of the screen from it out there and run the disk from my shed or some such. Though I might not as if he's outside I'd rather he was playing and not watching TV. I'm going to put in a window and door, maybe some steps to an upstairs. It just depends how the wood pans out. Anyway I hope he'll like it.

Helen is suffering. She is bigger this time than last, it's causing her other issues too so it's fate that I was to return home sooner. I've been chasing up the work admin. It appears that one of my business partners (currently overseas investigating a war crime) has 'forgotten' to bill someone for our work. It's just a few thousand but should have been in my bank account not theirs by now. How cavalier are we that we love the work so much the money is forgotten? I am sure the sarcasm is dripping from the email I've sent him. H provisionally has given me the OK for London for Remembrance, so I'm now letting a couple of mates know I'd like to see them there. Still not sure about the plan for the day but it will come to me.

Junior J Mk2 is any time 24th Oct to 5th Nov. I'd like 24th, 31st, or 5th please for my father, H and me. I was praying James would wait until after April 1st and bless him he did.

So that's it really. I'm enjoying being home, am getting things done around house which is having a massive positive effect on my head – doldrums breed doldrums, I find. The company work is looking exciting though I'm going to miss a lot doing the Uni thing. H is managing, and studying for her exam. My boy is just a perfect joy. Even the tax man has admitted I don't owe him anything, although I still haven't sent them last year's return as they still have not sent me an access code and that will remain that way until they do something about it. No one needs to die today.

24 JULY

TROLL

This is one of those nights where I used to be able to write. Annoyingly, the file I had where I kept a record of the ones I'd sent is not here. I'll find it tomorrow. I'll stick two on the end, I know you've not had one. I've hated it, as it was a very young Troll who wrote it. Modified it tonight, hate it less.

I've clearly got something on my mind.

I've had this recent external stress, the admin and so on, and despite thinking you have left it all behind, it is this which brings you back to where you once were. It is this that they don't fix and they most likely don't understand. People think they can abuse you by virtue of their position, whereas I never abused anyone I worked with because I considered all those I worked with to be trained killers. I guess I got away with a lot because I out shot them all and had a good back catalogue, compared to most they knew.

I am silently angry, (and having typed my thoughts I now find I cannot send them). Your shrink in the cells [*in the play 'Later, After'*] would think she was seeing inside, but she's not; she's seeing only that which makes it to the surface. They poke and they prod but they will only ever see that which we allow to come out. As with all soldiers, we have control beyond control. I am a man without limits, and those two words do not do justice to what a dedicated man is capable of ... our definitions differ and that's the difference between 'reactive' people and the intelligent world.

I want your character to have more depth. I don't know if it is relevant to your story and if not please ignore it.

One of my young soldiers, he was a soft kid, (was in the van that crashed into me with the idiot bleep), we met, we worked together, I tried to be a good boss, and he moved on. He in his turn became an operator, we met in passing and I remember telling him good luck when he progressed from junior to senior operator. He did his tour in Afghanistan. I next met him at a royal visit, he joined me and told me that people thought him soft and weak, he would pick fights in bars, he would pretend to be drunk and show a fat wallet to try and get mugged and so on. He'd then destroy those who tried it on. There was much more but it was all the same style of live now as you die tomorrow and see threats everywhere. I told the Regimental SAT that as a TRIM assessor this lad was in need of help. The SAT said he knew.

They medically discharged him. He was no more broken than me, probably less so, but I grew into my issues; he was young and thrown into his.

I'd feel the need for a drink away from those who knew me. I walked into town to a pub and drank, but looked for those who would talk. I told a group that I was a soldier and did EOD. The girl said she didn't believe me. I walked home and got my scrap book, came back to pub and showed them all the pictures including all the dead. Madness, in hindsight, but symptomatic all the same.

When I met the docs, I'd assess what their agenda was. Those who were 'Slap around the head and get back to work' were obvious and easy to lie to. Others were, 'does he need sacking' and were pathetic, unprofessional types, but needed to be spoken to carefully. They'd use anything to stab you and sack you. The rest were genuine, but equally flawed; most were 'observers' – they understood you were broken but really had no idea how to fix you. Some tried tablets, some tried breathing exercises, sleep programmes, CDs and so on. All of it is fine for a time, (usually measured in minutes or days rather than anything useful), but your condition would adapt and destroy it. It is a self-destructive condition and no one can save you as well as you can destroy yourself.

Generally, I looked at them as targets, weighed up their risk before anything else and tried to get into their heads before they got into mine. The last doc was very professional. I know very little about her, and she gave up personal facts (she had a son), before she gave up thoughts. I never understood why one of them tried to tell me all about Iraq because 'he'd been there'... yeah? And killed who, you cunt?

Fundamentally, no matter how clever (and many were), they could not keep up; you cannot keep up when a man cannot speak as fast as his mind is raging.

If I was sat in a cell and a 'fucking quack' – especially one working for the coppers – came to test me, she'd be lucky if I didn't tell her I'd eat her liver with beans. No soldier is going to be on side with anyone in a cell, especially not an ATO who has met head doctors before. I'd toy with her, I'd see what she was looking for and play up to the vulnerability she presumed before coming out with a comment that would make her piss her pants. Fucking quacks, you were no use selecting me and you're fuck all use on my way out.

What do I want? I want you to accept that without being me and being where I've been you have no way of knowing what will actually help. By all means, you are intelligent and offer your knowledge of the effects of stress and combat, but after that, unless you can fix me, you need to be looking for what can fix me rather than trying to make what 'has fixed other people' fit me.

Generally, know that at best you're the enemy and I'd have no problem, and at worst you'll kill me yourself trying to do good.

Talk to me in a cell, or the police station or anywhere other than outside in a park, why would I be anything other than hostile with you as the enemy? You consider the gross horror of seeing a broken and dismembered body, but you're not even close because we consider that, those who respond, those who did it, those who support it, condone it. We are the shrink that goes inside the head of the psychopath.

And we're not trained to cope, only to survive and go on to the next task. I am sure the shrinks that select us know that we are the type that would never back away from a fatal task, and I am sure they know what the work does to us, how it is like a slow poison working its way into us long after we've stopped.

Anyway, enough ranting, I thought it might be helpful.

25 July

Troll

You're welcome to use the poem as long as it doesn't stop me being able to use it myself one day, if I ever get that far. I wrote to you because these days I recognise the symptoms. It's passed now, although remind me to tell you about the tax office another day.

I'll read properly and reply later but just as an aside, look at the date of the mail? About 3 days ago was it? Then the proximity of the full moon; I know it was close.

All is well, house needs work for my boy, so more important things to worry about.

Thanks for replying.

CHAPTER 29
AUGUST 2013

17 August

TROLL

I booked a hotel for Remembrance today and for some insane reason I applied for a ticket to march in the parade. I booked somewhere near Victoria as its closer to the AT pub post- the parade and it's near the National Army Museum in case I get the chance to go and see the IED display.

Just a little bit more about the ceasefire tour. I'm struggling to write about some stuff so I guess I'm working around the rest as it comes to mind.

CHAPTER 30
JUNE 2015

Troll

Did I ever write that I was in an airport going to Ireland and I saw a woman with a baby? As remote as I was from people, I remember thinking that I was happy to do my job to make NI better for the baby.

When I watched *Kajaki*, I remembered something I had forgotten. I remembered how I stopped caring about the rules and was prepared to go to any lengths, to take any risks if it meant saving just a single soldier's life.

I remember deliberately fragging myself (very minor fragmentation injuries) to complete a task, and now I remember why.

I'm not sure I could face watching it again. God knows how much you'd feel if the faces even look familiar.

CHAPTER 31

OUT OF THE ARMY

JHB: What did you do the first day out of the Army?

Troll: Unpacked the world on a stick that was like mt 4th load of kit from Colchester and crammed it into all the spaces in the house.

jhb: Eloquent. Second sentence?

Troll: Drove home

TROLL

The transition from Army to civilian? It's simple really: you're addicted to it. You might not know exactly what it is, what it is might change, but you know that you only really get it on Ops. On tour, on task, doing stuff, it's that feeling of being at the front. I'm guessing (because I still don't really know) that it's adrenaline. You train to be good, and the better you get the more you want it. They (the army) do nothing to bring you down, why would they? They want you at your fighting peak for as long as possible. I've read that the ideal mental age for a soldier is 17, so the environment is designed not to make you grow up. All deductions from your wages are taken out before you get them, your food and accommodation are subsidised – you are protected from growing up. Me, personally, I have no issue with any of it. I loved my job and I would still be doing it if I could make time stand still. I have never felt so alive, and leaving it behind with the thought that you'd never feel that again, I have cruelly described to loved ones as 'worse than death'. A very selfish feeling.

It feels like you're a spring and you've been overstretched, you will never go back to how you were. In my writing, I try and explain what causes this, but I came back from Iraq and desperately didn't want to come home. If I had the choice again, I'd have stayed out there far longer. Eventually, I guess, I would have tired and then they could send me home, but as it was, they sent me home to a standing stop when I was going flat out. My friends on my team had been captured and murdered, my best friend had died trying to save an Iraqi family, and I'd killed people. I should have died myself probably. There was no way I was going to adjust and the idiots waiting for me back in the UK just made things worse. I have no doubt the shrinks would label it survivor guilt but I think it was more. It had more to do with addiction, and not knowing the details of how addicts are, I would not be surprised if they had the same symptoms from different causes.

So you try to deaden the pain: more of the same, volunteer for duty all the time ... drink, phys/sex (same thing), fighting, fast cars/bikes, loud rock music, parachuting or adrenaline sports...

I'm aware that others did drugs but I know what my choices were. As avenues became blocked to you, you do the others more, and it was at this point, after Iraq I, found my musical choice tended towards the female vocalist with the lilting tones. I've always liked music and mapped my life by what was regular on my play list. Evanescence was top after Iraq, and the words to 'Bring Me To Life' took on an ever important role. I'm aware the band lead, Amy Lee, is religious and you can hear that in her songs. I'm not hugely religious, but I do have a faith. I desperately wanted to die. I had conquered my fear long ago, so death had no hold on me. I spent many days determined to kill myself but I also knew I could never give up. I was tortured. I would play the song over and over, the louder the better. To me, I felt it was orders, a demand to come back to my real life, some strength from someone else to do it when I had none left myself. I feel no shame in how I was, and I'm content that Amy Lee saved my life. If so, she's not the only one in my history.

When you risk your life, there must be a reason for it. I've not listed my ideas as they are probably different for each person. But again it's selfish, you risk everything that you are to all your family and loved ones for ... well, for something, and no matter the rewards you think you're doing it for, you will have to atone for your actions in the future. While I was single, it was easy, atonement was done selfishly with little regards for my parents and siblings. Now I've got my own family, that callous behaviour has come back to haunt me, and even still I have that addiction.

I've volunteered to go away, a selfish need to go and prove I still can, under the lying guise of doing it for the money that will support my family. The fear has returned only to be destroyed by me as I had trained myself to do, but in the back of my mind is the knowledge that I'm leaving my wife, my son and my unborn child. A part of me is afraid, not of the work, but of being a family man.

How is it leaving the Army? It's easy. The army on the most part is shit. It's your mates that make it – leaving them is terrible, like losing your family. If I had replaced this one family with the other, I would be rehabilitated or cured, and every doubt that enters my head makes me feel like a worthless human being. But it's my choices and my burden.

NIGHTMARES

I don't suffer too much from my nightmares, I have them, I wake up and realise it's a dream. I go back to sleep.

Sometimes I have night sweats and wake in a sweat-soaked bed.

I dreamt I had no hands, not bloody stumps like just after the explosion, but healed stumps, years on. I had made a mistake on a job in Northern Ireland. I had chosen to break the rules because I thought it was the right thing at the time, and while I was working, there had been an explosion. I had the suit on, I was saved, but the small bomb took both my heads. I cried in my sleep that I'd made a mistake. I woke, and in the near darkness, I saw my hands. *Thank fuck, I have my hands.*

I crawled through the burning building. I'd been pulling the bombs from the smoke-filled rooms and putting them on the path outside. As I was crawling, the fire had released the electrical cables from the plaster ceiling, so as I crawled they went underneath my armoured plate and pulled burning plaster down onto the back of my suit. As it happened, although I got a few hot spots, I survived pretty much intact, but in my dream I get tangled in the wires. I burn, and having seen the dead following a fire, I know they crunch up, their arms and legs draw to their body. In my dreams, I see my hands blacken, my fingers curl, then I'm outside my body watching myself burn. I wake. Usually this is accompanied by a soaking bed.

I'm not yet ready to write about the bridge job.

I spoke to a few DCMH specialists. It's quite hard going, and you really have to earn my trust (as a doctor who might take my job away from me) before I will open up. One or two were okay, the rest were shit.

Letter from Libya

The captain seems to represent a rather large swathe of current military. The cuts have destroyed the military, and it seems there are two camps: those who want to bluff their way through, and the remainder who pick up the work.

The Squadron has three detachments, currently manned with 9 - 8 - 3 operators. The Sergeant Major was an idiot when I joined, and despised by all us professional Sergeant Majors. How he was promoted can only be down to an agenda, but that's a different story. He has no man management; his boss used to work for me, and was completely spineless back then. Bottom line is, how he can let one of his troops run with three men while the others have so many staff? It isn't anything short of criminal ineptitude.

I'm sorry I left because I could do a better job asleep than those two clowns could manage at their best.

Always happy to chat if you're about. My head isn't fit for uni work or story writing at the moment, so I'm mostly monging in front of the TV, hating the TV.

CHAPTER 32

THE MANCHESTER BOMB, 22 MAY 2017

MY FLIGHT HOME WAS UNEVENTFUL. I had utilised my usual technique of a melatonin tablet, ear plugs and a blindfold.

I didn't sleep properly, but instead drifted on the edge of sleep, waking to shift my position or as people passed my seat and disturbed me. The course [in the US] had been well received due to some good instructors, but stressful as I had fought to control my urge to kill people with the apathetic ineptitude of the supplier. I was looking forward to getting home and seeing the family.

That changed when I turned on my phone. All my messages were of concern about the incident in Manchester. A quick google revealed that a suicide bomber had attacked a music concert, casualties were already in double figures. I know that I have friends at the concert, and that H will in all likelihood be at home looking after the children. My assessment keeps me calm as I dial her number. It takes seconds for her to answer, but in those seconds my mind flashes through my past.

In my time, I have defused twelve suicide vests and attended seven suicide bombings. It's impossible for me not to draw comparisons between what I have seen and what must be going on in Manchester.

Obviously, the first thing I remember is the smell, that sticky metallic smell that hits you when you first get on scene, but that is quickly followed by burning. Pieces of burnt flesh are stuck to every surface, up the walls, on the vehicles and on every facing surface so that you can quickly identify where the blast originated. I realise that the humanity of these scenes is lost on me as I'm only interested in where the blast happened, much of the human tragedy of these incidents passed me by.

A dull thump in the distance and an almost imperceptible ground shake would signal another atrocity had occurred. I'd rally the team, don kit and head to the Ops Room. By the time we had permission to deploy, the team would be waiting with the QRF and our stolen Snatch Land Rover. The QBOs (Quick Battle Orders) were always the same, half the team with gloves and bags to pick up the debris and evidence from the scene, the other half and the QRF are eyes out watching for the second suicide bomber. We arrive as the locals are ferrying their dead and wounded from the scene. People are crying and others are angry. How do you spot a suicide bomber amongst all this? The best you can hope for is that he's trying to be calm. He's emotionally unaffected by the scene. I'm looking for my own self in the crowd.

Or else he hates us and is trying to kill us, and you're hoping that you can tell the difference between his angry face and that of those on scene who have lost loved ones or are just angry that this has happened because the fucking British have come back to Afghanistan.

Once the casualties have been ferried to what passes as a hospital out there in the back of pickups and beat up cars, you're left with what remains. The locals have an annoying habit of sweeping the scene into the gutters, and on more than one occasion, I have had to delve into the Afghan sewers to recover a piece of potential evidence. It's that grim an activity, I have told the team to look but not touch and call me to recover things they find. Makes me fucking gag, and I have the constituency of a goat, so I figure they'd puke if I made them do it. As the team do their thing, I'm doing mine. My job is to PiD (Positively Identify) the attacker.

Amongst all the blood, body parts and guts, I have to find a piece that is positively the bomber. The purpose being to trace through DNA where he came from, and by knowing his country of origin, maybe how he transited to Afghanistan. From evidence we collected on my first tour, we received back reports that identified six UK-living Pakistani nationals who had been in Afghanistan firing weapons at our troops, and two families related to suicide bombers. Every scene I attend returns to me as I remember the political lies while our MPs tried to think of a reason why they sent us to Afghanistan. It was to fight terrorism; it was to destroy the drug trade; it was to hunt AQ. It was better that we fought the enemy overseas to prevent them bringing the fight to our shores...

That lie failed in July 2005 with the attacks in London – the enemy's intention to bring this barbarism to the UK.

I return to Manchester and pity the teams who have to respond. I visualise the dead and wounded, and I rage.

This feels familiar – anger is so common to who we are and what we do. Hatred is something they cultivate in us to enable us to do what we do, and sometimes I think our rage would be better spent on our MPs. Those feckless wankers who prioritise open borders and their own agendas over the lives of our citizens. Beyond the reach of the common man ... but not beyond the reach of us, and for a moment I remember the training we gave to the SAS on the Advanced Demolitions course, where we trained them to assassinate VIPs. For a moment, I smile at the thought they should fear the common man...

"Hello..."

Her answer snaps me back to now, and the plane, and my real concerns. She's okay, the children are okay, and my friend and his family are okay. She spoke to them as soon as she heard of the attack.

My reality returns to normal, and I'm gutted to no longer be in a job where I protected people from this reality, compounded when she tells me that she has been called into work and will be leaving as soon as I get home to take over child care.

CHAPTER 33

TRAINING IN THE USA

August 2017

It is currently 32 degrees, my hat is soaked through and the sweat runs constantly down my back. I am uncomfortable. No, that does not do it justice ... I have been bitten by a swarm of fucking insects so much so I look like I have leprosy, my groin is on fire from the abrasion of the trouser material, and I am soaked from top to toe. I fucking hate this moment ... but my focus remains.

The students complain about the heat, and every instructor disdains them for the fact they would not survive. This place is 20 degrees cooler than Afghanistan, you do not have body armour on, no one is shooting at you ... and you are bleating it's hot? You have no idea.

What did asking me to talk about the heat prompt? An understanding of the weather.

It does not matter what the weather is. I remember the rain in NI, that same miserable feeling of waking up during training, sometimes in a dry sleeping bag, to find the pitter patter of rain meeting you. You know you're going to get wet, no question about it, but what is the alternative? Say no to the platoon Sergeant? Suicide, quite simply. So you crawl out of your sleeping bag, bitching about the fact your boots pushed the bag out from under the poncho so the bottom of the bag is now soaked. You pull your rig on and tramp through some dank wood on some deliberately miserable training area and assume the position on sentry. Nothing moves, nothing happens, there is nothing to see except the drips falling from the front of your helmet. It keeps your head dry so you don't notice the rain so much, that is until the drips soak down the back and falls down your collar, then you notice. But there is nowhere to go, no way to escape. Your only option is to shift position and let the drips soak some previously un-wet place on your body.

So how does Wales in 1989 prepare you for Afghanistan in 2009? Choice. You chose to be there, you still chose to be here. So regardless of the misery, you accept the weather. It simply does not matter if it is freezing cold, baking hot, or pissing with rain – a soldier knows his only choice is just to accept it. He has more important things to worry about, and the weather is just a fact that he acknowledges. The only chance he will notice it, is if it might affect his shot or his drills, and even than all he will do is adjust to accommodate.

The heat out there is nothing short of blistering, you simply can't understand it – even the blast of heat opening an oven door only emulates it for a second. You leave your tent (with its – occasionally – working air con), and walk down a plastic mat corridor. The exit flap pulled aside, the furnace heat hits you.

Afghanistan has to be one of the worst places on earth to fight. Norway and the Arctic are grim, you have to be skilled to cope, but there is always a way to stay warm... ish.

There is no escaping the heat. Afghans call this place 'the furnace', and they are not wrong. We do so many things wrong out here, we carry so much kit, we get so hot ... no wonder the Afghans often come close to outflanking us. Light clothes, no body armour and an AK with a few mags, it weighs a tenth of our kit. But we kid ourselves we're okay because we are stronger, and fitter ... and we are ... but that doesn't equal out under a furnace sun.

I remember the heat as we patrolled Afghan; the cold, freezing cold of Bosnia; and the drudging misery of the wet in Ireland. I remember it all, and the only feeling it prompts is acceptance and the desire to bitch about it.

The weather simply means nothing to us, you just accept it, adjust for it if needed, and carry on.

I have a lot more to write about this, like how you know which bits of you are going to get wet and cold depending on which work you do, or how you ignore sunburn and just decide you are going to be fine every day under a burning sun.

However, I owe some writing, so I started.

Currently, I know this heat is different to anything I have experienced before. I avoided jungle/tropic theatres, by design.

The fucking sweat runs from me from about 07:00 until I quit work; any exposed skin is already tanned brown. The sweat runs so fast that my boots fill and fluid squelches out through the canvas as I walk. I have to mop my face with my hat every 5 minutes to keep my eyes clear. The heat here is not Afghanistan. Afghanistan is so blisteringly hot there is no moisture in the air, except that evaporating off us. This is a heavy heat, thick and cloying, even standing and watching the students, sees us dripping with sweat.

I don't mind, simply because it is different. If it was Afghan heat, or NI rain, I would hate it, but this time it is simply work, and because it is work, I can make it irrelevant. The same as we ignore the weather on an op, I can ignore this weather at work.

POSTSCRIPT

Jane Harvey-Berrick

The play *Later, After* was born from a desire to do something. At the time, 2012, Camp Bastion was still home to tens of thousands of British troops, and the US Camp Leatherneck was larger than many American towns.

Another 19 year old had been killed by an IED, another had lost his legs. Olaf 'Oz' Schmidt's wife had been in the news, talking about her husband who had lost his life whilst neutralizing a bomb.

I wondered what it would take to do a job like that.

Since then, Afghanistan has been left to the people who were born there, and we can only hope it all meant something.

But what about the men and women who fought for that patch of dust on the other side of the world? What was their reality when they came home to a country that didn't believe in the war they fought, where soldiers were and are advised to hide the uniforms that they once wore with pride?

What comes next? What comes later, after?

This was the question I asked myself. And as I read more about the new reality of life after the military, the ugly truths that affected too many of those who had served, and their families, there was another question, a naïve question: what can I do to help?

Because I'm a writer, the answer was to write something and to make it matter.

So *Later, After* began life as a filmscript, with little hope that it would ever see the light of day, but it felt important to write it. It felt like doing something. How arrogant.

But I'm not a military person, and at the time, I had no friends or acquaintances who had current military service. And there were technical questions that needed to be addressed.

I contacted *Felix Fund: the UK bomb disposal charity* and explained to the then CEO, Holly Davies, that I needed help, and could she suggest anyone who might be interested in correcting my script.

She put me in touch with Troll, recently retired from EOD, also a writer, and more importantly, willing to help a naïve, but well-meaning stranger.

Over the next few months, we built up trust. It took time, and we both had other projects on which we were working, but finally we had something that looked and felt like a real script: one that would probably never be made into a film, considering the subject matter and parlous state of the British film industry.

But then I sent it to my long-time friend, Elizabeth Thick – Libby to her friends – who was looking for a directing project.

"Turn it into a play," she said, "and I'll take it on. I know an actor who might be interested."

She organised a read-through with the experienced TV and stage actor, Neil Anthony. He had a couple of suggestions for changes, nothing too contentious. We rewrote a few sections, and then we met up.

"I want to take this play to the stage," he said. "This play needs to be seen, and I'll make that happen."

The words every writer longs to hear.

Troll and I didn't realise that the script was challenging, a two-person play with circular dialogue that was a feat of memory.

There was little about the process that was smooth. There was money to be found or saved, logistics to be worked out, grant applications to be looked at and then discarded as being too long-winded, too interminable.

Funding it entirely ourselves, we booked the theatres directly, and went into rehearsals. We had an enormous stroke of luck when Libby and Neil auditioned the ferociously talented Flora Sowerby, astonished to find that she was only recently graduated with a Masters in Acting for Classical and Contemporary Text from the Royal Conservatoire of Scotland.

Our first performance took place in the Wardroom at RNAS Culdrose, organised by Lieutenant Mark Taylor, a keen theatre-goer and actor himself.

From there, we played at the Acorn Arts Centre in Penzance, a week at the Drayton Arms Theatre in London, and our final performance was at the Marlborough Barracks in Kineton, guests of EOD operator, Major Chris Saunders.

Where it was seen – which wasn't many places – it got great reviews. But one of the most important one was from an older couple who approached Troll after the play.

"Our son was an ATO. He's estranged from his wife and we never see him. But now we understand a little bit of what he's gone through, we're going to try and get in touch with him again."

Reviews don't come better than that.

The play became a record of our efforts to do something that mattered, however small, but more than that, it was a journey towards an unlikely, but lasting friendship between a romance novelist and a bomb disposal expert.

Troll, my friend, never completed his memoirs, and his family watched him die from brain cancer. But seven months before his death, he ran a 10k race for charity, because that's the kind of man he was.

Justin J. Bell

31.7.72 – 22.6.19 RIP

POETRY

Our lives are the same but different

Our lives the same but different, my selfishness
    becomes my pain.
I miss you my closest friend, and want our time
    again.
We face our fate with open eyes, we go to war we
    will not die.
My friend of years at my side, our friendship is my
    pride.

Our deeds made us immortal, those acts that made
    us men.
My days hurt with you gone, and I wait to see you
    again.
Loyal boys with mischief eyes, we go to war we
    can't die.
We joke about time after, our destiny met with
    laughter.
My mind relives your leaving, seeking a cause for
    hope.
Disbelief and denial my reason, my only way to
    cope.

Warrior men with fiery eyes, we went to war.
This fury clouds my mind, so much life so little
    time.

I'm alone in my desert mind, your task I wish I'd
    shared.
No more to fight beside you, our story ends unfair.
Younger men with older eyes, we went to war so we
    could die.
Time pains me now, your desert sands ran out.

A soldier's return

The mind of a child torn without grace,
And cast without fear into this nightmarish place,
The body is safe it's surface unmarked,
The soul now in torment is emotionally scarred,
Returned to his homeland his spirit felt strong,
But weakened beyond sight by the things that went
  wrong,
To spare her his pain, he never looked back,
But the weight overcomes him, his life is turned
  black,
His lover comes to him and a stranger he seems,
Only time and her love heals the scars in his
  dreams.

You fight without thinking
You fight without thinking,
You maim with no cares,
You kill loved ones and family,
And leave naught but nightmares,
Your time here should end,
This Army won't beat you, nor me,
But a people that want their peace,
Is sick of you and now can see,
The end is in sight,
For black hoods and heavy boots,
I'll fight for a time without,
Irish violence from religious roots.

I look to the distance

I look to the distance with my unseeing eyes
I remember my time of a blood red rage
With un-cried tears travelling foreign shores
I wrote my friend's life's last page
Hearts on fire, never learned to breathe.
Men of steel, who never learned to grieve.
Gaze no more, at the setting sun.
Rage no more, your time is done.
Remember that time, a calmer place.
See in the mirror, that young boys face.
Remember who you were, so far in your past.
Let go your pain, find peace in your life at last.

Abaddon

Their kit's checked and ready,
This patrol's about to go,
Along Armagh's roads and hedgerows,
Quiet sounds, on the ground, the players know.
Search around the farmland,
Mind that gateway, don't use the track.
The professional soldier who's my friend,
Can't know his mistake or hear the thunder clap.
I've torn myself in half,
At my failure to save your life.
You were beyond our reach as you left the camp,
How will anyone face your wife?
The long dead eyes of a friend,
Stare accusingly at my face.
His lifeless body's a rag on this roadside,
Ireland's a godforsaken place.

To only live my life as I did that day
To only live my life as I did that day,
How I long again for the feeling,
After all my hard fought tours you'd think,
The sound of death knells pealing,
Would be something that I'd know.

The smell of death from all those sins,
Have numbed me till I'm blind,
My addictions clear only to me I think,
But I recognise others of my kind,
We all deserve better.

If words could replace my feelings,
Then, 'I miss my friend', could suffice,
If pain could only ease my sorrow,
Then to finally cry would be nice.
But who remembers how?

Check the time, grab your gat,

Check the time, grab your gat,
Another rush job, for Felix the cat.

Got to drive again, this armour feels so heavy,
Little hint of the job, my kit's prepped and ready.

Engine racing in the van, out the gate then right,
Worrying if we're lost, Ireland on a rainy night.

Arrive at the checkpoint, no time for the RUC,
All stood around talking, their eyes are now on me.

Barrow's off up the road, hope I can cross this
    dump,
Weapons ready on the wire, det cord cuts it with a
    thump.

No time to draw a breath, get the boss into his suit,
He's off on the Long Walk, concerned I watch his
    route.

The boss shows the SOCO, the bomb in the
    wheelie bin,
The task is safe and finished, time to get the kit
    back in.

Pack the van again, get the team to move,
Quiet thanks from the boss, that job was fairly
    smooth.

Back to the Detachment, all busy no-one asking,
If I need a little help, to be ready for our next
    tasking.

It took a complete day, yet you'd think it hadn't
    mattered,
I know a soldier walks safe, but I'm fucking
    shattered.

I could never look back when I went away

I could never look back when I went away,
Was it because I had already left?
Did you understand that I never came back?
And my life was somehow bereft.

You knew my time was hard and bloody,
They asked, and we always gave,
Even though it cost us so,
We always fought to be brave.

Something in my eyes was gone,
Some scars that you would never see,
Had changed your friend forever,
I never came back as me.

Each day we merely carry on,
We fight now merely to survive,
We saved our share by our hands,
But did we really come back alive?

THE EXTRAORDINARY CASE OF
THE LOST DADDY

Troll was working in Libya in May 2013, de-mining and ridding the country of unexploded ordnance.

His son, James, was then just three years old and missing his daddy.

I suggested that Troll could write him a story about why he had to go away. This is the poem he wrote.

jhb

The Extraordinary Case of the Lost Daddy

A little boy called James
Would play his best games,
With a monkey-friend all of his own.
But Daddy had some monkeys, too,
And they were fully grown.

Where was Daddy's special task?
Who on earth could monkey ask,
To set his worried mind at rest?
Because nothing's better than a cuddle,
And Daddy's hugs are special – double!

While monkeys are fairly rare,

There are lots and lots of teddy bears.
Monkey asked his teddy friend.
"Our mission is – find James's daddy.
That's the message we must send!"

Teddies are a special kind,
Blessed with such a clever mind.
Others rallied to the call,
Passing the word from bear to bear,
Looking for Daddy, one and all.

In front of big computers perched,
Travel plans were now researched,
As teddies pondered where to start.
Could the airport play a part?
Boy, oh boy! Those bears were smart.

But at the airport the trail went cold.
One little bear was soon told,
"We won't give up our searching plan
Across the land by any means.
Undaunted we, the teddy clan."

James had ridden in Daddy's car.
Teddies now drove them very far.
Searching, leaning out the side,
With ruffling their fur,
Scouring landscapes far and wide.

They travelled the river as well as the roads.
They asked little fishes and even the toads.
Along waterways the little bears floated,
And every new lead was carefully noted.

Teddies soon were everywhere,
Seeking Daddy here and there.
Asking people on the train,
Hoping for a little clue.
But their quest was still in vain.

They asked a policeman who carefully said,
"Have you thought to look under the bed?"
But Daddy always went by plane.
A new plan of action was needed again.

They asked the Army for some new tactics
Who stopped for a moment their military antics.
"We do camping, if it's searching you need,
Try Aeroplanes with their superior speed."

"Of course!" cried teddy, taking heed.
"A pilot is just the chap we need!
He'll know best how to gain a good view.
We'll fly up high, we'll find a clue."

First there was a teddy up in a balloon,
Then came planes and parachutes really soon.
Parachuting teddies are really quite tough,
But it still was not nearly high enough.

The last idea in the bear's little pocket –
What could possibly go higher than a rocket?
So with a call to their astronaut moon base
Was handed the job of the Lost Daddy Case.

High above the earth, those astro-bears went,
Seeking out the route that James's Daddy was sent.
A mission success, just as they planned –
Daddy was there, in that desert land.

His location now found, it was mission ahead,
The journey was tricky, it had to be said.
As camel riders, bears are well versed,
But travelling through desert was definitely worse.

When Daddy saw teddy, he wanted to cheer,
He was missing his family, so it brought forth a tear.
"But, teddy," he said, "you must understand,
I'm good at my job and I'm lending a hand."

The big, brave bears had travelled through the land,
Others now worked with Daddy, clearing the sand.
With their message passed bear to face,
Teddy knew Daddy's making this a safer place.

Teddy came home, with his news,
Hoping monkey would share his views.
When Daddy left James with his toys,
It was to save other girls and boys.

With his answers, Monkey now slept.
By James's side, he was always kept.
But in the dark, as is often the case,
A teddy stood guard in Daddy's place.

Soon it was, the time had passed,
The days and weeks had not gone fast.
At his heart, the teddy had tugged.
To James and Mummy, Daddy came home.
Best of all, a family hugged.

JUSTIN BELL, QGM

Justin joined the British Army in the late 1980s and quickly qualified as an Ammunition Technician within the Royal Army Ordnance Corps. He completed 23 years' service as a Bomb Disposal Operator, seeing service in three major conflicts. He completed tours in Northern Ireland, Iraq and Afghanistan; supporting over two decades of front line UK counter-terrorism activity, including responding to the 2005 London bombings.

Justin finished his service as a Senior Explosive Ordnance Disposal Soldier responsible for the supervision and provision of EOD teams across a third of the UK in support of National Contingency Operations. During his service he received a bravery award for his EOD activities, and was subsequently rewarded a second time on the Queen's New Year Honours list on his retirement.

Identifying that the psychological well-being of EOD Operators was being largely ignored, he was instrumental in the implementation within EOD Units of the Trauma Risk Management programme, originally instigated by the Royal Marines. He retired in 2009 to spend more time with his family and currently has a career lecturing.

* *Previously published in the programme for 'Later, After', 2016, and credited as 'Mike Speirs'.*